THE FILMS OF
Theo Angelopoulos

PRINCETON MODERN GREEK STUDIES

This series is sponsored by the Princeton University Program in Hellenic Studies under the auspices of the Stanley J. Seeger Hellenic Fund.

Firewalking and Religious Healing: The Anastenaria of Greece and the American Firewalking Movement *by Loring M. Danforth*

Kazantzakis: Politics of the Spirit *by Peter Bien*

Dance and the Body Politic in Northern Greece *by Jane K. Cowan*

Yannis Ritsos: Repetitions, Testimonies, Parentheses *edited and translated by Edmund Keeley*

Contested Identities: Gender and Kinship in Modern Greece *edited by Peter Loizos and Evthymios Papataxiarchis*

A Place in History: Social and Monumental Time in a Cretan Town *by Michael Herzfeld*

Demons and the Devil: Moral Imagination in Modern Greek Culture *by Charles Stewart*

The Enlightenment as Social Criticism: Iosipos Moisiodax and Greek Culture in the Eighteenth Century *by Paschalis M. Kitromilides*

C. P. Cavafy: Collected Poems *translated by Edmund Keeley and Philip Sherrard; edited by George Savidis*

The Fourth Dimension *by Yannis Ritsos. Peter Green and Beverly Bardsley, translators*

George Seferis: Collected Poems, Revised Edition *translated, edited, and introduced by Edmund Keeley and Philip Sherrard*

In a Different Place: Pilgrimage, Gender, and Politics at a Greek Island Shrine *by Jill Dubisch*

Cavafy's Alexandria, Revised Edition *by Edmund Keeley*

The Films of Theo Angelopoulos: A Cinema of Contemplation *by Andrew Horton*

THE FILMS OF
Theo Angelopoulos

A Cinema of Contemplation

ANDREW HORTON

PRINCETON UNIVERSITY PRESS · PRINCETON, NEW JERSEY

Library of Congress Cataloging-in-Publication Data

Horton, Andrew.
  The films of Theo Angelopoulos : a cinema of contemplation /
Andrew Horton.
    p.   cm. — (Princeton modern Greek studies)
Includes bibliographical references and index.
ISBN 0-691-01141-9 (cl : alk. paper)
1. Angelopoulos, Thodōros, 1935– —Criticism and interpretation.
I. Title. II. Series.
PN1998.3.A53H67   1997
791.43'0233'092—dc20   96-20087   CIP

Publication of this book has been aided by a grant from the
Princeton University Program in Hellenic Studies under
the auspices of the Stanley J. Seeger Hellenic Fund

This book has been composed in Sabon with Helvetica

10 9 8 7 6 5 4 3 2 1

To my mother, Ann Griffith Horton

And to all who are seeking peace in the Balkans

———————————————————

*A*nd we who had nothing shall teach them peace.

▬▬▬▬▬▬▬▬ (George Seferis, from "Mythical Story")

Contents

Preface

I HAVE written this book because the films of Theo Angelopoulos matter.

They matter because they dare to cross a number of borders: between nations; between history and myth, the past and the present, voyaging and stasis; between betrayal and a sense of community, chance and individual fate, realism and surrealism, silence and sound; between what is seen and what is withheld or not seen; and between what is "Greek" and what is not. In short, Angelopoulos can be counted as one of the few filmmakers in cinema's first hundred years who compel us to redefine what we feel cinema is and can be. But there is more. His films open us to an even larger question that becomes personal to each of us: how do we *see* the world within us and around us? Bill Nichols has recently written about our media-deluged times (and he includes the computer- and Internet-driven spheres as well) that the "information age" is perhaps misnamed. More than information, we need narratives that can structure and focus it all. "The global reach and structural complexity of late twentieth century reality," Nichols writes, "calls for story telling that can appear to encompass it [information]" (ix). Angelopoulos's films go a long way toward meeting such a late-twentieth-century need.

This book has grown out of a personal involvement with Greek cinema in general and Theo Angelopoulos in particular for more than twenty-five years. And if I had to choose a moment when it became clear that I would someday write this book, it was the night *The Travelling Players* premiered in Greece in 1975. At the time I had been living and teaching in Greece for over four and a half years, covering Greek cinema as the first film critic for the English-language monthly the *Athenian*. I had interviewed Angelopoulos and invited him to visit film classes I was teaching at Deree College in Athens.

I remember being impressed then as I have continued to be with Angelopoulos the man as well as Angelopoulos the filmmaker. Born in Athens in 1935, a student of law in Athens, a practicing film critic (he hated the experience!), teacher, and student of film in France, Angelopoulos in 1975 seemed to me, on the eve of his well-deserved success with *The Travelling Players*, a man at peace with himself. That is not something that can be said about most filmmakers. The very nature of the struggle to make films invites the dangers of excessive ego, exhaustion, self-doubt, nervous tension, and lack of patience with others and with oneself. But before me in 1975 was a man quietly intense, completely focused on each student during that class visit, and able to respond to even the most trivial of inquiries with humor, insight, fresh vision.

No meeting with him since has diminished that first impression.

Since then I have met a lot of filmmakers, seen more films than I care to admit, and written a growing number of books about filmmakers around the world. But I have also stayed in touch with Theo Angelopoulos, maintaining my awareness of his films and his career. And in early 1990 I realized I was ready to write a book on his work for at least three reasons that are important to me: (1) his films have stayed with me over the years in a way that few films have; (2) most of my American friends, colleagues, and students have not heard of him but, after their first exposure, have been most enthusiastic, not to mention *persistent*, about wanting to see more of his work; and (3) while there is unquestionably a "universal" dimension to his work, so much of it stems from his ongoing dialogue with Greek culture—past and present—that it seemed important to help point out what some of those cultural (historical, mythical, political, religious, musical, cinematic, popular, and folk) intersections and echoes might be.

No book in English exists on his work. And while European critics and commentators in Greece, of course, have written both books and articles (see bibliography), no such detailed analysis as this one, combining film studies and a familiarity with the Greek language and culture, has yet come out. Nikos Kolovos's book-length study *Thodoros Angelopoulos* (1990) in Greek helped to break the ground in this direction, particularly in his understanding of Angelopoulos's use of Greek history.

In Parts Two and Three, the chapters offer a close look at six of Angelopoulos's films. In each case I have provided an extensive annotated synopsis of the film combined with commentary because, since they are not in general release, I realize that many readers may not have seen the films discussed. Also, even if one has seen a particular Angelopoulos film, there is the need to refresh one's memory: his films are longer than conventional commercial films and do not follow conventional narrative structures. The *New York Times* review of *The Travelling Players* includes a line that has become stereotypic of reviewers trying to convey some sense of Angelopoulos's cinema to readers who have not previously seen him: "There is no space to begin to enumerate the many marvelous things that are accomplished" (Eder). Clearly it is my mission to provide the necessary details so that even those who have not seen individual films will begin to appreciate Angelopoulos's filmmaking more fully.

My hope is that this volume will make it possible for Angelopoulos's films to be better understood and appreciated by English-speaking audiences everywhere. In approach, I have tried to follow the effort my Russian friend and coauthor Michael Brashinsky and I undertook to contextualize Soviet cinema in a cultural/historical perspective in *The Zero Hour: Glasnost and Soviet Cinema in Transition* (Princeton University Press, 1992).

Acknowledgments

SPECIAL thanks to Theo Angelopoulos for all of his help, support, cooperation, and long-term friendship.

This book would not have been possible without research grants from the National Endowment for the Humanities (summer 1993) and the Loyola Faculty Research Committee (1993). The Greek Film Centre in Athens and especially Elly Petrides of the Centre helped set up screenings, gathered information, and gave permission for the stills used in this study. Friends in Athens—Ariane Cotsis, Penny Apostolidis, Ellen-Athena Catsekeas, Katerina Zarocosta—aided this project in numerous ways they themselves may not be aware of. Thanks to the island of Kea, where much of this was written, and to my Greek friends there such as Argiris and Vasso, Nikos, Stephanos, and Katerina who made me and my family feel welcome. Thanks also to friends in New Zealand where one chapter was written in June 1995: Charles Steiner, Joy Gray, and Julianne Brabant. My wife, Odette, offered solid advice and put up with hours of my silence at the computer in Greece and in New Orleans.

At Princeton University Press I wish to thank the generous outside readers who so enthusiastically recommended the manuscript for publication.

But especially I appreciate my editor at Princeton, Mary Murrell, for taking on a project that at first must have seemed incredibly removed from the mainline discourses of film studies. And the manuscript would not have become a book without the levelheaded advice and help of assistant editor Deborah Malmud and the careful readings made by Lauren Lepow, senior manuscript editor at Princeton.

THE FILMS OF
Theo Angelopoulos

The Voyage beyond the Borders

The world needs cinema now more than ever. It may be the last important form of resistance to the deteriorating world in which we live. In dealing with borders, boundaries, the mixing of languages and cultures today, I am trying to seek a new humanism, a new way.
(Theo Angelopoulos)

Refuse the life of anarchy;
Refuse the life devoted to one master.
(The Chorus, Aeschylus's *Eumenides*)

A CINEMA WITHOUT COMPROMISE

IT IS a cool September evening in 1975 in Thessaloniki, Greece's second-largest city. A noisy standing-room-only crowd is packed into the major cinema of the annual Greek Film Festival. The lights dim and director Theo Angelopoulos's third feature film, *The Travelling Players*, begins. It is a three-hour-and-forty-minute epic about Greece from 1939 through World War II and the subsequent civil war up to the beginning of 1952. The film has no main character and is shot almost entirely in long shots that are also long takes, often lasting several minutes. Add to this the fact that most of the film is shot during the pale light and colors of dawn or dusk in northern Greece, particularly during winter. Immediately the crowd understood that in content and form this is a work as unlike the world's dominant form of cinema—Hollywood—as could be imagined.

Would more than a handful of true cineasts respond to such a demanding project? Several hours later the answer was clear from the standing ovation that lasted some ten minutes.

That evening was memorable for all present, including myself. *The Travelling Players* was an immediate sensation. In less than a year, it went on to become the largest-selling Greek film ever, to win numerous international awards, and eventually to be voted by the Italian Film Critics Association as the most important film in the world for the decade of the 1970s as well as one of the top films of the history of cinema by the International Film Critics Association (FRIPESCI).

Seven features have followed for a total of ten: *Reconstruction* (1970), *Days of '36* (1972), *The Travelling Players* (1975), *The Hunters* (1977), *Megalexandros* (1980), *Voyage to Cythera* (1984), *The Beekeeper* (1986), *Landscape in the Mist* (1988), *The Suspended Step of the Stork* (1991), and *Ulysses' Gaze* (1995). Six of these, furthermore, belong to trilogies that Angelopoulos himself has acknowledged. His "historical" trilogy—*Days of '36*, *The Travelling Players*, and *Megalexandros*—covers Greek history from the turn of the century through 1952; its "epilogue," *The Hunters*, jumps to the present (the 1970s) to suggest how the past has haunted contemporary Greece. And Angelopoulos has dubbed *Voyage to Cythera*, *The Beekeeper*, and *Landscape in the Mist* his trilogy of "silence."

What effect has this filmmaker from Greece had on others? The *New York Times* wrote of *Landscape in the Mist*, "There are sights in the film that once seen cannot be forgotten" (Holden). Raymond Durgnat states, "Angelopoulos' long takes approach, in their despair, their counterparts in Tarkovsky." Another critic writes that Angelopoulos's "shattering power resists conventional naming" (Murphy 42), while Michael Wilmington calls Angelopoulos "one of the cinema's great unsolved mysteries": a filmmaker working far from Hollywood in every sense who suddenly bursts "upon us full force" (32). But it was in May of 1995, when he won the Cannes Film Festival's Grand Prix for *Ulysses' Gaze*, that he began to receive wider attention in the United States in particular. Richard Corliss wrote in *Time* magazine, "The intelligence behind the camera is matched by the aching humanity in front. *Ulysses' Gaze* surely deserved to win the Palme d'Or"(an even higher award than the Grand Prix). And David Stratton in his *Variety* review praised the film as "a devastating statement about the tragic Bosnian conflict."

Few filmmakers have ever shared such honors and touched such nerves within their home cultures. What Angelopoulos succeeded in accomplishing in 1975, before, and since is our concern in this study. More specifically, I wish to explore his cinema in the context of his Greek heritage, including Greek history, myth, literature, folk culture, music, and cinema. And I am interested in the wider *cinematic* context of Angelopoulos's resistance to Hollywood narrative and style as well as his subsequent relationship to world cinema.

In Greece there is a dedicated following for Angelopoulos's work. But it should be added that as Greece's best-known and most critically acclaimed director abroad, Angelopoulos has, in contrast, often had to face indifference and opposition at home as well. Some Greeks interviewed, for instance, who greatly appreciated *The Travelling Players*, have accused Angelopoulos of being too uncompromising in exposing the darker corners of the Greek experience. Others admire his talent but on a very practical level say, "When you've worked hard all day, and you want to go to the cinema in the evening, it's hard to get into the frame of mind necessary to 'enjoy' the length and intensity of an Angelopoulos film."

Angelopoulos smiles when asked about such reactions. "I am in a very strange position in Greece," he comments. "I have fanatic enemies and fanatic followers. That's all that I can say!" (Horton, "National Culture" 29).

TWELVE CHARACTERISTICS OF ANGELOPOULOS'S CINEMA

> *History is not dead: it is only taking a nap.*
> (Theo Angelopoulos)

> *The best of them [writers/artists] are realistic, and paint life as it is, but because every line is permeated, as with sap, by the consciousness of a purpose, you are aware not only of life as it is, but of life as it ought to be, and that captivates you.*
> (Anton Chekhov)

Two shots. First: A desolate village appears on the screen in black and white as an unidentified narrator explains that this village in northern Epirus, near Albania, had a population of 1,250 in 1939 and 85 in 1965.

The second shot: what appears to be a jerky black-and-white silent film from the turn of the century. On the screen we see an actor playing Odysseus, climbing out of the sea, washed up at long last on the shore of Ithaca. He pauses and looks out at the camera and thus at us, "living at the end of the twentieth century," as the screenplay says for this moment.

Theo Angelopoulos has emerged as one of the most original voices in world cinema in a remarkable series of ten feature films made since 1970. That he remains virtually unknown in the United States despite so many international awards and a major retrospective at the Museum of Modern Art in New York in 1992 simply adds to the need for a study that attempts to account for the enduring importance of his work. For he is both a contemporary voice within Greek culture and a filmmaker within the context of world cinema sharing influences and affinities with individuals as divergent as Jean Renoir, Ozu, Tarkovsky, Jancsó, Antonioni, and the creators of the Hollywood musical, as we shall explore in chapter 3.

The two shots mentioned embrace his first feature, *Reconstruction* (1970), and his latest, *Ulysses' Gaze* (1995). But more important, they point to the duality of Angelopoulos's vision, which both "documents" (thus the documentary look and statistical sound track to the opening shot) and fictionalizes, alluding to and building on a Greek past (Odysseus as captured in a silent film at the beginning of the twentieth century). This particular tension between the image and its suggestive power, a realistic base and an effect of that which is beyond realism, can perhaps be most usefully described as a poetic realism. Such a term can help us account for the unusual style and content of Angelopoulos's uncompromising approach that continually, for instance, mixes echoes of history and myth, the individual and the group, the past and the present.

That history and myth cross in complicated and provocative ways in Angelopoulos's films is clear from the context of the silent Odysseus shot. The film-within-the-film is being screened in a bombed-out cinema in Sarajevo in 1995 while bombs burst around the building. And the person viewing that film is a Greek-American film director (Harvey Keitel) who has searched throughout the Balkans for this missing film, which he has been told was the first made in the Balkans. In a single shot, contemporary horror (the Bosnian war), individual destiny, myth (Odysseus), and the history of cinema (the first Balkan film) come together. (Note: This shot occurs in the screenplay to *Ulysses' Gaze* and indeed was made but, finally, not used in the film. Instead, this moment when Odysseus actually gazes into the camera and thus at us at the end of the twentieth century became the final shot of the cinematic centennial celebration film *Lumière and Company* (1995), in which thirty-nine directors from around the world were asked to shoot a fifty-two-second piece—the length of the first film ever made by the Lumière brothers—using one of their original cameras.)

Angelopoulos stands apart even within his own culture. We search in vain for the straightforward strong drama, comedy, and tragedy found in Jules Dassin's *Never on Sunday* (1960) or Michael Cacoyannis's *A Girl in Black* (1957), *Zorba the Greek* (1962), or *Iphigenia* (1978), or the riveting pace and simple dogmatism of a film such as Costa-Gavras's *Z* (1969). There is none of the bright blue cinematography and romantic stereotyping of Greece found in films such as *Mediterraneo* and *Shirley Valentine* in which Greece serves as a pastoral ideal for foreigners discovering true sexual liberation and personal happiness on sunbathed shores.

The Greece seen in Angelopoulos's films represents a very different perspective, focus, direction. The following twelve characteristics found in his work are not the only characteristics to be found. But they suggest points of entry that will be explored to various degrees throughout this text.

1. *Angelopoulos helps to "reinvent" cinema with each film because of his concern for cinema as an aesthetic as well as a cultural medium.* His films evoke powerful and essential cinematic questions beginning with, "What is an *image*?" And what does an image mean or suggest?

It is one of Angelopoulos's traits and, we might add, virtues that he does not "explain" or preach. The image is simply there, intriguing in its own right, open to multiple readings, and evoking a number of emotions. But clearly the filmmaker has orchestrated form and content to *invite* us or even *compel* us to go beyond the image itself and establish "meaning." As Nikos Kolovos has noted in his book-length study of these films, Angelopoulos believes in treating each image with "lucidité": like a poet, selecting his images carefully, but letting the image speak for itself (16).

Such a presentation of images suggests what W.J.T. Mitchell has described as the original concept of the image in his study *Iconology: Image, Text, Ideology*. Image, he explains, originally was understood in Greek, Hebrew, and Latin "not as 'picture' but as 'likeness,' a matter of spiritual similarity" (31). Exploring the history of religious meanings attached to images, Mitchell observes that by definition an image embodies a "tension between the appeals of spiritual likeness and material image" (35). Angelopoulos is setting forth no orthodox religious messages such as those described by Mitchell. But these remarks regarding a tension between the material reality of an image and something other (the spiritual or that which transcends the material world) do help us describe the effect on the viewer of Angelopoulos's cinematography, both in individual shots and in complete films.

A photograph implies likeness. But an image includes a sense of "difference from" at the same time that there is a similarity. The tree that appears at the end of *Landscape in the Mist* is clearly a tree in a misty landscape. But given the narrative that has gone before, we cannot help but see the tree as something much more powerful and important for the two young children in search of their father, and thus for us as well.

I have had the pleasure of sharing with a number of viewers their first Angelopoulos film. And the result is always the same: before talking about characters, ideas, or story, viewers wish to speak about the beauty and power of his images. We should mention that he has been blessed with one of the truly great cinematographers in the world, Giorgos Arvanitis, who has been with Angelopoulos from the very beginning and who is now in great demand throughout Europe. Thus, to be perfectly accurate, we should acknowledge the combined talents of Angelopoulos as director and Arvanitis as director of photography, for artists such as these who have worked so closely together for so long obviously share the creative act in ways of which either or both may not be completely aware.

Angelopoulos's respect for and fascination with the single frame has meant that he has developed a form of cinematic narration dependent on long, uninterrupted takes, often involving extended tracking shots. While the average American feature film is made up of six hundred to two thousand individual shots in a ninety-minute narrative, Angelopoulos characteristically uses fewer than one-tenth as many shots in the two to three hours of his films. His deliberate effort both to stretch out a shot and to leave it uninterrupted means, of course, that he calls on the audience not only to follow what is going on *but to be aware of the process of the unfolding of a moment or moments as they occur in time and space*. In an age of ever increasing rapidity of editing, in film, TV commercials, and MTV music videos, Angelopoulos's films force the audience to return to zero and see the moving image with new eyes. Critic Wolfram Schutte puts it this way: "His poetic medium is time. This allows the viewer to make his own images from what is projected on the screen—yes, it almost forces him to—while he remains critically aware of the technical means employed: the long shots, sequence shots, slow pans and long takes. They are scenes from a voyage through the world. Their complex structure sends the viewer on his own inner journey."

But we should view Angelopoulos's preoccupation with the "continuous image" on at least two other levels. First, one can consider his films as "silent" films. There is very little dialogue in his movies. The result is that we have extended moments when we must concentrate on the image *completely*. There is frequently also a strong musical score—in recent years done by the impressive Greek composer Eleni Karaindrou—for us to respond to in concert with the image before us. For instance, in *The Suspended Step of the Stork*, the camera tracks past a stationary train of open boxcars in northern Greece near the border. Karaindrou's score is richly orchestrated as we watch a different refugee family in the doorway of each boxcar. The image is like some endless modern fresco of unrelenting grief, with music adding powerfully to the effect. As we watch this continuous tableau, without dialogue, we "get" the scene Angelopoulos wishes to show us. We comprehend the environment in which the rest of his narrative will unfold as a story about borders/boundaries and barriers, personal and national, contemporary and ancient.

And we also keenly feel a pleasure in *the shot itself*, which has made it possible for us to see not only into the image but "through" it as well. Angelopoulos's depiction of the refugee condition thus far transcends the simple close-ups on CNN or ABC and contrasts with the personalized, dialogue-centered narratives that the American tradition of cinematic storytelling would point toward.

We can also note that Angelopoulos's vote for the continuous image is a ballot cast in the opposite direction from that developed by Soviet cinema, most obviously by Sergei Eisenstein and Dziga Vertov in their emphasis on montage. Music videos as well as television commercials are dedicated to fragmenting images shot at the viewer in ever increasing rapidity, and Hollywood films are also cut to what the studios feel is an attention-gripping pace.

Angelopoulos's films work against all of this, both in pace and in resistance to the fragmentation that montage demands by definition. Chapter 3 explores the influences on Angelopoulos's devotion to the imagistic language of film and suggests the implications of his film aesthetics.

2. *Angelopoulos has throughout his career been completely fascinated with history.* Of course since all of his films until *Ulysses' Gaze* have been made in Greece, the history depicted is Greek history. But as we shall see, while "factual" events are suggested—the German Occupation of Greece in *The Travelling Players*, for instance—Angelopoulos's use and (re)presentation of such events avoid any simple or traditional depiction of history. For his cinema leads us to question both what history itself is and what it means to be Greek or, for that matter, an individual within any state.

Chapter 2 is devoted to a detailed consideration of how Angelopoulos forces us to reconceptualize history as he has worked to present repressed and forgotten histories on the screen.

3. *Angelopoulos has a deep fascination with Greek myth and culture and the echoes of Greece's past: classical, Byzantine, and beyond.* The legends of Odysseus and his wanderings and of Agamemnon and his tragic homecoming are the two most frequently used motifs in Angelopoulos's films. The "players," for example, in *The Travelling Players* bear the names of figures in the *Oresteia* cycle, including Agamemnon, Clytemnestra, Orestes, and Electra. And Spyros, the old Greek communist who has been living in Russia for over thirty-five years since the civil war, finally, like Odysseus, returns home in *Voyage to Cythera*.

But visual "fragments" abound as well. Early on in the same film, a film director, Alexander, is discussing his new project, "Voyage to Cythera," while stagehands walk by carrying an "ancient" statue (horizontally, thus giving it an odd perspective). And when the outlaw dictator protagonist of *Megalexandros* is finally destroyed by a mob of his former followers, all that remains is a bust of Alexander the Great, as if some magical transfiguration had taken place. Chapter 1 contextualizes Angelopoulos's films from a Greek cultural perspective.

4. *We can also describe Angelopoulos's films as a cinema of meditation.* The deliberate effort to fly in the face of traditional cinematic form and narrative forces the spectator into the role of coauthor and covoyager as he or she must meditate on the images and events that unfold on the screen. The viewer must thus mediate among levels of reality and presentation that are neither "closed" nor totally mapped out. While Greek history and myth intertwine in often surprising and subtle ways in these films, no simplistic or reductionist meanings are given to their relations with or influences on individual destinies depicted. A character in *Mega-*

lexandros speaks a line that actually derives from a well-known poem by Greece's Nobel Prize–winning poet George Seferis: "I awoke with this marble head in my hands which exhausts my elbows and I do not know where to set it down." We feel strongly in Angelopoulos's films that Greek history and myth are a *presence* for the individuals we follow, but, more often than not, that presence points to an *absence* of cultural/historical connection, strength, continuity. For as Greek cultural critic Vasilis Rafalidis has noted in discussing Angelopoulos's involvement with Greek culture, "Greece is like a circle with many intersections and no center" (23). Viewers thus must do what Angelopoulos has obviously done—that is, not only must we experience various realities, but we must meditate on them. One feels this contemplative dimension within a film by Angelopoulos even more strongly as one begins to see more of his work.

Compare this approach, once more, to the dominant Hollywood cinema, which is quite clearly "action" based. But it is still not enough simply to say that even critically acclaimed Hollywood films such as *Thelma and Louise* or *Schindler's List* have "a lot going on" in them while, by comparison, very little ever "happens" in an Angelopoulos film. Rather, we should emphasize that the meditative quality of his work is a product of all of the characteristics outlined above and below, together with an unusual tension generated between what is present in the extended images we view and that which is absent from the screen.

A list of what we do *not* see or hear on the screen or throughout an Angelopoulos film is long. But primarily his ability to leave things out has the reverse effect of opening up his films for us to complete in our own minds. Again, the point of comparison is the traditional American film that presents us enough narrative and character information so that we feel we know everything by film's end.

We can be even more specific. Since Angelopoulos's films appear so different in every way from traditional narrative films, we too as viewers begin to experience topics and issues as well as characters and stories from a fresh perspective. This disruption of traditional perspectives thus creates the gap that can be bridged only by meditation. Each chapter explores some of the meditations his films evoke.

5. Angelopoulos has his own conception of "character." He is concerned with individuals, but his above mentioned interest in suggesting how history and myth cross or do not cross paths with individual destinies has led him to go beyond the concepts of psychology, which has been the basis of so much of Western experience this century. Hollywood's demand, for instance, for strong "character" is actually in direct line with Aristotle's call for clear motivation and cause-and-effect depiction of inner struggle centered on certain given conflicts that must be faced and resolved. Add to Aristotle Freud's contribution in our century to the conscious and unconscious workings of character and we realize how much of what Western cultures consider character has been shaped by these particular inner-directed perspectives.

Angelopoulos's depiction of character stands clearly at odds with two thousand years of character presentation in the West. In Angelopoulos's works, we have no self-conscious soul-searching dialogues, no simple "Freudian" motivations (Tom Cruise must become a "top gun" in *Top Gun* because we know his dead father was one. The mission and the need—to become a man—are never in doubt within such a Hollywood narrative).

Typical of Angelopoulos's presentation of character would be the returning husband—the Agamemnon figure—in his first feature, *Reconstruction*, a guest worker who has been away in Germany for many years like hundreds of thousands of other Greek men in the 1950s. We never hear a word of what he feels or thinks or believes. We simply see him return, share a meal with his family, and then we learn he has been murdered.

Angelopoulos presents character *from the outside*, forcing us to search, to study, to view other possibilities that make up an identity, an individuality, beyond those that have been more readily offered in the past. Greece is quite clearly the place where East meets West. And in Angelopoulos's cinema, the concept of character perhaps suggests a dominance of the East in that meeting. "The characters are human signs and not psychological figures," notes Greek critic Nikos Kolovos (20). We have only to think how dialogue-centered most films—even action movies—are, including especially Hollywood offerings, to realize, in contrast, how unusual Angelopoulos's *image-centered* work remains.

6. *In terms of location, Angelopoulos is purposely on an odyssey to explore his characters and narratives through the lens of rural Greece, especially the northern territories of Epirus (near Albania), Macedonia (near the former Yugoslavia), and Thrace (bordering both Turkey and Bulgaria).* Even more specifically, he is occupied with the past, present, and possible future of the Greek village.

This focus needs to be placed in context. Greece is a nation of almost ten million, almost half of whom live in one city, Athens. Greece, in a real sense, can thus be considered as two countries: Athens and everywhere else. It is important to realize that the gap between the two is great and growing with each year, each technological breakthrough, each contemporary urban glitch—pollution, crime, and the like—that appears on the horizon.

Angelopoulos has thus consciously turned his back on the city and culture he grew up in. For he is not from the north or from a village. He is in this sense always the outsider, the foreigner within his own country in search of what he cannot find in Athens or the culture he has known. He has put it this way: "The village is a complete world in miniature. The old Greek villages had a spirit, a life, full of work and play and festivity. . . . We need to return to those places to find much of what is still important, authentic to our lives" (interview, Athens, July 1993).

It is, therefore, with something deeper than mere pride that Angelopoulos enjoys telling those he meets that he has visited every village in mainland Greece.

7. *While Angelopoulos points to no simple truths, messages, or solutions, his cinema does suggest a desire to* transcend. *The Suspended Step of the Stork* ends with a series of telephone repairmen in yellow rain gear ascending poles and trying to connect or perhaps reconnect wires that go "across the border." And *Landscape in the Mist* ends almost mystically as the young girl and her brother, who have been searching throughout the film for their father whom they have never met, hug a tree "across the border" (they have been told their father is across the border in Germany).

History and myth, documentary and lyrical moments thus appear in Angelopoulos, forcing each viewer to recast everything else he or she has seen (or heard) in a new light. Near the end of *Landscape in the Mist*, in the port of Thessaloniki at dawn, the young girl and her brother, together with a former actor, Orestes, stand motionless as a huge marble hand with a missing index finger rises from the sea. At first it appears as some sort of miracle. But then we see it is being transported by a large military helicopter to an unknown destination. What is the hand? Where did it come from? Where is it going? What does it mean? Commentators are swift to suggest it does represent a classical past that no longer "connects" with a Greek present. And yet the *experience* of watching the hand emerge and rise creates something of a feeling of awe, of mystery, of *potential*.

Greek critic Yannis Bacoyannopoulos underscores the complex echoes in Greek cinema shared by Angelopoulos and perceived as definitely "foreign" to non-Greek viewers. He states that Greek cinema shows "an attachment to the eastern, Greek orthodox tradition, to folk and popular values, customs, songs, dances, together with a distant idealized recollection of antiquity" (15). It is just that in Angelopoulos's cinema, the tension between the form (and technology) of filmmaking and its cultural content is even greater. Thus the urge to transcend the gap and search for what Angelopoulos calls "a new humanism, a new way."

In the spirit of Chekhov's words quoted above, not only does Angelopoulos depict realities we can identify, but we also feel his films are permeated "by the consciousness of a purpose." This is the sense behind his feeling that cinema "may be the last important form of resistance to the deteriorating world in which we live." Theo Angelopoulos is a serious maker of films: "uncompromising" is the adjective often assigned to him by critics and audiences alike. This is to say that he is, ultimately, using cinema, working in the medium, with "other" intentions.

I remember being asked in Moscow in 1988 by eager "kino club" viewers who I thought the *spiritual* leader of American cinema was at the moment. Spielberg, Scorsese, Woody Allen, Spike Lee? Of course they had an answer for Soviet cinema: Andrei Tarkovsky. It was no use trying to explain that nobody in Los Angeles or Culver City would understand the question, let alone try to answer it.

But the question does originate from a very different concept of what "serious" cinema offers an audience. Within such a framework, Angelopoulos has served, if not as a spiritual leader, at least as an outspoken artist who has looked deeply into Greek culture and created films that follow Plato's dictum quoted in the beginning of Angelopoulos's latest film, *Ulysses' Gaze*: "To know a soul, a soul must look into a soul."

What that looking has brought forth for Angelopoulos and those who appreciate him is a vision of "the other Greece," the one that has been neglected, repressed, rejected, covered up. It is a Greece of rural spaces, long silences, mythic echoes, missed connections, winter landscapes, wanderers, refugees, actors without a stage or audience, lonely expressways at night, depopulated villages, cheap cafés, and crumbling hotel rooms. This is not the Greece on travel posters, of the Parthenon, or of a small country trying to hold its own in an emerging united European community.

The Greece in Angelopoulos's films is clearly "somewhere else," somewhere other than Athens and the centers of tourism. Furthermore, by extension, this "other Greece" is the other life that each of us would rather sweep under the rug, put under lock and key, turn our backs on.

8. Beyond Greece itself, Angelopoulos stands apart as a director and "contemporary citizen" deeply concerned with the past and present of the Balkans *as geographical, cultural, and spiritual territories.* He is painfully aware that the borders have always shifted in the Balkans. And he knows that it has never been easy to simply say one is "Greek." Robert D. Kaplan has been even stronger in his book, *Balkan Ghosts*, about the importance of the area: "Twentieth-century history came from the Balkans. Here men have been isolated by poverty and ethnic rivalry, dooming them to hate. Here politics has been reduced to a level of near anarchy that from time to time in history has flowed up the Danube into Central Europe" (xxiii).

Angelopoulos knows this and attempts to go deeper than history. "How many borders do we have to cross before we can get home?" asks the character in *The Suspended Step of the Stork*, a line repeated in his most recent film, *Ulysses' Gaze*. What Angelopoulos realizes clearly is that all of the countries that make up the Balkans share much of a similar past, particularly as it relates to having been under Turkish domination for hundreds of years. It is, therefore, no surprise that *Ulysses' Gaze*, made while the Bosnian war was still raging on and the "Macedonian Question" remained unresolved, embraces rather than avoids these territories. The plot brings its protagonist through northern Greece, Albania, Skopje (the Greek name for the Former Yugoslav Republic of Macedonia), Bulgaria, Romania, and Serbia, and ends in war-torn Sarajevo. As Angelopoulos has said:

> It's impossible for us to understand why, at the end of the twentieth century, we are killing each other. Do professional politicians anywhere really care? Many nations, including Greece, are climbing over the bodies of murdered innocent people—most recently in Greece I am referring to slaughtered Albanians who wish to leave home—in order to make some *political* advantage? I want a new politics in the world with vision. And this will not be a simple matter of balancing an economy and the military. It must be a new form of communication between people. (Horton, "National Culture" 29)

9. *Angelopoulos plays with notions of "reconstruction" to force us to consider the fictive boundaries of any presentation.* The Travelling Players begins with a closed theater curtain, then proceeds to open the curtain and our narrative to the "real" lives of the "players." *Voyage to Cythera* begins as a filmmaker's attempt to cast a film about an old man "like" his father and then quickly blurs reality and film as an old man (Manos Katrakis) appears who may or may not be the filmmaker's father. *Ulysses' Gaze* introduces many poignant moments drawn from the current crises in the Balkans, but it is centered on a search for a missing "first Balkan film." And *The Hunters* "reconstructs" the Greek civil war when the body of a Partisan is found frozen in the snow during a hunting trip in the 1970s. Even in the largely realistic *Landscape in the Mist*, many scenes point toward the "theatrical" or "unreal," such as an early scene in which a whole town empties into the street to stand motionless and transfixed as snow falls (as if they had never seen it before). And when the retired schoolteacher in *The Beekeeper* makes love with a young girl, they do so in an abandoned cinema, onstage, in front of a blank screen, while Alexander, the film director protagonist in *Voyage to Cythera*, makes love to his actress-mistress in her theater after it empties one evening. Simply put, we feel the fictive in reality and the reality of fiction simultaneously in Angelopoulos's work, with this "tag" note: while Angelopoulos often refers to Brecht and the need for an audience to think as well as feel in theater and cinema, we do not experience anything close to what could be called an "alienation effect" in Brechtian terms. To the contrary, the mix-

ing of theatricality and reality in his films often leads us into a deeper, fuller emotional bond with the film—one that, we could say, embraces our thinking mind as well.

10. *We can point to the Faulknerian interconnections among themes, characters, locations that run throughout his works.* The traveling players themselves show up in *Landscape in the Mist*—granted, much aged, but still traveling—and major characters named "Alexander" weave their way through films including *Megalexandros, Voyage to Cythera,* and *Landscape in the Mist.* And *Ulysses' Gaze* even begins with clips from *The Suspended Step of the Stork* and with a main character named, simply, "A," which naturally points us toward Angelopoulos himself. So much in Angelopoulos is about the breakdown of relationships, nations, beliefs, causes. The recycled figures, names, themes within Angelopoulos's work thus function to do what art has always been able to do: go beyond history itself to suggest connections, echoes, relationships. The main character in *Voyage to Cythera* is the film director Alexander and his sister is Voula. And in *Landscape in the Mist,* the young girl and boy are Voula and Alexander as well. Of course *Megalexandros* announces immediately that "Alexander" is not only an assumed name (the real name of the bandit-protagonist is never established) but a legend growing out of history. What connections, if any, are there among all of these? Angelopoulos remains silent, letting the accumulative effect of his films begin to form, for the viewer, one "metatext," one "megafilm" in which the echoes from one play off against those in another.

11. *In many ways, Angelopoulos's fascination with some accounting of and for history as crossed with culture and myth is a study in the nature and dangers of the violent abuse of power.* Put another way, all of his films suggest the dangers of a lack of tolerance and encourage acceptance of diversity in beliefs, attitudes, practices.

Beginning with a close look at the rigidity of village morality in *Reconstruction* and continuing with a depiction of various forms of fascism in *The Travelling Players,* Angelopoulos has shown, in each work, how so much suffering has been caused by a failure to reach out and accept or attempt to understand *difference.* Nowhere is this more apparent than in his most recent film, *Ulysses' Gaze,* which takes us to the heart of some of the most disturbing trouble of our times: Sarajevo, Bosnia, and the fierce struggle for survival in the midst of hatreds that appear to transcend all value systems.

Angelopoulos's decoding of fascism, furthermore, often takes startling original forms. In *The Travelling Players,* for instance, the young Electra invites a young fascist soldier into a hotel room (see chapter 5) and asks him to strip for her. Immediately, of course, we are struck by the gender reversal of the clichéd moment when men ask women to strip for their pleasure. But Angelopoulos takes the scene further. The soldier, not quite sure what is going on, nevertheless obliges Electra and strips, standing, finally, before her and thus before us with full frontal nudity.

This scene alone is memorable as a "first" in my recollection for Greek cinema. But the final impact comes as Electra simply begins to laugh, and we and the originally unsuspecting soldier begin to catch on that she has intentionally played out this moment to embarrass the young fascist.

Part of what is so fresh in this scene as a deconstruction of power is its purposeful ambiguity. Angelopoulos paints no simple stereotype of a macho fascist who abuses women. Quite the contrary, the soldier seems like a very ordinary young man and, in fact, shows some spark in his ability to play Electra's game (until, of course, he discovers he is the punch line of her joke!). Because we are not prepared for Electra's manipulation of the scene and we have no dialogue or follow up to "explain" it, we never learn exactly why she has decided to humiliate him in this way or exactly what it is she hopes to accomplish through this surprise action.

What emerges, finally, might be called "fascism with a human face." That is, Angelopoulos makes us aware that those who become fascists are not necessarily cruel tyrants or bullies, but that the lure of adventure and a paycheck, not to mention a uniform and a degree of power, may be enough to call up thousands or millions of young men.

The scene seems quite out of place, functioning merely as a diversion from the rest of the narrative in *The Travelling Players*, until, as we shall discuss in chapter 5, Electra is gang-raped by fascist plainclothesmen wearing masks. While Electra's action against the young soldier was individual and playful—mean, yes, but playful—the gang rape emerges as perhaps the single most horrifying event in the film on all levels including the sexual and the political.

12. Finally, much concerning Angelopoulos's films could be embraced in one question: how can one establish a community *where individuals flourish without fear and repression?* The Greek community in *Voyage to Cythera* cannot accept Spyros, the old exile, back home. Voula and Alexander in *Landscape in the Mist* are abused and betrayed by all communities they come in contact with in Greece and, finally, find solace in their own journey away from the communities they have known. And the film director in *Ulysses' Gaze* travels through several troubled Balkan nations (communities) trying to establish a different kind of community: a relationship with the past of the Balkan cinematic community. This foregrounding of the question of the individual and the community is, of course, at the center of the ancient Greek experience as well.

For what the Greeks have given the rest of the world is, in large part, a concern for the *polis*, that is, the city-state, and an ongoing democratic dialogue on how that concern can best be expressed.

The polis means, of course, the life of the group. "In all of my films there exists a *group*," Angelopoulos has said (Kolovos 18). This aspect of his character depiction is also important. *The Travelling Players* announces the group in the title, of course. But even in a film such as *The Suspended Step of the Stork*, which appears to be, on one level, simply one journalist's search for one missing Greek politician, the groups exist. The journalist, first of all, is not alone: he has brought a television crew with him to make this documentary. But the important group turns out to be that of contemporary refugees from all over the Balkans and the Middle East, huddled on the border, searching and waiting for a new life. In terms of character, the group appears faceless, a combined mass, which works against individuality. But paradoxically what we come to feel through Angelopoulos's unusual way of presenting groups is a sympathy for these people and a collective sense of individuality different from the ways we have experienced groups in the past. The group itself has a character that, rather than being faceless, is one of multiple faces.

Angelopoulos's films show us both the failure of past communities and the possibilities of newly formed groups in a world that both changes and remains the same.

At last we return to the *experience* of watching movies in general and Angelopoulos in particular.

During the summer of 1994, I arranged a screening in Athens of *Landscape in the Mist* for a group of American film students and professors who had never seen an Angelopoulos film before. When the final freeze-frame of the young girl and boy hugging a tree in an otherwise empty landscape faded from the screen, with Eleni Karaindrou's haunting score still playing in full Dolby sound, the house lights came on. We had originally planned to have a discussion of the film afterwards. But the group, almost all of whom were in tears, asked to postpone a discussion till later—that is, until they had time to reorient themselves and think over the strong emotional odyssey Angelopoulos's film had just released them from.

Milan Kundera in *The Art of the Novel* explains that he feels the purpose of a novel is to "discover what only the novel can discover" (5). Angelopoulos's films work in a similar fashion: they discover for us what only cinema can and, we should add, seldom does discover. That those discoveries can often be overwhelming, especially for audiences used to fast-paced, plot-oriented Hollywood fare, is demonstrated by the group's reaction to that summer morning's screening of *Landscape in the Mist*. It is the purpose of this book to explore a number of the discoveries Angelopoulos's films have brought to a world audience.

ANGELOPOULOS: THE MAN

There is an autobiographical level to Angelopoulos's work that goes beyond a Hitchcockian walk-through or an auteur's wink at his or her followers. It has to do, once again, with his whole concept of cinema as a "reconstruction." In his first feature, *Reconstruction*, he is one of the journalists who descend upon (or ascend upon, to be more accurate!) the mountain village to "cover" the murder story. In *Voyage to Cythera*, it is Angelopoulos's voice we hear every time the main character, the film director Alexandros, speaks, and in *Ulysses' Gaze*, the protagonist is once more a film director simply named "A" (in the script), clips of whose last film are heard, but not seen, in the opening scene. The film they are from? *The Suspended Step of the Stork*. Angelopoulos makes no press conference announcements about this level of his work.

In fact, he is extremely quiet about it. But it is a motif, a strand in his work that recurs so frequently that it does suggest a significant way in which he views his chosen medium of communication. On this level, we might say that there is a certain similarity between Angelopoulos and early Jean-Luc Godard, who used to describe his films as "essays on film," playing with the root meaning of "essay," "to attempt." Similarly, there is a sense in Angelopoulos's films that these are "attempts" to make films, to form a kind of communication, to follow through one way of "reconstructing" reality, imagination, history, and myth.

But what of Angelopoulos the person, the man?

He was born in Athens, on April 27, 1935, to a family of merchants. His father, Spyros, came from Ambeliona, a small village in the Peloponnese nestled between two ancient sacred places, Olympia and the temple of Apollo. He ran several small shops in Athens. Angelopoulos describes his father as "an extremely quiet man, and a very good man" (interview, Athens, July 1995) from whom he learned and appreciated much. But it was his mother, Katerina, he explains, who "ran the home and the family as a loving dictator or matriarch" (ibid).

He has a brother, Nikos, who has become a successful businessman and two sisters, Haroula, eleven years younger, and Voula, who died of an illness when he was thirteen, an event that changed his life. "I wasn't the same person afterwards," he says quite simply but with all the force of a memory that is still painful to recall (ibid.).

During World War II, politics and hunger affected his family as they did all Greeks. His father was condemned to death by ELAS, the Greek Communist Party, in 1944 during the German Occupation for not supporting their party. He can remember going with his mother to look for his father's body, wandering past many murdered Greeks. His father escaped, but only "by luck."

1. Theo Angelopoulos

After the Greek civil war, Angelopoulos studied law at the University of Athens from 1953 to 1957. He also wrote poems in a romantic vein influenced by Byron and later by George Seferis and Constantine Cavafy (see chapter 1). After his military service (1959–1960), he went to Paris in 1961 and studied with Claude Lévi-Strauss at the Sorbonne. He next entered IDHEC, the French film academy, from which he claims he was expelled for arguing with one of his professors. Nevertheless, he spent many hours in Langlois's Cinémathèque where an earlier generation— Truffaut, Godard, and others—had gained their film education as well. Perhaps his latest film, *Ulysses' Gaze*, got its seed, the search for an undeveloped first film in the Balkans, from Angelopoulos's first film experience. He shot a short film but was never able to get it back from the lab because he ran out of money. Angelopoulos describes this "lost" film as a black-and-white nod to film noir, that is, Hollywood crime films of the 1940s and 1950s, set in Paris.

He feels his political education traces back to 1964 when he was clubbed by the police at a pro-Papandreou (left-wing) rally and subsequently decided to stay in Greece and work for the next three years on the left-wing newspaper *Democratic Power*. Although identified as a radical, he was not imprisoned when the Greek colonels Papadopoulos and Pattakos established a dictatorship in 1967. With others who became the leading figures of a new wave of filmmaking in Greece, he formed a film community whose members met regularly to plan films that could get by the totalitarian censors and yet still have political "bite."

His first completed film was a twenty-three-minute production entitled *The Broadcast* shot over a two-year period, 1966–1968, or, put another way, begun before the Junta of 1967 and finished afterwards. This youthful black-and-white film is told with sly humor and a solid eye for detail, especially young faces captured in a variety of styles; he sees this as a wholly experimental film in which he tried out a lot of ideas. The film took so long to make partially because of his lack of funding and also because he depended on the help of friends as actors and as assistants in shooting. In fact, he describes this period in his life as that of belonging to the "free cinema," or experimental cinema, movement. Then, with *Reconstruction* in 1969–1970, his feature filmmaking career began.

He notes that his father died during the summer of 1974 when he was shooting *The Travelling Players*. For this reason he stopped production for some time before finishing the film. Angelopoulos adds that after his father's death, he went through an old trunk of his father's and found passionate letters he had written Angelopoulos's mother when they were courting. Never having been aware of his quiet father's literary interests, he was startled to find, as well, a French grammar book, a biography of Napoleon, Balzac's works, and other volumes. "I was so surprised," comments Angelopoulos, "because my father was a man who never spoke!" (interview, Athens, July 1995).

Later, for a number of years he lived with actress Eva Kotamanidou, who played Electra in *The Travelling Players*, among other roles. But since 1979, he has lived with Phoebe Economopoulou, who grew up in a Greek family very much involved in cinema production. She has served as line producer on all of his subsequent films, helping out particularly with finances and the running of the office, but also with many other aspects of production. They have three daughters—Anna, Katerina, and Elleni—who all appear in the New Year's Eve scene in *Ulysses' Gaze*.

P a r t O n e . . . . .

CULTURE, HISTORY, CINEMA

*What do our souls seek journeying
on the decks of decayed ships?*

(George Seferis, from "Mythical Story")

*Grant meaning to these appearances
good, yet not without evil.*

(The Night Watchman, Aeschylus's *Agamemnon*)

Chapter One

Cinema and the Borders of Greek Culture

There are times when fear is good.
(The Chorus in Aeschylus's *Eumenides*)

To become true to himself, he had to shed the superficial traits which in every country are seized upon and cultivated to make national dance groups and propagate national culture.
(Peter Brook, *The Shifting Point*)

ONE need not study Hitchcock's relationship to British culture to understand *Rear Window* or *Psycho*, or John Ford's Irish roots to appreciate *Stagecoach* or *The Searchers*. But some filmmakers, artists, and writers need to be understood in the context of their cultures if their works are to be appreciated on a more than superficial level. It is difficult to understand Luis Buñuel's cine-surrealism without an awareness of his Spanish small-town, quasi-medieval Catholic upbringing, and though we can laugh at Woody Allen movies without a grasp of New York Jewish culture and humor, we laugh even more if we do have some insight into Woody's cultural background.

Angelopoulos belongs to this latter group. Compare Angelopoulos, in his films' overall relationship to Greek culture, to a director critics have often mentioned in discussing his work, Andrei Tarkovsky, whose immersion is in Russian culture. Each stands as a major filmmaker, recognized for going beyond the conventional cinema in any country to establish his own distinct voice. The striking originality of each forces us to reconsider our whole notion of both cinema and the way we view the world. And each is taken as speaking through and about his particular culture. Furthermore, each has remained so distinct that there can be no close followers or imitators.

But the differences between these two filmmakers are also clear. Tarkovsky tried several genres in different countries. While *Andrei Rublov* and *The Mirror* feel completely "Russian," for instance, *Nostalgia* was made in Italy, *Sacrifice* in Sweden. *Solaris* offered Tarkovsky's meditation on sci-fi, while *Stalker* becomes an abstract morality tale with futuristic implications. All of Angelopoulos's films, in contrast, have been made in and about Greece, with the recent "expansion" seen in *Ulysses'*

Gaze, which travels beyond the borders of Greece into the neighboring Balkan nations.

To more clearly appreciate Angelopoulos's accomplishment, let us examine how he has reflected his country's ancient, Hellenistic, Byzantine, and Turkish Occupation cultures, as well as its modern, contemporary, and folk cultures, to create films that bring forth "the other Greece."

Byzantine Culture and Iconography in Angelopoulos's Vision and Visual Style

> *You cannot help but be influenced by a place and its culture when you grow up there, especially at a particular time, as I did, when the church was an important part of my cultural (not necessarily religious) life.*
> (Theo Angelopoulos)

What strikes one most immediately in an Angelopoulos film is the visual composition and duration of individual shots. While it is possible to speak of other cinematic influences on this visual style (see chapter 3), Angelopoulos is in significant ways making use of the long tradition of Byzantine iconography. Angelopoulos acknowledges these influences. In fact, he remarks that *Megalexandros* (1980) in particular was "completely a Greek Orthodox or Byzantine work, because it is constructed on many elements of the Orthodox liturgy, combining music, ritual and the catharsis through blood. And of course the role of the icon in all of this" (Horton, "National Culture" 30). Thus the need to more carefully consider this "Byzantine connection."

The period least well known or understood by those outside of Greece is the thousand-year-long span of the Byzantine Empire and its subsequent influence. One might expect to see a study of Angelopoulos's cultural roots begin with the classical period. But "ancient Greece" is a more distant influence on Greeks today. On a day-to-day basis, the traditions that are strongest for contemporary Greeks are those handed down from Byzantium. For this empire, which held sway longer than any other empire in history, was a multinational, multiracial network spanning the Balkans, Turkey, and much of the Middle East. What made the empire cohere for so long was the strength of the Greek language, the Orthodox religion, and the individual nuclear family (Kazhdan). And for the almost four hundred years of Turkish rule that followed the collapse of Constantinople, the "capital" of Byzantium, in 1453, these three ingredients—language, family, and religion—provided Greeks with a purpose, a center, an identity. Furthermore, it is so to this day, though the pressures of contemporary world culture—especially American pop culture with its related consumerism—have become, along with Balkan political unrest, unsettling signs of the times eroding all three cornerstones.

Add to the above considerations the fact that the empire was basically constructed of small households united as small villages in the countryside, far from The City (Constantinople) or any city for that matter. Except for the special few living in the Polis (as Constantinople was known), most were considered "country folk." The gap therefore between city and village life was at least as great as the one that exists today between Athens and the typical Greek village.

The "Byzantine" echoes in Angelopoulos are numerous. Like inhabitants of the Byzantine Empire of old, Angelopoulos's characters come from across or near a variety of borders. And though, in his films, silence itself has for the most part replaced speech, the Greek language is the language of communication among these various peoples despite their various origins. Families, broken and dysfunctional as they may be, from *Reconstruction* to *The Suspended Step of the Stork*, are at the heart of Angelopoulos's narratives, as they were (see below) in the world of myth and legend. Needless to say, as in Byzantine times and as during the subsequent Turkish domination, Angelopoulos's figures live in villages and small towns in the countryside.

Finally, while his films are not Orthodox or religious in any formal sense, Angelopoulos has been influenced by the Orthodox tradition of icon painting. Angelopoulos's inclusion of "magical" moments and unexplained phenomena, for instance, suggests the Orthodox tradition. Robert D. Kaplan helps us understand how different Western religions and the Orthodox faith are in their approaches to spiritual experience: "While Western religions emphasize ideas and deeds, Eastern religions emphasize beauty and magic" (25). The phrase "beauty and magic" well describes many of the most memorable moments in Angelopoulos's works, and without an understanding of how "Eastern" such a perspective of conception and composition is, the full effect of his films will be missed.

Annette Michelson has convincingly demonstrated that some of Soviet cinema, especially in its early years, can be seen as strongly influenced by Russian Orthodox iconography together with the religious implications that go with such an influence. In particular she has explored how Dziga Vertov's *Three Songs of Lenin* (1934) derives from Russian icons depicting the mourning and adoration of the dead Savior—with Lenin, the revolutionary "savior" in the place of Christ.

Angelopoulos's similar debt to the Byzantine Orthodox iconic tradition is not apparent immediately. But like the overall effect of his films, it emerges quietly yet steadily for those aware of the tradition. Let us focus on its contribution to *The Travelling Players*.

Consider the framing of the traveling players (fig. 2) by Angelopoulos alongside the Byzantine mosaics from Palermo and the Cathedral of Cefalu of Christ Pantocrator. Of course superficially the film and the mosaics are a study in contrast: the mosaics are depictions of spiritual power while the traveling players appear as simple folk of simple means. Yet the *concept of presentation* is the same.

In Byzantine art, figures are generally presented in such flat or two-dimensional poses that de-emphasize action and the dramatic. Otto Demus, the eminent Byzantine art historian, has noted that Byzantine art makes its appeal "to the beholder not as an individual human being, a soul to be saved, as it were, but as a member of the Church, with his own assigned place in the hierarchical organization" (6). Thus every aspect of Byzantine art is subject to a three-part doctrine of images. As Demus observes, this doctrine holds that if each picture is done in the "right manner," it is a magical image of the prototype and so has an identity with it; the image of a holy person is worthy of worship and respect; and every image has its place in a continuous hierarchy.

According to such beliefs, the "correct" way to depict a holy person is frontally, for this is the way we most clearly come to recognize and thus identify with the subject. Angelopoulos presents his actor-characters in *The Travelling Players* with the same respect for clarity and frontal depiction and with the same middle-distance "shot." "Everything must be clear for the beholder to perceive" (251), notes Demus.

Furthermore, Byzantine art de-emphasizes background to highlight the figures presented but also to separate the subjects further from "worldliness" (in most mosaics, the background is a simple gold). Angelopoulos's characters are in no way religious figures. His whole point is that they are representatives of common men and women though their names reflect mythical and ancient aristocrats. But Angelopoulos similarly isolates his characters in space so that they stand out both as a *group* (our first impression) and as the individual members of the group that they are. The pale, bland blues and grays of the sky in these shots help to etch the foregrounded figures more clearly in such a Byzantine-influenced style.

The lack of dramatic tension in Byzantine art was a further effort to suggest the spiritual as opposed to the worldly. Again, while Angelopoulos's figures share a similar disinterest in the dramatic (all the more ironic since they are actors!), his purpose differs from that of the Orthodox tradition. Such a distancing effect from the everyday world of action invites us to consider their lives on a more reflective level, beyond the world of passion, action, drama, and strife.

2. *The Travelling Players*: the troupe seen in a "Byzantine icon" lineup in the snow

The environment in which these characters function is violent enough. What Angelopoulos allows the viewer is the same respite from the world of everyday events that the Byzantine church allowed its members through its icons, frescoes, and mosaic patterns and programs (related series of biblical stories and figures). In this sense, this Greek film—*The Travelling Players*—like the Greek church, is not a *retreat* from life but a means of *transcending* the continual stimulation and confusion of daily "history." Both allow the individual a chance to gain a perspective on his or her life.

Furthermore, the parallels between film and mosaic composition seem obvious but worth reviewing. A film is the sum of its individual shots as a mosaic is constituted by its tesserae—the small individual squares used for composition in mosaic building.

Beyond the framing of individual shots in *The Travelling Players*, there is the structuring of scenes in both Byzantine art and Angelopoulos's film to create a program, which we shall consider in chapter 5.

Finally, we should consider *duration* and the Byzantine iconic tradition. Viewed from the Byzantine perspective, Angelopoulos's extremely long takes, often lasting up to ten minutes, suggest the "continuous" relationship between Byzantine art and the observer: one could stand and gaze at an icon, a program, or a scene as long as one wished. In this sense it was the observer who controlled how long his or her experience would last. While a viewer in cinema is locked into the forward flow of images, the lack of classical editing and traditional narrative film pacing seen in Angelopoulos's work means that his films are unique in allowing audiences time to "look around" within each scene as they please. Such a lack of narrative drive results in the establishment of a more personal and contemplative relationship between the film and the viewer, much like that between the observer and the icons in an Orthodox setting.

Even with so many similarities, the skeptical filmgoer may feel that the parallels between Byzantine iconography and Angelopoulos's cinema are more fanciful or coincidental than real. Granting the possibility of such lingering doubt, I offer a further dimension that I suggest links the two. In *The Travelling Players*, but even more strongly in *The Hunters*, death and the ritual need to transcend it are represented with echoes of Orthodox art and ritual.

In the Orthodox tradition, the Resurrection has always played a greater role than has the Nativity. For the Byzantines, it was Christ's victory over death that was most memorable. For this reason, Easter has always been a more significant celebration than Christmas. Likewise, especially in rural Greece, the rituals connected with death are detailed and elaborate. "Christos anesti" (Christ is risen) is the joyful cry of the Orthodox congregation down through the ages at the culmination of the midnight liturgy on Easter Saturday each year.

Death, Ritual, and Resurrection

The power of the Orthodox faith is best exhibited in the Easter service and the rituals of death. The artwork on the walls and in the dome, the incense burning throughout the church, the haunting effect of the Byzantine chants and the light of candles flickering throughout all add up to a "magical" experience that lifts one beyond the triviality of self, society, history, and even life. Rebecca West has captured well the logic and feeling of the Orthodox orientation: she explains that because the empire was continually invaded by barbarians and fellow Christians alike, the Byzantine "genius" "turned away from speculative thought to art, and its Church preserved its dogma without developing it and concentrated its forces on the glory of the Mass which gave a magic protection against evils that were unknown as well as those that were known" (641). But it must be stressed how unlike Western societies this orientation of Byzantium is. For the Byzantines, their religion, including Christ's triumph over death, was expressed primarily through visual and aural effects rather than through the written word of the Bible and biblical exegesis. But the particular emphasis is on the visual. The artwork and the liturgy become the "text," serving the function performed by written dogma in Western European religions. The celebration of Christ's death and resurrection thus becomes the most important of all the liturgies, for it is through this "magic" that personal salvation is possible.

Angelopoulos's *The Hunters* (1977) provides a good case study of how such rituals are reflected in his work. In that film, a group of hunters in the 1970s must decide what to do with a "Partisan" who appears to have been killed in 1949 but whose body is miraculously preserved so that he seems to be quite recently dead. The film becomes a biting commentary on the hunters, who represent a cross section of 1970s Greece in political as well as social terms because of their inability to decide what to do with or about the body. Taking the Byzantine tradition into consideration as outlined above, we can see Angelopoulos's film from yet another perspective. The bearded Partisan has a Christ-like appearance, and his placement on a table in the hunting lodge as the center of attention throughout the film both echoes and parodies the Mourning of Christ in Byzantine art and the Orthodox tradition. These hunters are not in mourning so much as in acute embarrassment: how can they cover up a past they thought had ended after the Greek civil war?

In short, there is no possible resurrection in Angelopoulos's sequel to *The Travelling Players*. The body is returned to the spot where it was found in a snowy landscape; the circularity of the narrative resembles a Byzantine program, which "circles" the interior of the church. Instead of the "magic" of the Byzantine liturgy, which protects believers against known and unknown fears, we see a series of scenes acted out in front of the corpse in a manner that is, like Byzantine art, half realistic, half stylized, and thus symbolic. And as Christ is the center of attention in an Orthodox church, so the corpse is the main presence in Angelopoulos's film.

While Angelopoulos's central metaphor is quite apparent, many of the ironies of the situation are, as in *The Travelling Players*, much more subtle. For instance, it is possible to read in Angelopoulos's images a degree of hope and resurrection. While the Greek Partisan-Marxist cause met a final "death," that death has still not been acknowledged properly, fully, ritually. Old communists have often sold out while neofascists and the wealthy continue to exploit others as they enjoy themselves at the expense of their once strongly felt political beliefs. Still, the reality of the corpse with its fresh blood (a miracle!) exists to haunt them all. And thus it becomes "resurrected" in their memories. What matters for us is that Angelopoulos is, like Vertov and the early Soviet filmmakers, playing off of a rich and complex religious tradition both for effects of form and to suggest meanings that echo these traditions while establishing their own resonances.

The Greek tradition is particularly rich in death rituals. While we have previously established the role of death and resurrection for the Byzantine tradition, we need now to focus even more sharply on the Greek rural tradition, which is a particular branch of the vast Byzantine Orthodox faith and one with which Angelopoulos is concerned since his films take place almost entirely in rural Greece.

Loring M. Danforth builds on various anthropological perspectives concerning death to better understand the role of death rituals in rural Greece. He documents these rituals as a "passage" between two worlds. He not only captures the format of the initial funeral service with all of the events leading up to it, but he devotes considerable attention to the second phase of mourning, the "rites of transition" (32).

Within this framework, *The Hunters* represents a bitterly ironic corruption of the traditional rites of passage from life to death as an eternal finality. The exhumation process and ceremony are particularly significant for the rural Greeks as a means of both accepting the finality of death and reorienting themselves toward their own lives again. In *The Hunters*, the rituals of mourning and death become a sham. There can be no traditional mourning since the body has not decomposed. Clearly the transitional stage of death has not been completed. Instead of taking this preservation as a kind of miracle, as people would have done in days gone by, the living hunters think only of themselves and the threat that the corpse of the past revolutionary spirit poses for their careers, lifestyles, and present nonrevolutionary conservative ideologies.

We will meet other "resurrections" in our study that similarly appear ambiguous, hopeful, and tinged with the magic Rebecca West found so much a part of these rituals. After all, even the effort to "reconstruct" a life and a death in *Reconstruction* can be viewed as a resurrection. *The Travelling Players* echoes rural ritual as the troupe stands over Orestes' grave and begins to applaud as if his spirit had somehow triumphed or at least escaped the tribulations the rest of the group must continue to endure. Spyros's dance on the grave of his old Partisan friend in *Voyage to Cythera* is purely an expression of personal grief and joy shaped through rural folk ritual and custom dating back centuries and centuries. And the final viewing of the "missing" early Balkan film at the end of *Ulysses' Gaze* is a resurrection of a text long since thought "dead."

ANGELOPOULOS AND THE HERITAGE OF CLASSICAL GREECE

Angelopoulos's films are filled with echoes and fragments from Greece's long classical past. The intersection with such a past occurs on three levels:

1. visual cues such as that of the huge marble hand rising from the sea in *Landscape in the Mist*;

2. the verbal, as in the use of the George Seferis quotation, "I awoke with this marble head in my hands which exhausts my elbows and I do not know where to set it down"; and

3. the narrative, as in the use of the *Oresteia* cycle of Aeschylus and Homer's *Odyssey* in many of his films.

On the most obvious level, the invocation of such a past suggests a contrast with a supposedly glorious "golden age." Of course, such a contrast emphasizes discontinuity with the past and underscores the insignificance of the modern and contemporary. Much contemporary classical study, however, has supported a considerably more realistic view of the classical age.

No simple golden age ever existed. By no means a unified culture expressing continuity of its heritage, classical Greece, like Greece of any period, was characterized by its attempt to balance—usually unsuccessfully—diverse influences with a constant threat of a complete breakdown of all order: social, political, religious, personal. The so-called golden age, we are now aware in our multicultural, multiethnic world, was to a certain degree the willful invention of European scholars, particularly of the nineteenth century, who bypassed fifteen hundred years of Greek culture to give their own interpretation of what they "saw" of ancient Greece.

What actually existed was a much more fragile culture in which the irrational powers of Dionysos ruled more frequently than the ordering forces of Apollo, to paraphrase Nietzsche's descriptive analysis of the Greek "tension of opposites" in *The Birth of Tragedy*. The description of Greek tragedy could serve equally well to describe the classical period: "The rationality of the form of Greek tragedy only sets off the irrationality that it reveals just below the surface of myth, cult, and other social forms" (Segal 25).

In this sense, we can say that Angelopoulos reflects visions of the irrational but that what has changed particularly is the *form* of presentation. Greek tragedy is characterized by its concise clarity and brevity. Each classical tragedy, for instance, took less than two hours to present. Angelopoulos's cinematic narratives, in stark contrast, are often double the length and offer no direct access to the characters' inner world such as is given by the characters and the chorus in tragedy.

Even here, however, we must be careful not to suggest a simple contrast between "then" and "now" as reflected in Angelopoulos's films. For he himself is very conscious that his use of off-camera action is influenced by Greek tragedy. The actual murder in *Reconstruction* occurs inside the house while we focus on the exterior. The rape of the young girl, Voula, in *Landscape in the Mist* occurs inside the back of the truck while we remain outside by the highway.

Angelopoulos did not have to work with his classical past. As a filmmaker and thus as a storyteller, he could easily have opted to construct narratives that completely avoided any allusions to or reflections of a classical past. But he has not chosen to do so. Clearly he feels very strongly that he is not just a filmmaker but a *Greek* filmmaker. As such he cannot help but be in dialogue with his culture. His "Greekness," however, he views as a characteristic that helps his films transcend their national culture. "I feel the deeper one goes into one's particular place— Greece for me—the more universal it will become for others," he comments. "What I don't like are those films that try to please everyone with a little bit of everything, Hollywood included, but which wind up being nothing in particular. We call such films Euro-puddings!"

WHERE TO LAY THE MARBLE HEAD?

The quotation of the Nobel Prize–winning Greek poet George Seferis, which Angelopoulos uses in *Megalexandros*, targets not only the modern Greeks' cultural "problem" but also that of Greeks stretching all the way back to the classical period: "I awoke with this marble head in my hands which exhausts my elbows and I do not know where to set it down." With such a long and varied history and richly diverse heritage of story, song, drama, art, music, poetry, architecture, religion, how does one make use of and sense of that tradition?

It is worth quoting the entire poem because of the issues raised and because Angelopoulos has made it clear that Seferis is his favorite poet. The poem is part of a twenty-four-poem series entitled "Mythical Story," which, taken as a whole, suggests "an effort to find contemporary significance in the long heritage of Greece for a modern Greek poet writing with a knowledge not only of his own country's past, but of the twentieth century's record of two world wars and other disasters" (Horton, "The Poetry of George Seferis and Constantine Cavafy" 38). Labeled simply as number 3, the poem begins with a quotation from Aeschylus's *The Liba-*

tion Bearers, "Remember the bath by which you were slain," a line that, of course, evokes the Agamemnon myth discussed below in this chapter. The poem then follows:

> I awoke with this marble head in my hands
> which exhausts my elbows and I do not know where to set it down.
> It was falling into the dream as I was coming out of the dream
> so our lives joined and it will be very difficult to part them.
>
> I look at the eyes: neither open nor closed.
> I speak to the mouth which keeps trying to speak.
> I hold the cheeks which have passed beyond the skin
> I have no more strength.
>
> My hands disappear and come back to me mutilated.
>
> (Translation by Edmund Keeley and Philip Sherrard,
> from *Four Greek Poets* 44)

Angelopoulos has verified that the spirit of his films absolutely reflects the spirit of this poem. As Seferis suggests, the modern Greek is surrounded by bits and pieces and echoes of the past. But what to do with them? What significance to give them? And, we should note, both Seferis and Angelopoulos suggest that this question has arisen not in a waking reality but in a dream, and that the result of this metareality has been that the past and the present consciousness have joined, "and it will be very difficult to part them."

In comparison, we in the United States can point to a very brief history and a seemingly shorter cultural heritage (of course, our scope broadens immediately when we include the Native American traditions and those of the divergent ethnic groups that inhabit our country). Thus it is no wonder that one of our major poets, T. S. Eliot, originally from St. Louis, spent a lifetime acquiring a European-based cultural heritage that he could not find in his native city or state or country.

The situation for the Greeks has been the opposite. There is so much that reminds them of the past in so many ways that each must make his or her own peace with how to interact with that past in the present and in planning a future, and *there is no one unified way to see or use this past.*

Consider the Greek myths as we have received them from Homer and classical tragedy. The legends of Odysseus and Agamemnon existed in a variety of forms before they were "fixed" in the literary genres—oral epic and tragedy—that have come down to us. Furthermore, these ancient stories predate the authors by many centuries. Homer composed his epics about a culture that had ceased to exist hundreds of years before him, and of course over three hundred years separated Homer from fifth-century Athens and the classical period of drama, architecture, philosophy, and art when his epics were finally collected and written down.

Remember, too, that fifth-century Athens was a democracy (granted, a limited democracy at best, since women and slaves did not vote) that did not favor the system of monarchy and blood feuds highlighted in the myths of King Odysseus and King Agamemnon and the others. The center of life in fifth-century Athens was the polis—the city—and the health, commerce, and culture of that city. The Greek myths, in contrast, were about family feuds: Zeus and his family on Olympus, and, on earth, the various royal families. Thus as Charles Segal has suggested, the myths as represented in the tragedies perform a very complex function for the audience of the polis. As he notes, "the hero of Greek tragedy stands at the point where the boundaries of opposing identities meet" (34).

At the center of Greek myths and tragedy itself lie ambiguity, destruction, chaos. Segal writes that "Greek tragedy is remarkable for its ability to face the disintegration of the cosmic, social, or psychological order without losing all sense of coherence" (45). The myths suggest, put another way, what happens when the hierarchy of power embracing nature, god, and man comes unstrung. For Angelopoulos, that sense of ambiguity and disintegration is also present, but amplified many times over, for there is no suggestion of any clear contact with "the gods," and nature, while a presence, is an indifferent one.

Mythic, Lyric, and Historical Truth

Bruno Snell, in *The Discovery of the Mind: The Greek Origins of European Thought*, makes it clear that for the ancient Greeks, the oral epics of Homer were taken as "true." History in any form did not exist, and, in a culture without a written language but with an oral tradition, the stories told contain "mythic truth": the characters are known, remembered, believed in, and passed on from generation to generation. Homer's form of epic poetry gave myths a special form for that "truth." Once tragedy developed, hundreds of years later, poetry became dramatic, lyrical, and, above all else, *representational*. Audiences knew that it was not really Agamemnon on the stage or Medea in Euripides' play, but an actor impersonating that character. Truth at that point took on a different meaning, becoming "lyrical truth": true in its sound and beauty and *suggestive* powers but different from mythic or epic truth when the thing or person spoken about could exist only in one's imagination.

Once history began to be recorded, as we shall discuss in chapter 2, yet another form of "truth" came into being: that of the witnessed event or word. Thus by the time drama flourished in Athens, "truth" existed in a number of forms that might best be described as overlapping rather than as existing in conflict or competition with each other.

In our own time, we are aware that cinema itself offers yet another level of "truth": that of the visual image (and sound) projected. Clearly cinema is a representational medium, for the figures represented are not actually present. In this sense, "cinema truth" exists as a special form of "lyrical truth" with the power to evoke "mythic truth" as well, for while in theater there are actually actors in a space before an audience, such is not the case in cinema. In terms of Greek culture, therefore, cinema occupies a particularly evocative position between the power of oral epic to call up the elemental force of myths and that of drama to create strong lyrical moments.

Angelopoulos seems, in his constructions, framing, scope, and execution of each film, quite aware of how to make cinema work for him to express these various levels. And of the two—lyric and mythic—I would say he favors the mythic simply because he mutes all performances so that drama as we conceive it in terms of our Western theatrical tradition barely exists or, in many scenes, does not exist at all. In *Landscape in the Mist*, for instance, when the young girl and her brother are walking along a highway in northern Greece, we are left to consider these two figures *as simply a young girl and young boy walking in a vast, dark landscape*. The minimalism involved—no speech, little action—leads us to dwell upon the scene in our own minds, to open it up to interpretation, meditation, exploration, and thus to consider the mythic dimensions of these two characters' lives.

Consider one other view of the role of myth. Claude Lévi-Strauss has explained that myths are culturally charged narratives embodying basic contradictory value systems that cannot be resolved. Myths have power, therefore, because they touch our deepest fears and needs and give them narrative shape and thus consciousness. But we are not always conscious of how myth works and in what ways certain myths overlap. There is thus a large degree within Greek myth systems of what Charles Segal calls "meta-literary consciousness" (50). On this level, myths offer what can be described as "more or less subconscious patterns or deep structures or displaced forms which tales of a given type share with each other" (Segal 52).

"Meta-literary consciousness" applies well to cinema, for in going beyond the spoken word to present images within specific contexts, films can imply and evoke myths *without* speaking.

THE JOURNEY HOME

Given the context suggested above, what can we say about the legends that Angelopoulos draws upon most—Agamemnon and Odysseus? They are both about men returning from war, searching for home, *nostos*. The difference in the traditional narratives is, however, that Agamemnon returned from Troy relatively swiftly to meet his death at his wife's hand, while Odysseus had a true "odyssey"—a journey lasting years because it was an exile (he was condemned by the sea-god Poseidon and held against his will by the goddess Calypso)—before reaching home and successfully reestablishing himself as a king, father, and husband.

The journey and the need for a home—personal, political, aesthetic, historical, and geographic—stand at the center of each Angelopoulos film. *The Travelling Players* announces the journey in its title, as does *Voyage to Cythera*, an island that, as it turns out, is never reached in the film. And so on for each of his films, for the ancient myths of Greece simply mirror the timeless reality of Greeks: they have been, are, and, one suspects, always will be a nation of travelers, either by choice or by chance. This central narrative pattern and theme in Angelopoulos's films thus echoes a basic mythic and historic pattern for him and his culture.

ODYSSEUS AND THE DIFFICULTIES OF HOMECOMING

The homecoming of Odysseus after the Trojan War as captured in Homer's *Odyssey* has occupied many authors', painters', and musicians' attention over the years. In our century alone we need only mention James Joyce's *Ulysses* and, in Greece, Nikos Kazantzakis's *The Odyssey: A Modern Sequel*, which literally picks up where Homer left off and traces Odysseus's restless wanderings past Greece through Africa and on, at journey's end, to the furthermost frozen tip of Antarctica. W. B. Stanford documents in his fine study, *The Ulysses Theme*, several major reasons why the story has had such resonance over the centuries.

Of more immediate importance to modern Greeks would be the much loved poem of the Alexandrian poet C. P. Cavafy, a contemporary of T. S. Eliot, whose "Ithaca" many Greeks today know by heart:

> When you start on your journey to Ithaca,
> then pray that the road is long,
> full of adventure, full of knowledge.
> Do not fear the Lestrygonians

and the Cyclops and the angry Poseidon.
You will never meet such as these on your path,
if your thoughts remain lofty, if a fine
emotion touches your body and your spirit.
You will never meet the Lestrygonians,
the Cyclops and the fierce Poseidon,
if you do not carry them within your soul,
if your soul does not raise them up before you.

Then pray that the road is long.
That the summer mornings are many,
that you will enter ports seen for the first time
with such pleasure, with such joy!
Stop at Phoenician markets,
and purchase fine merchandise,
mother of pearl and corals, amber and ebony,
and pleasurable perfumes of all kinds,
buy as many pleasurable perfumes as you can;
visit hosts of Egyptian cities,
to learn and learn from those who have knowledge.

Always keep Ithaca fixed in your mind.
To arrive there is your ultimate goal.
But do not hurry the voyage at all.
It is better to let it last for long years;
and even to anchor at the isle when you are old,
rich with all that you have gained on the way,
not expecting that Ithaca will offer you riches.

Ithaca has given you the beautiful voyage.
Without her you would never have taken the road.
But she has nothing more to give you.

And if you find her poor, Ithaca has not defrauded you.
With the great wisdom you have gained, with so much experience,
you must surely have understood by then what Ithacas mean.
        (Translated by Rae Dalven, from *The Complete Poems of C. P. Cavafy*)

Several features are prominent in Cavafy's version of the *Odyssey*. He
has, first of all, presented it as a "reconstruction" since the narrator is
clearly an older person who has already completed (or almost completed)
his or her journey. And this modern odyssey is an internalized one rather
than an actual trip. "Ithaca" itself, therefore, becomes a metaphorical
space, not an actual place. Finally, Homer's theme—that of a man who
wishes to get home but is prevented—is reversed: "Pray that the road is

long." This odyssey becomes self-willed, self-initiated, and self-controlled as well.

Angelopoulos does not choose Odysseus figures because of an appreciation of Cavafy. But I have discussed this Alexandrian Greek's contribution since it illustrates how central to the Greek experience the concept of the troubled journey is, and suggests that the modern poet feels both the pleasure and the necessity of altering Homer's view. Angelopoulos's use of the Odysseus theme suggests a similar allegorical and individualistic artistic approach.

Of course Angelopoulos's most overt nod to Odysseus is in *Ulysses' Gaze* as we have a literal representation of Odysseus in the final scene, captured in the first film ever made in the Balkans. But this literal representation is directly related to the main narrative of the film: the film director protagonist's odyssey in search of his cinematic Ithaca, which takes him throughout the troubled contemporary shifting Balkan borders and cultures.

Similarly, Spyros, the returning old communist in *Voyage to Cythera*, and the old schoolteacher played by Marcello Mastroianni in *The Beekeeper* (see fig. 3) are on odysseys in search of home. As we shall see, in each case, the return to the physical location of home ends either in rejection and exile once more (*Voyage to Cythera*) or in death on the protagonist's home island (*The Beekeeper*).

The Suspended Step of the Stork and *Landscape in the Mist* echo the Odysseus theme, but as seen from the major subplot of Homer's epic: Telemachus's search for his father. Homer thus offers a double tale: the father's return and a coming-of-age tale for the child. To become a man, the son must find his father, receive his blessing, and help his father complete his homecoming. It is part of the deep pleasure and satisfaction of Homer's tale that all of these narrative strands are successfully completed, as in a fairy tale.

The contemporary refractions of this ancient narrative strand work out quite differently in Angelopoulos, of course. *Landscape in the Mist* presents both a daughter and a son in search of the father. But their search is doomed, for, as we learn from their uncle (their mother's brother), their mother has no idea who their father is; unlike Penelope, she has slept around freely. Part of the devastating effect of viewing the film is the sense of total hopelessness this *Odyssey* without an Odysseus generates in the viewer. We feel the accumulative effect of the father's absence on these children without considering the *Odyssey* parallel. But our realization of such an echo within a culture brought up on this narrative is even more troubling.

The impact of *The Suspended Step of the Stork* on us is all the more significant when we see Homer's Telemachus patterns reflected in the

3. Mastroianni as the retired teacher in *The Beekeeper*

journalist's search for the fatherlike Greek politician who has disappeared near the border. The young man is not actually related to the politician, but Angelopoulos's narrative once more gains in both texture and
significance as we see this relationship as yet another failed father search.
Unlike *Landscape in the Mist*, of course, this film does depict the finding
of a father figure. But in *The Suspended Step of the Stork* the father-son
reunion produces no Homeric victory over the forces destroying the
homeland. No such simple borders can be found in Angelopoulos's version of this ancient myth. And yet we can point to a kind of connection
that the mere awareness of such a similar mythic pattern repeated, despite
differences, creates for the viewer. A similarly implied pattern occurs in
Voyage to Cythera in which Alexandros, the filmmaker, can be seen as
both the actual son and the would-be son of "the old man" as he, Alexandros, either creates a fiction film with the stranger playing his father or we
follow the filmmaker actually following his father. The boundaries between these two possibilities become so completely blurred that we cannot tell which choice is the "truth."
     This level of felt implication of ancient myth is in no way treated by

Angelopoulos in a heavy-handed manner. Nowhere in *Voyage to Cythera*, for instance, is Spyros called "an Odysseus." But for anyone anywhere who has come into contact with Homer, it would be difficult to imagine a viewer's seeing the film without being aware of the parallels and similarities and thus, as well, the differences. That Spyros's end sets up a contrast with Homer's version would be an understatement. Spyros is rejected by his village and, finally, by Greece itself, as he is set afloat on a raft to drift away into the mist since not even a Russian ship will take him back. That Angelopoulos had yet another version of the Odysseus myth in mind when he wrote and shot the film is clear from his own comments: "Spyros as Odysseus is much closer to Dante's vision of him than to Homer's. For Dante really draws from a much earlier tradition of the Odysseus myth than did Homer. As you remember, Homer has a 'happy ending' whereas Dante emphasizes that Odysseus continues to wander and that he dies at sea" (interview, Athens, July 1993).

It does not matter to the overall impact of the film that few viewers would get such a point. But that Angelopoulos consciously wove in such implications suggests his desire to play with his ancient heritage rather than simply reconstruct it.

AGAMEMNON, FURIES, AND THE FORCES OF DISORDER

Two-thirds of the way through *The Travelling Players*, the young actor Orestes walks onstage as the troupe is performing *Golpho*, a popular turn-of-the-century Greek lyrical romantic melodrama about village life, and, using a real pistol, shoots his mother, Clytemnestra, and her lover, Aegisthus, dead. Instead of hearing shouts of horror from the rural small-town audience, we suddenly hear loud applause and cheers of "bravo" as the curtain closes on the bodies of the slain.

The moment has all of the characteristics of Angelopoulos's work as I have outlined them in the introduction. In particular we sense, of course, the blurring of theater and reality (applause for real murders), and, furthermore, between history and myth. For the modern individuals bear the ancient names of the Agamemnon myth, but they are caught up within the history of their times. The time of the murder is during the German Occupation of World War II, and Orestes has joined the communist "Partisan" resistance while Aegisthus has aligned himself, as a traitor, with antidemocratic forces including the Nazis. Furthermore, it should be noted that the play which the traveling players try to perform throughout the film, *Golpho, the Lover of the Shepherdess*, written in 1894 by Spyros Peressaides, went on to become both an extremely popular melodrama and also, in 1914, *Greece's first feature film, now lost*.

The murders are drained of any possible "tragic" or even dramatic effect. In fact, the suddenness of the killings followed by the applause takes us by surprise, leading many in the audience to laugh out loud as the "bravos" echo behind the curtain.

The Agamemnon myth is the other legend Angelopoulos treats frequently. But while the Odysseus myth necessarily takes us back to Homer, Agamemnon—although he appears as an important motif in the *Odyssey* and a major character in the *Iliad*—suggests the *Oresteia* cycle of tragedies by Aeschylus. We need, therefore, to consider Aeschylus's treatment through tragedy of the legend.

"Reading the *Oresteia* makes one afraid for one's life!" remarks Brian Vickers in *Towards Greek Tragedy* (425). We see that, like most of Greek tragedy, the story does treat royalty and a family feud that has gone on for several generations. But beyond being a domestic tragedy, it is also, as translator and commentator David Grene has noted, a "tragedy of war" (15). And Charles Segal goes further to suggest that, ultimately, what we see in this cycle is an eternal conflict and gap between male and female or, in the terms of these plays, the city (*polis*) and nature (*physis*).

The legend can be briefly told. Pelops of Argos had two sons, Atreus and Thyestes, who came into conflict when Thyestes seduced Atreus's wife. Atreus, to gain revenge (*ergon*), murdered Thyestes' children and served them up to his brother in a thick stew. Only one son survived this slaughter: Aegisthus, who brought down a curse on the house of Atreus. Atreus's son Agamemnon married Clytemnestra, sister to that Helen whose abduction caused the Trojan War. In exchange for favorable winds for the sea voyage to Troy, Agamemnon was told he must sacrifice his daughter, Iphigenia—an act he carried out, much to Clytemnestra's horror (legend has it that Iphigenia was swept away by the gods at the last moment and became a priestess or a minor goddess herself in Asia Minor). With such a background, Clytemnestra and Aegisthus became lovers and, after Agamemnon's murder, rulers. Then Orestes returned and, with his sister Electra's help, avenged his father's death.

The tragedy is, once more, a double one. It is the story of a family in deep trouble, but it is also a tragedy of war. Because in "overdestroying" Troy—instead of simply accepting the defeat of the Trojans, the Greeks under Agamemnon laid waste the whole city and committed wholesale slaughter and looting—Agamemnon is guilty of bringing destruction to his own country and people. The myth thus becomes political as well as personal. For it touches on the basic issue of how peoples should live together and govern their affairs.

We must remember that Aeschylus was living and writing during the heyday of Athenian democracy. Thus what emerges in the *Oresteia* is, ultimately, a hymn of praise and hope for democracy and collective life under the rule of law. Let us be more specific. Aeschylus treats the death of Agamemnon in *Agamemnon*, the murder of Clytemnestra and Aegisthus by Orestes in *The Libation Bearers*, and the resolution of the blood curse on the house of Atreus by Athena in *The Eumenides*. For our purposes, it is most important to consider how a tale that Vickers feels should make one "afraid for one's life" is resolved. At the beginning of *The Eumenides*, Orestes is hounded by the Furies, those ancient spirits descended from, ultimately, mother Earth, and thus aligned with and protective of all mothers. They have the right to hound Orestes for murdering his mother. Orestes, on the other hand, has the right to avenge his father's death. Thus the threshing floor of tragedy where, as Segal says, "the boundaries of opposing identities meet."

Note that the conflict is not between good and evil but between right and right, or, more particularly, between an ancient female right and a more contemporary male right. Aeschylus builds his drama beginning at Delphi where he swiftly traces the history of the oracle, noting its female origins: Earth, Themis, and Phoebe, all ruling in turn before Apollo and then Bromius (Dionysos) arrived. But it is Apollo who sanctioned Orestes' deed and who continues to back him up.

The resolution to this clash occurs in a lengthy trial held in Athens with Athena presiding. Aeschylus gives each side its due. The chorus of Furies are articulate about their role as "the gloomy children of the night" (line 330). They create *fear*, but

> There are times when fear is good.
> It must keep its watchful place
> at the heart's controls. There is advantage
> in the wisdom won from pain.
>
> (Lines 517–20)

Athena hears both sides and rules in favor of releasing Orestes: she must favor men since she was born from "a father without a mother." Her skills as a mediating judge are clear, however, for she finally succeeds in pleasing the Furies. She has them enshrined as official spirits of the Athenian community, arguing, in the spirit of their above quoted speech, "What man who fears nothing at all is ever righteous?" (line 699).

The conclusion to Aeschylus's version of this terrifying tale of war and family feuding is clear. Athens as a community (polis) ruled by law wins out against disorder, primitivism, blood feuds, as well as family and royal squabbles. The resolution is thus not tragic at all, but triumphant, celebratory, even joyful. Aeschylus, having acknowledged and powerfully evoked the spirits of the irrational, of destruction and chaos, of conflicting rights, offers a dreamed-for "happy ending" that turns personal into communal, pain into triumph, and destruction into the construction of a new order under democratic law.

Angelopoulos's reflections of the Agamemnon legend offer a strong contrast to Aeschylus's ultimate optimism. No goddess Athena exists to settle the affairs of the modern traveling players, and there is clearly no suggestion that Athens is a city of law and order and celebrated peace. But it is perhaps helpful to acknowledge how "terrifying" are the forces of disorder evoked in Aeschylus. It is not as if he were unaware of what his characters were up against. And thus we can see that Angelopoulos has shown us, in effect, the *Oresteia* with an emphasis on the disorder, not the imposed Aeschylean ending.

The Agamemnon tale is, as we shall see, the mythic pattern behind Angelopoulos's first feature, *Reconstruction*, as well. The murder of the returned guest-worker husband in a small, nearly deserted northern Greek village once again evokes the ancient myth. But as with Angelopoulos's return to a pre-Homeric version of the Odysseus tale, so his version of the Agamemnon legend here is more in keeping with a pre-Aeschylean formulation. As Eleni, the Clytemnestra figure, is being taken away from the village by the police in a Jeep at the end of the film, she is literally attacked by a screaming pack of old women in black sounding very much like Furies. At least Aeschylus allows Clytemnestra and Aegisthus a moment of imagined glory as they are in control of the kingdom at the end of *Agamemnon*. Not so in *Reconstruction*. By film's end she has been apprehended, betrayed by her lover, and hounded by village harpies, who, ironically, appear in their anger and fury to be upholding the constricting patriarchal customs of rural Greece.

Such ancient patterns as those of the Agamemnon myth often function in Angelopoulos's films simultaneously with other legends. I am thinking particularly of *Megalexandros*. The dominant legend represented in the title, as well as in theme, narrative, and characterization, is that of Alexander the Great. The bandit–Robin Hood central character even rides a white horse that resembles Alexander's famous steed and wears a helmet modeled closely on Alexander's.

But the Agamemnon legend is also evoked. At a certain point this would-be Utopian leader sacrifices his daughter in a situation mirroring the Iphigenia sacrifice, and his homecoming to his village leads ultimately to his murder, not by a single Clytemnestra, but by the village as a collective whole in a transformed analogy. Note that in all of these narratives, as in Greek tragedy, the personal family problem becomes a political and public issue as well, a crossroads "where the boundaries of opposing identities meet."

GREEK TRAGEDY AND BEYOND

Angelopoulos's relationship to ancient tragedy is quite complex. As we have suggested, to evoke the Agamemnon cycle is also to call up Aeschylus and the ancient stage. On one hand, we see that Angelopoulos is concerned with the theatrical and with reconstruction on many levels. But we have also noted that Angelopoulos drains the theatrical of its dramatic effect: the murders of Clytemnestra and Aegisthus, for instance, become absurd rather than tragic, and almost comic rather than frightening.

Such an effect directly resembles Brecht's approach to theater, an approach that Angelopoulos approves of. Raymond Durgnat observes, "The long take, as a 'local unity,' can suggest a 'traveling stage.' And Angelopoulos' long shots, meditative action, riddles, and uncertainties can evoke Brecht's search for spectatorial contemplation, detached criticism and alienation" (45). Angelopoulos has added that he hopes, through his films, to create a new kind of audience, "not just a consumer who uses only his emotions, but a person who uses his mind; a viewer such as the one Brecht was trying to find for his work" (Stenzel, "An Interview with Thodoros Angelopoulos" 34).

Tragedy became a particularly rich and dramatically charged form of *language*. Here again, we see Angelopoulos working in contrast to the tradition. His films present us with the moment between words and action, to become through the long shots and long takes a cinema of spaces, of gestures, and of off-camera realities. Yet even this is not always the case. For in *The Travelling Players*, for instance, part of the film's structuring has to do with the use of direct camera monologues delivered by the protagonists. At these brief moments the characters open up, acknowledge us, and *connect their lives with ours*.

But they do not do so through such characterization techniques as are most familiar to a contemporary audience. Angelopoulos is in fact closer to the spirit of Aeschylus's conception of character than to that of Sophocles and Euripides, with their emphasis on the revelation of internal conflict and psychological cause and effect. David Grene notes that the *Oresteia* as a whole does not follow a "logical" or even "dramatic" course in its development and that its characters are much more public symbols than individuals with inner lives. Agamemnon, for instance, hardly appears in *Agamemnon*, and Clytemnestra is portrayed as a much more complex figure than her husband: we simply do not completely understand who she is and why she commits the murder. Contrast Aeschylus's handling of tragedy with Euripides'. There is no doubt by play's end why Medea killed her children in *Medea* or why Pentheus had to die in *The Bacchae*.

We never get to know any of Angelopoulos's characters "personally," and, because of the mythic and legendary names and/or narrative patterns attached to his protagonists, we feel they are just as much signs as they are individuals. As far away from the intensity of tragedy on the stage as Angelopoulos appears to be, there are, however, surprising parallels with Aeschylus. Like the ancient presentation of *Agamemnon*, Angelopoulos's *Reconstruction* tells us much more about Clytemnestra (Eleni) than about Agamemnon (Costa) but leaves us, finally, outside her deepest feelings, motives, thoughts.

Even the seeming contrast between ancient tragedy and Angelopoulos's visual emphasis share a common basis. The images that make up Angelopoulos's films are his *language* and, like Greek tragedy, they are offered to the viewer not just as entertainment but as both a critique and a celebration of the culture they spring from.

Angelopoulos and Greek Popular and Folk Culture

Angelopoulos's films are not hymns to the simplicity and strength of folkloric traditions. But there are those echoes and gestures which originate in Greek popular and folk cultures. We will briefly consider some of the more important uses of these echoes here.

Folk Songs and Dance

In *Voyage to Cythera* when Spyros, the old communist who has been exiled to Russia for over thirty years, returns to his native village in Macedonia, he dances a Ponti dance (Ponti being a region on the Black Sea from which many Greeks immigrated to Macedonia in the 1920s) on the grave of a departed Partisan friend, singing a traditional folk song.

The song is a simple folk tune of the north, "Forty Red Apples." It is one of those haunting and melancholy tunes about "drying up" in old age, and the song becomes a motif throughout the rest of the film. At the very end of this, Angelopoulos's sixth feature, as Spyros is being placed on a raft by Greek authorities and pushed out to sea, abandoned by his culture and former friends, he begins singing the song again.

As for the dance Spyros does on his dead friend's mountaintop grave, it too comes from a very old folk tradition. The style of dancing—swift short steps with arms raised—is "Pontiko." According to the customs of this region, such a dance serves a purpose similar to that of dancing in New Orleans at a jazz funeral. Death is viewed not just as sorrow but as a joyful liberation of the soul from the body. It is a moment of celebration.

We will meet many other expressions of Greek folk culture in our discussion of Angelopoulos's work, including the folk tune that frames the opening and closing of his first film, *Reconstruction*. What we need to understand is the importance such a culture has in Greece. We have noted that the non-Greek considering the country immediately envisions the classical period and possesses almost no knowledge or understanding of the other cultures that have existed on Greek soil.

But the Greek folk heritage is significant and mixes elements of the Orthodox with simple village "pagan" traditions. While I have suggested some of the implications of the classical echoes in Angelopoulos, we should be aware that the folk tradition represents a rural and *oral* tradition of, for the most part, illiterate Greeks. The folk tradition is of further significance as a bearer of Greek culture in the face of hundreds of years of the Turkish Occupation as well. No matter that most rural Greeks were illiterate: they were not acultural—they had their customs, their dances, and their songs *in Greek*.

Thus it is doubly significant that the "language" Spyros chooses to use upon his homecoming is that of the folk culture he once knew and lived. That he is cast away, literally, on a raft and continues to sing his folk song ironically suggests a casting away of so much of folk culture and the past by the contemporary villagers who are trying to turn a quick profit by selling their land to developers. It is an ironic echo that many Greeks would therefore perceive that while these customs, songs, and dances survived hundreds of years of Turkish rule, they may disappear under the new international "Euro-capitalism."

Angelopoulos is not heavy-handed in pointing up such a possible reading. It is simply there for those who are familiar with the culture.

Popular Music: Rebetika, Bouzouki, Rock

In *The Travelling Players*, before any of the characters speak to each other, they define their political and personal orientations by the songs they sing in a darkly lit taverna. One thespian is softly singing a popular love song of the 1930s when he is suddenly interrupted by the traitor Aegisthus, who stands on the table and belts out a nationalist right-wing hymn while military songs and chants are heard from outside in the square.

Angelopoulos has said that Hollywood's biggest influence on him came in the form of musicals (interview, Athens, July 1993). Half joking but serious as well, he has noted that *The Travelling Players* can be considered "a kind of musical" (ibid.). But while Hollywood musicals may have been deep in the back of his mind while he was writing and shooting *The Travelling Players*, Angelopoulos is much more clearly building on popular Greek social behavior: people gathered in tavernas sharing long meals inevitably start singing. Furthermore, they sing bits of old songs and pieces of new ones. Ballads mix with pop songs and so forth in a musical montage. Given this context, Angelopoulos draws from at least four musical traditions beyond that of traditional folk songs mentioned above.

First, there is the rebetika music of the 1920s from Asia Minor. Experts have labeled this form of music "the Greek blues" (Butterworth and Schneider 11), for like the blues, these songs are almost always down-and-out songs about love lost, hard times, drugs and booze, and life at the bottom. Because these songs and musicians came to Greece from Asia Minor in the population exchanges of the period (see chapter 2), the music immediately evokes the East, immigrants, and "the other Greece." Typical of a rebetika song would be the following:

IN PIRAEUS IT'S CLOUDY

I light my cigarette and the rain puts it out;
I knock on the door I love and it doesn't open.
In Piraeus it's cloudy and in Athens it's raining
one guy lost love and another guy found love.

I see fancy cars passing on the avenue
and I know you're laughing at my pain.
I'm standing by a lamppost and it's getting dark;
I don't give a damn for the rain, let it pour.

(Butterworth and Schneider 79)

As with the blues, rebetika is not just a form of music but a way of life as well. "Rhembetes," as the singer-musicians were called, lived and loved and sang hard, staying up all night at the clubs. Rebetika music thus represents a subculture associated with petty criminals, drug addicts (opium was the drug most frequented in Asia Minor where fields of poppy flowers still grow), and social outcasts. Furthermore, the style of presentation became quite codified: the true rhembetis would sit, not stand, and, except for his or her hand moving across a bouzouki (the popular mandolin-like Greek instrument, originally unamplified but since the 1960s amplified to earsplitting levels), would remain absolutely motionless and expressionless. All of the grief and emotion comes in the music, not the body.

Because rebetika scenes and music appear in a number of Angelopoulos's films, including *The Travelling Players* and *Voyage to Cythera* particularly, it is possible to speak of a kind of rebetika style that is reflected in Angelopoulos's presentation of characters. Like the rhembetes, the figures in Angelopoulos's films tend to be motionless and expressionless, with one additional characteristic: unlike the musicians, most of Ange-

lopoulos's characters have no clear form of communication. There is another important difference between the rhembetis's motionless stance and
that represented in Angelopoulos's films. For the rhembetis, such total
denial of expression and body motion becomes a form of manliness or
macho with a corresponding sense of "tough womanness" in the stance
of the female rhembetes. For Angelopoulos, however, his characters are
motionless and expressionless without such pretense: their stance cuts to
their core.

Once more, one can watch these films with no knowledge of Greek
rebetika culture. But clearly, to know, as any Greek watching these films
would, that these echoes are present and have implications which mix
with and/or work against the other cultural echoes is to enrichen our
viewing experience of these works.

Popular bouzouki tunes can also be heard throughout Angelopoulos's
films. In contrast to the Greek blues of rebetika, bouzouki is the Greek
pop music that emerged in the late 1950s. Bouzouki cuts across a much
larger segment of Greek society, from the working class to the Greek middle class, newly formed in the 1960s, and beyond. These are the tunes
most frequently played on the radio, on jukeboxes, and by bands in popular tavernas. As *Voyage to Cythera*, for instance, moves from the village
to the bland city dock area, it is predominantly bouzouki music we hear
at the cheap "cantina" and in the kafeneon (coffee shop). Here,
Angelopoulos is clearly pointing a contrast to the old folk tune, "Forty
Red Apples," that originates in the village. At other times, in *Landscape
in the Mist* and in *The Beekeeper* as well, bouzouki music is heard at
truck stops and in cheap restaurants, thus becoming connected, within
Angelopoulos's contemporary mythology, with a kind of manufactured
("electronic") and rootless Greek pop culture.

Foreign songs are used in a variety of ways, but all to herald a non-
Greek presence within a Greek context. In *The Travelling Players* we hear
British troops singing "It's a Long Way to Tipperary," which helps establish that a foreign force has now entered the Greek landscape. Similarly,
a group of low-level entertainers roll into the dockside kafeneon at the
end of *Voyage to Cythera* and proceed in their drunken poor English to
sing and play everything from "Alexander's Ragtime Band" to "In the
Mood" and even some old Tom Jones hits. The effect is jarring: Spyros is
about to be cast out of Greece as an undesirable alien but those "at
home" appear to be alienated creatures with no solid grasp of any culture, Greek or foreign.

Bland "Euro-rock" songs and sequences offer glimpses in several films,
including *The Suspended Step of the Stork* and *Landscape in the Mist* as
well as *The Beekeeper*, of a Greek youth depicted as being as bland as the

music they listen to. Even the great Beatles' tune "Let It Be" comes off, on purpose, sounding tepid and lifeless in *The Suspended Step of the Stork*. In *Landscape in the Mist*, Orestes, a young gay actor, befriends the young brother-and-sister travelers and takes them to a motorcyclists' hangout one evening. The decor is dungeonlike, and the music is an uninspired Euro-copy of Van Morrison's raw style. Rock music has offered a certain direct energy level to world popular culture. In Angelopoulos's rendering, however, it represents yet another form of alienation without pleasure or poetry.

At counterpoint to the musical examples listed above—Greek and foreign, folk and manufactured—stands the lyrical, haunting, and "post-Romantic" music of composer Eleni Karaindrou, who has done the music for all of his films beginning with *The Voyage to Cythera*. Karaindrou's music does not sound Greek. It is not particularly rooted in any national musical tradition though the feel of it is "European."

Karaindrou has emphasized herself that in her approach and under Angelopoulos's guidance, she has avoided sounding "folkloric," Greek, or even popular. "Classical" is not exactly fitting either, even though the orchestration of the sound track is quite rich and full. What seems important about a Karaindrou score is that it unifies the film—image and sound—in a meta-Greek landscape, joining the Greek-Balkan images we see with something larger, something beyond place and time. One might also add that Karaindrou's music helps create a "spiritual" level to the image. It is a music of interior space as well as of the landscapes we see.

Shadow Puppet Theater and Popular Greek Theater

The Greeks have a strong tradition of humorous folk shadow-puppet theater called, after the name of the protagonist, *Karaghiozis*. The name is a Greek corruption of the Turkish for "Dark Eyes" and suggests the origins of this centuries-old artform, which was easily transportable from village to village during the Turkish Occupation and on to the late 1950s.

The importance of this entertainment for Greeks, especially in rural areas, was great: quite simply, Karaghiozis suggested the survival of Greek culture under the oppression of foreign (Turkish) rule. Karaghiozis (see fig. 4) is an ugly, long-nosed, bug-eyed (thus his name), hunchbacked, poor, and ragged Greek who lives in a tumbledown shack represented at the far left of the brightly lit white "sheet" screen. On the other side of the screen lives the Turk in a palace. With folk humor—often quite scatological—Karaghiozis finally triumphs over his opponents, not through brute strength, but, like Odysseus himself, through cunning and trickery (*poneria*). Slapstick, folk music (with strong Turkish influences), comme-

4. Karaghiozis, the hero of Greek shadow-puppet theater

dia dell'arte–like stereotypic plots and characters, and bits and pieces of Greek folk culture and wisdom combine in these half scripted, half improvised presentations.

To this day, Karaghiozis theaters still exist and a half-hour Karaghiozis television show for children continues to draw large audiences for this deeply loved comic cultural antihero. In everyday speech, for instance, Greeks will say of someone who tried to trick them, "He/she played Karaghiozis with me." Karaghiozis shadow theater is far better known to the average Greek than is ancient comedy or tragedy or Homer's epics.

Angelopoulos does not present such a slapstick comic vision. But he has, especially in his visual framing, as well as thematically, played with elements of Karaghiozis theater that are quite familiar to Greek audiences. In *The Travelling Players* the line of the players standing in bright backlight at the taverna window doing their little preview song and dance is a direct reminder of the warm-up dance tune played at the beginning of every Karaghiozis presentation. And Angelopoulos has commented that *Days of '36* was heavily influenced by Karaghiozis (interview, Athens, July 1993).

There is one other characteristic at the heart of what Karaghiozis represents for Greeks, and that is the capacity to endure. Angelopoulos shares this spirit. Sometimes Karaghiozis wins, and just as often he is tricked and cheated and beaten himself. But he goes on. Similarly, the "framing" shot of the players in *The Travelling Players* standing, suitcases in hand, at the railroad station, but at two completely different time periods, suggests that they too keep on playing and keep on traveling.

Epitheorisis: In the Shadows of Greek Vaudeville

The tradition of Greek vaudeville, which is called *epitheorisis* in Greek, has clearly influenced Angelopoulos as well. On one level, for instance, this echo suggests a counterbalance to the "high" culture of classical Greece. The traveling players in their "real" lives have classical and thus mythical names. But the play they act is, as noted previously, *Golpho*, which typifies the most popular Greek theater *and cinema* genre, described by critic Yannis Bacoyannopoulos as "the bucolic drama." He characterizes the play and the genre as "romantic, sentimental, moralistic": "it idealized and prettified the rural past. The village, particularly the mountain village, with its shepherd and flocks, stern patriarchal fathers, fine young lads, pure morals, honor and virginity, forbidden love and tragic endings are themes which are repeated from film to film" (32). That the Greek popular theater and cinema centered on this particular play and its romantic and melodramatic vision is important for our understanding of the very different direction Angelopoulos has taken in his rendering of Greece and particularly life in rural mountain areas. In this light, *Reconstruction* becomes an even stronger debut film, for it flies completely in the face of the "folkloric" myth that so many Greeks wished to believe in.

The placement of *Golpho* within *The Travelling Players* opens up layers of irony. The play—complete with its bucolic fantasy of Greek village life—can never be performed *whole and complete* within the narrative of the film, for history in all of its forms between 1937 and 1952 interrupts it constantly. Of course, a question never asked is why the troupe does not present some other play, some more up-to-date work. But we are not allowed to ask this within the context of Angelopoulos's film. The continued impossibility of performing the complete *Golpho*, or any other play,

particularly over so many years, once more announces to us that Angelopoulos is not working within a tradition of strict realism but is pushing
beyond to a metaphorical level.

As actors and as people, the players seem unable to shed the past, unable to change the play, to change their approach, or to alter their vision.
They keep on keeping on, carrying their shabby suitcases from village to
village and small town to small town long past a time when traveling
players traveled.

Vaudeville died out in the United States during the 1930s, but in
Greece the epitheorisis, Greece's answer to vaudeville, has been going
strong throughout the century. And now in the 1990s, it seems, ironically, to be more popular with Greeks than cinema (during the summer of
1994, for instance, I noted that an island cinema had closed and the theater had been converted into a musical epitheorisis hall!).

Like vaudeville, the epitheorisis presents an evening of music, dance,
comedy, farce, and romantic melodrama all wrapped up in an opening
and closing theme song-and-dance routine involving the whole troupe.
And like vaudeville, the epitheorisis is an urban theatrical form that has
spread to the rural areas. Some of its main characteristics (also similar to
vaudeville) are worth remembering: (1) because the format is a loose col-
lection of vastly differing acts, the show is not "narrative" or plot driven
like a typical Hollywood film or a dramatic play; (2) because it is a "variety" show, we as audience are always aware of performance: so much of
the effect of the acts depends on the audience's *not* "suspending disbelief"
and thus joining in on the fun of playing with the conventions of theatricality; and (3) music plays an important role in defining character and
loosely uniting the troupe.

Angelopoulos has incorporated, in his fashion, elements of all three
characteristics of the epitheorisis. His films constantly play with the concept of theater, presentation, "reconstruction," and the presence of an
"audience" or "chorus." And, as we have discussed, music is used in both
subtle and direct ways to define and unite (and sometimes to divide) his
groups.

Finally, those familiar with the Greek cultural elements briefly noted in
this chapter can view much of Angelopoulos's work as both a frightening
and a moving "epitheorisis" of Greek life itself: a little bit of history, a
large pinch of myth, a dash of the musical past and present, a touch of
theater, and, beyond it all, the movie camera recording, adding its own
voice and perspective across the whole territory of Greek culture.

Chapter Two

The Moving Pattern of Images: Greek History

and Individual Perspectives

*A long life gives one to witness much, and experience much
oneself that one would not choose. . . .
Hence man is wholly accident.*
(Solon as reported by Herodotus, *History*)

HISTORY, CINEMA, ANGELOPOULOS

Myth translated into reality becomes history.
(Hegel)

A GROUP of actors walk through a town in northern Greece. The scene takes some ten minutes on the screen and is captured in a single tracking shot. But that is not all. At the beginning of the scene, it is 1952, and when the troupe reaches a taverna in the town, it is 1939: it is almost as if each minute of screen time takes them back a year in history.

The scene is from *The Travelling Players*, and it marks not only Angelopoulos's experimentation with the language of film but also his deep interest in history in general and Greek history in particular as seen through individual destinies. History itself becomes a major character for Angelopoulos. Few filmmakers anywhere have been so concerned and involved with history from such a variety of angles. We are cued to this fact because, as noted in the scene above from *The Travelling Players*, he so frames, shoots, and constructs his narratives that we cannot avoid thinking of time and of "the time" as it acts on and through the individual protagonists.

As Nikos Kolovos states, "These films are meditations on history, not historical films per se" (12). We should add that not only are Angelopoulos's films meditations on history, but they are exploratory acts of liberation concerned with histories beyond what had previously been accepted as Greek history. *The Travelling Players*, for example, was the first cinematic treatment of the Greek civil war of 1944–1950 from the perspective of the Left. In this sense Angelopoulos is concerned not just with canoni-

cal history, but with *repressed* histories that he obviously feels should become, through cinema, part of his culture's consciousness.

Filmmakers everywhere have made "historical" films. In Hollywood,
we can point to everything from *Birth of a Nation* and *Gone with the
Wind* to *Shane*, *Apocalypse Now*, and *Dances with Wolves*. In terming
these historical films, however, we simply mean that these are films with
narratives set in the past, either "bio pics"—screen portrayals of famous
people in such works as John Ford's *Young Abe Lincoln* or the television
film *Stalin* (1992)—or, as in *Dances with Wolves*, narratives constructed
around historically undocumented protagonists living through a particular time in the past. What we should note in such films, particularly as
created by Hollywood, is that these narratives highlight individual destinies, albeit set in the past and influenced by those times. But still, we sense
the presence of individuals who carry out their own destinies. At best, as
in David Lean's *Doctor Zhivago*, for instance, we can glimpse how
strongly the social, political, and cultural forces of history work through
individual destinies. At worst, history becomes a backdrop of relatively
little importance, a matter for set and costume design more than for thematic or narrative concern.

To understand how different Angelopoulos's concepts of history are
from those of even a "serious" American director, consider the historical
films of screenwriter-turned-director Oliver Stone. In films such as *JFK*
(1991), *Salvador* (1986), *Platoon* (1986), *Heaven and Earth* (1993), and
Nixon (1995), Stone has taken on major topics of contemporary historical conflict that most Hollywood directors would avoid: the assassination
of John F. Kennedy and the supposed conspiracies behind it, the CIA involvement in Latin American politics, the horror of the Vietnam experience from the average soldier's point of view, the Vietnam war experience
from the Vietnamese point of view, and, most recently, the Watergate
scandal of the Nixon presidency. Stone's trademarks for delivering history on film, furthermore, have become the use of strong dramatic conflicts, the depiction of extreme violence, and a heavy reliance on the montage of MTV-like editing (especially in *JFK*). Critics have often noted that
Stone's films continually assault the audience, allowing no time for contemplation or relaxation between one scene of violence and the next. Add
to this strong sound tracks that also bombard the audience with overstim-
ulation and you have a concept of history on the screen that is characterized by continual sensory stimulation built around narratives of individuals caught up in very dramatic plots; these plots, Stone often suggests, are
politically motivated and often reduce to us-against-them stories driven
by fear and paranoia.

In cinematic technique and in conceptual terms, nothing could be further from the cinema of Theo Angelopoulos than, say, the montage se-

quences of *JFK*. It is the function of this chapter to explore such differences. But to the contrast with Hollywood's representation of history we must also add Angelopoulos's position in relation to the "instant" histories that surround us in the form of twenty-four-hour CNN and similar news network coverage. Here again, in such news reporting, the emphasis is on drama, conflict, close-ups of action, noise, trauma, and tragedy, often caught in jarring, jiggling video images with the voice-over, and sometimes on-camera, running commentary of the newscaster, all of which heighten, of course, our sense of being vicariously "on the spot" as history unfolds. Angelopoulos's carefully composed and beautifully shot scenes are in strong contrast to the "CNNification" of contemporary history.

The history Angelopoulos has traced for more than a quarter of a century has been that of the twentieth century in Greece. He has specifically called three of his films his "historical trilogy": *Days of '36*, *The Travelling Players*, and *Megalexandros*. And his unique approach to the representation of history on the screen has not gone unnoticed by filmmakers around the world. It is true, for instance, that when Bernardo Bertolucci's historical film *1900* came out in 1977, he was asked in one interview if his attempt to capture much of Italian history of the twentieth century in one film was not somewhat like Theo Angelopoulos's *The Travelling Players*. "Yes," he replied, "but I am not as talented a director as he is," was the surprising answer. Taken collectively, Angelopoulos's films offer an attempt to see clearly through the dark window of Greek history of this century with all of its internal conflicts, external pressures, and ancient baggage from past empires and eras so that we experience, as Bertolucci hinted in his flattering tribute, how individuals and their destinies are absolutely woven into and from the fabric of their culture and their times.

Consider the historical center of Angelopoulos's projects. *Reconstruction* is based on a "true" story from the newspapers. *Days of '36*, *The Travelling Players*, and *Megalexandros* constitute his "historical trilogy," treating Greek history from 1936 to the mid 1970s. *Megalexandros* doubles back to focus on the period from the turn of the century up to the mid-1930s, and the "trilogy of silence" (Angelopoulos's designation) of *Voyage to Cythera*, *The Beekeeper*, and *Landscape in the Mist* treats the present, while *The Suspended Step of the Stork* and *Ulysses' Gaze* take on the most difficult "history" of all, the contenporary confusion, war, and suffering in the Balkans.

Angelopoulos's films are not historical documentaries. They are clearly fictions, but fictional narratives that reflect his perspective on the complex web of Greek history. Historian Hayden White has written about the importance of understanding the historical text as a "literary artifact." He has, of course, made traditional historians uncomfortable when he writes, for instance, that all historical narratives are "verbal fictions, the contents of which are as much invented as found and the forms of which have more in common with their counterparts in literature than they have with those in the sciences" (82). Explaining the redefinition of the very concept of history that has gone on during the past few decades around the world, White notes: "All historical narratives contain an irreducible and inexpungeable element of interpretation. The historian has to interpret his materials in order to construct *the moving pattern of images* in which the form of the historical process is to be mirrored. And this because the historical record is both too full and too sparse" (51, italics my own).

"The moving pattern of images" is certainly an accurate description of history as represented by Angelopoulos. We return to the long tracking shot mentioned in the opening of the chapter. The shot embraces the same individuals and seemingly the same march, but historical time has changed because of its representation in screen time. And the moving pattern of images does not lead to a chronological march forward as real time progresses, but to a doubling back to the past. Thus Angelopoulos's combination of long continuous shots with nonchronological time forces the viewer to be actively engaged in the process of "reading" the images that flow before him or her, both for their narrative importance and for their historical significance. Angelopoulos presents narratives that foreground the politics, wars, and conflicts of the times.

Angelopoulos, as I shall suggest, has a past of being involved with Greek Marxist thought and causes. But it is in part the purpose of this chapter to suggest that the history presented in his films defies any simple or didactic political message. Certainly to present historical subjects that have not been covered adequately in Greek histories—especially the Greek civil war—can, of course, be read as serving the interests of the Greek Left. Yet Angelopoulos's blending of the mythical, cultural, and even spiritual levels of the Greek experience as outlined in the previous chapter suggests that history and time are being examined outside the usual boundaries of linear narrative and traditional concepts of what is historical.

It is significant that Angelopoulos's political consciousness was formed during the 1960s in Greece when that country was experiencing not only the culture of the sixties but also its own political turmoil, which led to the takeover of the country by the Colonels in 1967. As noted in the introduction, he dates his "political education" to the moment he was clubbed in 1964 at a left-wing demonstration. Clearly his three-year stint as a journalist and, briefly, a film critic for a left-wing newspaper allowed him a chance to open up and investigate a number of historical issues.

Furthermore, it is important to remember that Angelopoulos began his filmmaking career under a dictatorship (1967–1975) that was quite severe in its censorship. Many of his generation, Angelopoulos included, postponed or abandoned whatever "normal" careers or plans they might have followed. It was the times themselves that forced many to ask hard questions about their country, themselves, and their relationship to an autocratic government which claimed to have "saved" Greece and which enjoyed a certain popularity at first, particularly in the countryside where new roads were built and electricity was brought in, among other benefits for the supporters.

But to better view Angelopoulos's approach to history, we should first go back to the source of Greek history itself: Thucydides and Herodotus.

THUCYDIDES, HERODOTUS, ANGELOPOULOS, AND THE HISTORICAL IMPULSE

> It may be your interest to be our masters, but how
> can it be ours to be your slaves?
> (The Melians' response to the Athenians
> in Thucydides' *The Sicilian Expedition*)

"History in its root sense means inquiry," writes M. I. Finley (1). It was an inquiry into how and why things happened as they did that led Thucydides and Herodotus to begin writing "histories," which varied drastically from a mythological or religious frame of mind in championing reason and observation over superstition and blind belief.

But no one can read the great works of these men without realizing that history as they wrote it was very far from being a scientific or objective undertaking. Herodotus, writing about the Persian Wars, had no access to records, and few who had lived during those times would have survived to Herodotus's day. Similarly, somewhat later, Thucydides, who was influenced by Herodotus, wrote his own "histories," having to depend on his own ability to sift through oral reports, often many times removed from actual events, and on his own powers of reasoning. Thus they re-created dialogue, wove events in narrative form, attempting, of course, to establish a sense of cause and effect but also, as revealed in the quotation from Herodotus at the chapter's opening, acknowledging the role of "chance" in men's lives. What resulted, therefore, was very much their individual view of what happened.

As Finley explains, perhaps the most important accomplishment of these early historians was to discover, as did Herodotus, that "one could

uncover moral problems and moral truths in history, in the concrete data
of experience, in a discourse which was neither freely imaginative like
that of the poets nor abstract like that of the philosophers" (6). For our
purposes we should highlight that reflecting on history was a way to
make sense of a culture's as well as an individual's existence in moral
terms, and that people wrote history by making use of imaginative as well
as observational and rational powers. History as practiced by the Greeks
embodied a wider field than did literature, myth, or religion.

Angelopoulos shares such a broad canvas with his ancient predeces-
sors. Like these early historians, he makes use of stories, myths, known
events, and figures and presents them so as to force us to go beyond the
events themselves to ask ourselves about their importance and meaning.
Unlike such historians, however, he does not attempt to draw or present
clear conclusions. This is the way Thucydides ends his account of the
Athenian campaign in Sicily: "Of all the Hellenic actions which took
place in this war, or indeed of all Hellenic actions which are on record,
this was the greatest—the most glorious to the victors, the most ruinous
to the vanquished; for they were utterly and at all points defeated, and
their sufferings were prodigious. Fleet and army perished from the face of
the earth; nothing was saved, and of the many who went forth, few returned home" (Finley 379). Angelopoulos has no such conclusions in any
of his films. As an artist/filmmaker working with history rather than a
historian making films, he is more concerned to capture something of the
moving flow of images he sees history to be, leaving the meanings for the
viewer to decide. But the difference between the ancient historians and
Angelopoulos as a modern artist goes beyond the difference in occupa-
tions. The early historians manifest a clear and perhaps naive belief in the
power of the rational individual. In Angelopoulos's films, however, no
such clear-sighted belief in the simple power of the rational mind is expressed. In fact, it can be argued that by crossing history with other cultural elements, including myth and the realm of the mysterious,
Angelopoulos not only is attempting to represent a repressed history, as
in the case of the Greek civil war, but also wishes to suggest the danger of
trying to draw simple conclusions from too narrow a range of history.

There is another way in which Angelopoulos differs from the early historians and all who have followed in their footsteps. He has avoided
doing docudramas about famous persons and particular well-known
events. Both Herodotus in dealing with the Persian War and Thucydides
in considering the Peloponnesian Wars, for instance, studied the major
campaigns and the most important leaders in their efforts to understand
what had happened. Angelopoulos is quite the opposite. His study of
Greek history from 1939 to 1952 in *The Travelling Players* is seen off the
battlefield, in the provinces, through the lives of unknown actors.

And yet the ancients and Angelopoulos are united in suggesting the importance of a moral dimension to human existence. The quotation above from Thucydides, the Melians' response to the Athenians, both underlines the eternal conflict between the oppressed and the oppressors—we feel the injustice being done the Melians—and aims criticism at Athens for its tyrannical behavior. The flow of moving images that Angelopoulos portrays twentieth-century Greek history to have been shares a similar dual vision, underlining the levels of injustice, personal and social, that exist in that time and place.

ANGELOPOULOS AND GREEK HISTORY FROM 1900 TO 1939

Two films focus on Greece before World War II. *Megalexandros* glimpses turn-of-the-century Greece up to the 1930s, and *Days of '36* takes us into the dictatorship of General Metaxas.

Megalexandros (*Alexander the Great*, in English) was Angelopoulos's most difficult film and, by general critical evaluation, "the most ambitious Greek film to date," as William Megalos noted in 1980 during production. The narrative has to do with a real Greek bandit of indefinite origins, a kind of Greek Robin Hood who was a friend of the peasants, was touched with ambitions of being a new Alexander the Great, and, at the turn of the century, escaped from prison with some of his men, captured some Englishmen and women, and seized a village in northern Greece. To his surprise, this isolated village had become something of a Utopian community realizing the ideas of the village schoolteacher. Property had been abolished, men and women had equal rights, and a communal warehouse had been set up so that all goods could be shared.

Alexandros takes over the village by force, and the rest of the film depicts his decline as he becomes a tyrant instead of a reincarnation of the great Macedonian of the past. He has the government committee, the teacher, and even the English hostages murdered by film's end, while the villagers in turn murder him only to be overrun by government troops. Only Alexandros's son, twelve-year-old Alexandros, escapes.

The main character is played by the Italian actor Omero Antonutti, who gained international recognition as the star of the Taviani brothers' *Padre Padrone* (1977). In that film, Antonutti played a violent and passionate patriarchal figure in a Sardinian family. Characteristically, Angelopoulos has Antonutti become a very muted Alexandros, framed most often in long shot.

Why, one might ask, would Angelopoulos cast an Italian for a Greek role when he, of all directors, is so totally involved in Greek history? The action sounds like a nod toward commercialism or Hollywood casting, for, after all, director Michael Cacoyannis has ironically commented, "I was considered an artist when I made my early Greek films, but when *Zorba the Greek* was cast with Anthony Quinn, a Mexican-American actor, and the film made money, I was considered from then on as a commercial director!" (interview, Athens, June 1994). Certainly one cannot deny that Antonutti's presence in the film made it a more visible work for European audiences. But the casting also makes sense in terms of the fact that the real bandit figure upon whom the story is based was of obscure origins. Antonutti's "Mediterranean" face suggests just that: he may be Greek or he may have some mixture of backgrounds. We simply do not know.

Angelopoulos's sense of history includes a strong desire for authenticity of location. In *Megalexandros* the location is absolutely authentic since Angelopoulos insisted on shooting mostly in winter in the remote village of Dotsiko, fifty kilometers from the town of Grevena in Greek Macedonia. Angelopoulos's passion for finding just the right location is clear from his claim that he has been to every village in mainland Greece (Megalos 23) and spent over a year finding this particular village. Hollywood has worked miracles, in contrast, making us believe, for instance, that the plains of Spain were actually the snow-swept steppes of Russia in *Dr. Zhivago*. But Angelopoulos feels strongly that location is both character and plot to a large degree, and that to be as close as possible to the place one is attempting to portray adds to the final flow of images on the screen. No one who has seen this film can deny the stunning power of the mountains in winter as shot by Arvanitis, Angelopoulos's cinematographer, and the haunting effect of this gray stone-constructed village.

Of course, feeling that history can be more accurately portrayed through authentic locations and actually making a film in such a spot are two different matters. The isolation of the village for a modern film crew did not prove to be the only difficulty, however. Angelopoulos had his art director, Mikis Karapiperis, virtually rebuild the village as it would have been at the turn of the century at great cost and in battle against logistics and nature as winter in the mountains made every action extremely taxing.

The film as it finally emerged embraced a number of Angelopoulos's interests: history is represented both as the reenactment of a particular event and as a re-creation of an important period—the turn of the century—as Greece is just about to enter the industrial revolution and thus experience the events that will lead to the death of village life as it had traditionally existed in Greece for centuries. The story also involves "the other Greece": rural, northern, isolated village life.

We should add that, viewed through the lens of the current serious conflict between Greece and the Former Yugoslav Republic of Macedonia, this 1980 film, which focuses attention on rural Macedonia, appears almost prophetic in capturing a sense of the complex history of conflicts that informs that area of the Balkans. Three more points need to be made regarding Angelopoulos's presentation of history in *Megalexandros*. First, there is the opening of the film in which a suffering Macedonian faces us (the camera) and begins to tell us the story of this outlaw Alexandros. In this sense, therefore, the whole film is a tale related through time (film) to a contemporary audience about an already completed series of events. In short, history becomes a form of oral literature, and the film we watch becomes the represented vision of this Macedonian's tale.

Second, when we first see Alexandros, he is in a forest clearing on a white horse much like Alexander the Great's famous horse. And he is wearing a cape and helmet with plume much like those associated with Alexander the Great. With the sun slanting through the mist and a strong eerie chanting on the sound track, it is as if we have been pulled into a myth or fairy tale. The complexity of the moment needs to be emphasized. The film appears as a story told by one Macedonian about a Macedonian bandit of the past who believed himself to be some kind of reincarnation of Alexander the Great—who was, of course, a historical figure but who became, perhaps even more important, much larger than history for the people of the troubled region embraced as "Macedonia." Alexander became myth and the myth embodies history, folktale, and religious dimensions.

That the turn-of-the-century Alexandros participates in this folk myth is clear when he finally reaches the mountain village where a feast is taking place as a folk tune is sung:

Alexander, you are the wind.
You are the dragon slayer.
Alexander, you are the sun.

The dragon slayer, of course, is traditionally St. George, one of the most respected saints in the Balkans. And the sunburst image was the symbol for Alexander the Great's empire. Folklore and folk song have thus done what they always do throughout the world: they have fused and transformed history, religion, and myth for their own reasons, their own needs. In this case, for these people, Alexander becomes a Christ figure, and the Second Coming of Alexander becomes one of the most powerful myths in the southern Balkans.

The third point is simply that Angelopoulos makes the most of the fact that these events are unfolding in 1900, the turn of the century. Before we meet Alexandros in the film, we are at a New Year's Eve celebration in Athens as Athenian royalty, government officials, and various British officials celebrate "the coming of the twentieth century." Clearly in this one film Angelopoulos is suggesting that the roots of many of this century's problems were present at that moment. These would include foreign intervention in Greece's destiny (the presence of the British, in this case), the gap between the government in Athens and the simple folk in the countryside, and the influence of foreign ideas. The Utopian experiment in the village is based on imported European ideas, and early on in the film, a group of Italian anarchists arrive to observe this "experiment" in "communistic" living, a forerunner, of course, of the communist movement that was to arise. There is also the failure of diplomacy to solve deep-rooted conflicts (for all the talk back and forth in the film, all of the hostages are killed, for instance), the whole issue, as already stated, of Macedonia and its past, present, and future, and, finally, the rise and fall of revolutionary movements. We watch in the beginning as Alexandros triumphantly enters the village much like a Christ figure celebrated by all. With each step of disillusionment with his rule, however, we come closer to his murder by these same villagers who had originally welcomed him.

The film ends with the villagers coming to find the body of Alexandros and discovering instead a statue: a bust of Alexander the Great with blood on it. Angelopoulos then cuts to a view of crowded, polluted contemporary Athens as a simple country flute plays on the sound track. Finally we hear the voice of the storytelling Macedonian man from the beginning finishing his tale by saying, "And that's how Alexandros got into the cities." History and folk myth have literally come home to the present in such a jarring jump cut of an ending.

I would argue that despite much of the visual beauty of the film and the effort to open up and explore the issues mentioned above, *Megalexandros* is finally one of Angelopoulos's least successful films because we feel he is trying to cover too much territory in one work (I have not even touched on the complicated "personal" or tragic level that unfolds between Alexandros and his daughter-in-law). The modern Athenian ending is, in this light, quite simply too didactic a cut to prove effective. Such "jumps" can be done well. Pier Paolo Pasolini, for instance, in his *Oedipus Rex* (1967) ends his retelling of the ancient drama with a jump cut to Oedipus as a blind beggar on the steps of the cathedral in contemporary Milan for an ironic closing that leaves us forced to contemplate how ancient tragedy could touch us in our contemporary lives. Angelopoulos's cut, however, appears as needlessly strained. It is enough that the real body has become a statue. To add the smog of Athens on top of this pushes Angelopoulos into a homiletic realm he does not enter in his other works.

Days of '36, Angelopoulos's second feature, is a study of Greek history shortly before the dictatorship of General Metaxas. The film suggests the corrupting forces within the government that would lead to the dictatorship. The narrative concerns a political prisoner, Sophianos, who holds a visiting politician hostage. At first the prison officials and later the entire conservative government are forced to deal with a situation they cannot control except, finally, with a bullet. Of course the narrative similarities to *Megalexandros*—politicians being held hostage and the government being unable to deal with the crisis effectively—are clear in this earlier work.

Shot in the muted colors of prison and dingy government offices, *Days of '36* emphasizes the silence between actions and satirizes all of the officials with an appealing visual sense of ironic humor. In one scene, for instance, a small group of officials and dignitaries is transported to an open field decorated with flags and a speaker's platform. As the officials arrive by car, a military band begins to play off-key. Once the small crowd—there is no audience of the public, only officials—assembles, a speech is given dedicating a new stadium. The event is made to appear as theater of the absurd as Angelopoulos's camera frames these formally dressed officials against an empty landscape. The scene is brief and appears merely as a humorous diversion from the seriousness of the hostage plot. Yet it is typical of Angelopoulos's exploration of Greek history that although such scenes are complete in themselves, they also reflect the whole. In this case, just as these foolish officials conduct their own ceremonies to please a small audience of their own choosing, so they have likewise ruled Greece without the support or understanding of the majority of simple Greeks.

Once again we see how Angelopoulos works against the traditional narrative modes of depicting what other filmmakers would use as highly dramatic moments in a historical event: a hostage situation in prison. French-Greek director Constantine Costa-Gavras, in contrast, won an Oscar for Best Foreign Film in 1969 with his political thriller Z, which critics were swift to realize used every possible Hollywood convention to create swiftly paced, tension-building scenes in his reenactment of a Kennedy-like assassination in Greece during the 1960s. Angelopoulos gives us no such tension or drama. We do not even witness the seizing of the hostage, an event that has occurred before the film begins. Thus subject matter and camera technique are well matched, for the lack of action in the film mirrors the lack of direction and action within the Greek government. In one scene as officials argue back and forth that "we must have a solution or the government will fall," Angelopoulos's camera circles them in a 360-degree motion, emphasizing the circularity of their positions.

The solution is for the government to send in an assassin and murder Sophianos, an event that, once again, happens off-camera as the camera lingers on the window of the cell. Angelopoulos's view of Greek history in this work is simple. The government was so weak and corrupt that the actions of one person almost brought it down. The government was also so incompetent that it could solve a problem only through murder.

Days of '36 in retrospect was clearly a film in which Angelopoulos was searching for his way to present history on-screen. Some of the techniques mentioned above became important ones for the films that followed. But the film also bears some flaws that Angelopoulos triumphed over in his subsequent work. Most notably, he quickly establishes that the government members are weak and ineffective, but since most of the film deals with them, there is a feeling of oversimplification such that the film plays too intensely on one level of meaning. Simply said, rather than history as "inquiry," as discussed above, we have history as biased reduction.

But even in this early work Angelopoulos deserves a lot of credit for opening up a large topic that Greeks have generally been uncomfortable discussing since Greece became a modern country in the early 1830s as it was liberated from the Turks: the question of Greek identity, collective and individual. Modern Greek history has not been just a question of who has been in control since the Greeks began to organize their own nation (and remember that what we call ancient Greece was never a unified country) but a deep issue of what it means to be Greek, particularly after almost five hundred years of foreign domination under the Turks. Mixed blood, mixed language, mixed customs, and continually shifting borders have meant that there really was no such person as a "pure Greek."

Of course these confusions run deep even at the unconscious level, as British historian C. M. Woodhouse has noted in *The Story of Modern Greece*, describing drastic changes that occurred at the beginning of the twentieth century in the territories now called Greece. As he has written of the confrontation with Italy in 1923, "The fumbling, agonized quest for peace involved the Greeks deeply in unconscious contradictions" (212). Greek film critic Vasilis Rafalidis describes it this way in writing about *Voyage to Cythera*:

> Greece is like a circle with many perimeters and no center. Such a circle is called vicious. The main body of Greeks inhabited or inhabit the perimeter: Ionia [Angelopoulos's references to Ionia are continuous], the Black Sea, Danubean sovereignties, Cyprus, Odessa, Egypt, Tashkent and today's Germany, Australia, Canada, etc. The "metropolis" is a space of shadows and of its inhabitant Greeks, half feel like immigrants and the other half feel like emigrants in their very own fatherland, which is in a state of continual internal occupation by birds of prey. (23)

What I have said in the introduction about Angelopoulos's approach to character depiction applies directly, of course, to this issue of Greek identity. And *Days of '36* makes it clear that a question which cuts deeper than politics and the events that surround "history" is "Who are we?" Greeks have been asking themselves this question (or, Angelopoulos would argue, in many cases, denying themselves) since modern Greece became an official nation.

ANGELOPOULOS AND 1939, WORLD WAR II, AND THE GREEK CIVIL WAR

Given the two films discussed above, we can see that Angelopoulos is very aware that Greece entered World War II both with a dictatorship and with an ongoing heritage of cultural and political confusion and turmoil. Woodhouse calls the period 1941–1952 "The Second National Crisis" (the first, 1908–1923, embraced the expansion of Greece in the Balkans through World War I, including the addition of Salonika and surrounding territory and conflicts with Italy). Woodhouse's second crisis involved not only the invasions by Italy and Germany and the constant outside control of Greece by the Allies, especially the British, but also the formation within Greece of various organizations—political and military— along differing ideological lines. Primary among these were EAM (National Liberation Front), made up particularly of communists, and ELAS (Greek National Liberation Army), a more broadly based antimonarchical, prosocialist movement, both of which have been well documented by Dominique Eudes, in *The Kapetanios: Partisans and Civil War in Greece, 1943–1949*.

While all Greek parties more or less united to oppose the German Occupation, the ending of World War II unleashed what became the Greek civil war as monarchists, supported by the Allies, sought to impose a government. The bloody war that followed, in which hundreds of thousands of Greeks died, is still a deeply felt wound that has neither completely healed nor been accurately and completely detailed by historians. As Eudes notes, in 1949 when the shooting finally stopped, "a tenth of the Greek population had perished since the beginning of the Second World War. 3,500 people had been condemned to death and 1,500 executed. Between 50,000 and 100,000 Greeks crossed the frontier and took refuge in the People's Democracies. But even that was not the end: the way forward was blocked. The counter-revolution was under way. It is still going on" (354).

The Travelling Players is Angelopoulos's meditation on the sweep of Greek history during this second crisis. The film moves from the dictatorship of Metaxas on to the Italian invasion of Greece; it subsequently depicts the German Occupation followed by the Nazis' defeat at the hands of combined Partisan communist forces (*andartes*) and Allied-backed royalist troops. Chapter 5 treats the film in close detail; here I will only highlight three issues concerned with Angelopoulos's presentation of history in the film.

In the opening of the chapter, I described the single march that embraced a number of years in one tracking shot. I have also discussed the impact of this film on Greeks when the film was released because it did dare to treat the "hidden" history of both World War II and the civil war, as told from a perspective of the Left. And I have suggested the "nondramatic" approach Angelopoulos champions. Here I wish to emphasize that *The Travelling Players* will remain one of the major accomplishments of world cinema for the wide scope of its narrative (1939 to 1952), for the breadth of its characters (a whole "troupe" rather than several central characters, as is customary in Hollywood films), and for its ability to portray individual destinies crossed by the currents of history.

Two further shots: The first is a lakeside scene at dawn as figures, including members of the acting troupe, stand by the shore. Slowly and beautifully a boat full of standing men crosses the mirror lake, approaching. What we come to realize is that this magical moment actually portrays a prison boat coming to pick up one of the actors who has been betrayed by a member of the group.

Any typical filmmaker would play the moment for all of its dramatic impact with dialogue, close-ups of tearful farewells, and strong music. Instead, Angelopoulos shoots in long shot and encourages us to absorb the beauty of the moment in juxtaposition with the meaning of the action: someone has betrayed his fellow actor and the latter is being taken away. This is not "history" as reenactment of the life of a famous Greek who suffered. It is, rather, a representation of the kind of moment that was reenacted thousands of times throughout Greece during those very troubled years. The horror is that there is no blood, no shouting, no demonstration. Instead, there is silence and a cold beauty. Angelopoulos's visual meditation on this piece of history, of course, is clear. Much of the horror for thousands of Greeks was a similar muted, undramatic betrayal, followed by a removal and the subsequent suffering.

The extended moment is also important. As we wait for the boat and then watch it leave, Angelopoulos emphasizes the importance of waiting and of watching, quite in contrast, once again, to the Hollywood dicta of "Cut from action to action" and "Keep it moving."

The second example involves speech. Punctuating such long visual and silent scenes are a series of direct camera monologues delivered by different members of the troupe, as if speaking to us personally. One of the main actors, Agamemnon (again, as noted in the previous chapter, each actor in "real life" has a name taken from Aeschylus's *Oresteia*), faces us on a train ride and simply tells us his life story. He explains that he arrived during 1922, when two million Greeks living in Turkey were allowed to leave and resettle in Greece. He tells us that he left Turkey in a boat, starving, and that he, like thousands of others, fell into the sea, "like sheep," and was at last pulled to safety and fed beans. Finally at night they reached Piraeus, the port city of Athens, and he went out the next day to seek work at the low pay of two drachmas a day. "All of this ate up my life," he says.

The speech gives him "character." It helps us see Agamemnon as an individual. But it does something else as well. His story is absolutely typical of most of the two million who came to Greece in the 1920s. Thus Angelopoulos captures history in such a representative story. And he does so, once again, without theatrics, without drama, without preaching. I would suggest that this approach of breaking up the flow of images with direct camera monologues achieves something else. These monologues lead us to realize that any character we see in the film could turn to us and reveal an equally complex and difficult story of his or her life. That they do not simply magnifies the film's potential in the viewer's eyes.

THE LEGACY OF THE CIVIL WAR

"What outsiders who come to Greece fail to understand," states Greek philosopher Ann Cacoullos, "is that Greece is still in the 1990s trying to get over the civil war of 1945–50."

No one is more aware of this fact than Angelopoulos. *The Travelling Players* brought many painful issues to the fore in 1975 and into the open as part of the dialogue of Greek culture with itself. And in *The Hunters* and *Voyage to Cythera* that past is reexamined from two differing perspectives.

The Hunters serves as an epilogue to Angelopoulos's trilogy about contemporary Greek history as viewed from the Left. Like *The Travelling Players*, *The Hunters* is framed as a cyclical view of history, beginning and ending with a similar shot. In *The Travelling Players* these framing shots depict the group standing before a train station about to begin another performance in another town. The implication was not, however, that history literally repeats itself, because these scenes represent different time periods, and the members of the troupe differ in age and composition from beginning to end. Similarly, *The Hunters* represents what Arnold Toynbee would call the spiral of history: events tend to repeat themselves in similar but not identical ways. The film opens with a bleak mountain snowscape in northern Greece as a group of hunters silently cross the landscape, etched in dark contrast against the snow, like the figures in a Karaghiozis puppet theater show. Suddenly they come upon the body of a Greek resistance fighter from the civil war. His blood has not yet frozen on the snow around him. One of the characters expresses shock: Had they not finished with this "story" in 1949–1950? How is it possible that the corpse of the civil war is still warm in 1977?

For over two and a half hours, Angelopoulos presents a variety of scenes suggesting Greek history from 1949 through 1965 in an effort to delineate something of what happened to the "corpse" of the bitter civil war. His message is simply that most of Greece sold out its revolutionary ideals for individual gain. The hunters represent a wide spectrum of Greek political views, from ex-leftist to arch-royalist. But the film literally revolves around the slain leader as scenes, ranging from police investigations (as in *Reconstruction*) to taverna celebrations, are acted out in the same room in which the body lies "in state" upon the table. This surreal but thematically clever device serves to guide the film through an ensemble of moments that are clearly more metaphorical than realistic. The film ends as the hunters return to the wintry mountain landscape to abandon the corpse. They cover it with snow, a burial that is obviously far from permanent, and then they disperse. We cannot help but be reminded, in terms of composition—characters in long shot against a stark landscape—of Renoir's *Grand Illusion* and von Stroheim's *Greed* (Death Valley replacing the snows of Greece!), films that similarly imply the futility of the characters' actions.

Voyage to Cythera (discussed in detail in chapter 6) takes the "corpse's" view. In this narrative of an old Partisan's return to Greece after more than thirty-five years in exile in the Soviet Union, Angelopoulos comes to the same conclusion as in *The Hunters*. Corpses, living or dead, from the civil war are not wanted in the new era of materialistic greed. Metaphorically in *Voyage* Angelopoulos suggests that rather than come to grips with the past—represented by Spyros, the returned andartis (Greek communist fighter)—Greece has preferred to try to "exile" it once more. Uniting the two films, Greek critic Vasilis Rafalidis has said that "the Spyros of *Voyage to Cythera* and the Rebel in *The Hunters* are two versions of the same legend" (22).

THE 1980S AND 1990S: THE BALKANS

It would be easy to see Angelopoulos's concern for Greek history and thus for the Greek sense of identity as interesting but still foreign to our American or any other non-Greek concerns. But Angelopoulos's increasing involvement with the history of Greece as tied to the history of the Balkans is of urgent importance to us all as the war in Bosnia, which threatens to spread, makes abundantly clear. As Daniel Schorr said in a

National Public Radio editorial as UN troops were being held hostage by Bosnian Serbs in May 1995, what is being tested is not just the authority and power of the United Nations in dealing with smaller warring nations but the whole idea of world order in a postcommunist world. And that, Schorr suggested, should make us all take note of Bosnia, for it affects us all.

The Suspended Step of the Stork (see chapter 8) and *Ulysses' Gaze* (see chapter 9) make us painfully aware of the complexity, pain, and, possibly, an emerging hope that exist in the Balkans, that cross section of East and West which includes northern Greece, Albania, Romania, Bulgaria, the former Yugoslavia, much of Turkey, parts of Hungary, and up to Austria. Both of these latest films can be seen as Angelopoulos's cinematic attempt to fulfill his personal wish for a new form of communication among Balkan peoples.

As we have noted, all of the Balkan territories were under Turkish domination for between four and five hundred years, a fact that, given the basically Orthodox religious cultures of most of these areas (with some Catholicism and a very small Jewish population in areas such as Thessaloniki and Sarajevo), has left complex wounds and scars that still have not healed, long after clear reasons for hatreds and certain behavioral patterns have ceased to exist.

It is enough to say at this point that both of these films speak directly with Greek history as a part of Balkan history and vice versa. Whatever the Greek character is and becomes is, Angelopoulos realizes, determined in part by this background that goes beyond the borders of Greece as outlined on geographic and political maps.

Furthermore, these two films can be seen to form a "Balkan Duo," with *The Suspended Step of the Stork* aimed at the political and social level and *Ulysses' Gaze* at the cultural implications of history in the Balkans at the end of the twentieth century. Both films, like almost all of Angelopoulos's films, are journey quests, and each is deeply concerned with considering the meanings of "borders" in the Balkans today. In *Suspended Step* there is an unforgettable tracking shot along a series of stationary boxcars that have become temporary shelters for homeless refugees from all over Europe, the Balkans, and the Middle East. As Angelopoulos's camera moves past open door after open door, we see Kurds, Turks, Albanians, and many others, families, couples, young and old, sitting and standing in the doorway, staring at us. It is a fresco in motion of those who are the victims of the confusion between nations at the end of the twentieth century. That the film is set in a northern Greek town, on the border, further highlights the "in between" condition the film explores. The search in the film begins as the young television reporter's search for a missing Greek politician (played by Marcello Mastroianni) who simply "dropped out" to do a kind of Greek "unsolved mysteries" coverage. What happens ultimately, of course, is that the reporter discovers not just an individual destiny but that of all refugees, for it is the Mastroianni figure who utters the line quoted in the introduction: "How many borders do we have to cross to get home?" The search for Citizen Kane becomes in this case the discovery of what has become an emblem of our times: the citizen at large as refugee.

Angelopoulos's most recent film, *Ulysses' Gaze*, literally picks up where the previous film left off, for Angelopoulos has included a clip from *The Suspended Step of the Stork* in the beginning of this latest film. But this search is not for a lost politician. Rather it is for a lost film, claimed to be one of the first films made in the Balkans, and Ulysses is this time not a reporter but a filmmaker who has lost his courage to make films. This odyssey takes the protagonist (Harvey Keitel) across the borders set up in *Suspended Step*, through all of the Balkan nations today, ending in war-ravaged Bosnia. The conclusion is once again the portrayal of an individual destiny—the director's as he finds the first film—and the destiny of the multitudes, since the director's fate is clearly linked to that of all of the Balkan peoples. That the first film is about Odysseus further highlights that the odyssey of the Balkans has yet to be completed.

Angelopoulos is not acting as a historian or a sociologist or a psychotherapist. He is instead a powerful filmmaker. But as an artist keenly aware of his times and the area of the world he lives in, he has succeeded more completely than any other filmmaker I am familiar with in reflecting the dispiritedness of this territory—a land that has been repressed for generation after generation to the point that solutions cannot be found until the questions and the issues can be articulately formed and shaped.

Robert Sklar has written about history and film, considering, in particular, the efforts of Brazilian filmmakers to establish a historic and national voice of their own: "The concept of the national, however, is hardly unproblematic. Quite apart from the historical ambiguities of nationalism—the slippage between its original meaning as racial group and its later meaning as politically organized entity, the oscillation between its progressive and regressive poles—there are also cultural and intellectual ambiguities at work" (281). Angelopoulos's films, ironically, clearly reflect such historical and national ambiguities.

What is finally significant about Angelopoulos's depiction of history as "the moving pattern of images" is that he has not given in to despair. Beyond the melancholy and silence and inaction, and the betrayal of individuals and ideas and traditions, there is still a sense of wonder, of innocence that cannot be totally destroyed, and thus of hope.

Chapter Three

Angelopoulos, the Continuous Image,

and Cinema

> *Build your film on white, on silence, and on stillness.*
> (Robert Bresson, *Notes on Cinematography*)

A NGELOPOULOS'S films suggest a concern with the form and potential of cinema itself. "Cinema has not yet been invented,"
André Bazin used to say in an effort to make viewers, filmmakers,
and critics alike understand that far too many films have settled for too
little in concept and execution. This chapter concerns the cinematic dimension of Angelopoulos's work, that element which most immediately
draws attention to itself. For Angelopoulos belongs to that small handful
of feature filmmakers who have continually redefined cinema with each
film they have made. In that sense we should have discussed the "cinematic" first, before delving into cultural echoes and connections. But, as
I hope the previous chapters have made clear, to discuss the aesthetics and
cinematic form of his work before understanding its historical and cultural context would be a mistake.

We should realize, however, that Angelopoulos is an unusual paradox
in the history of cinema: he is very clearly "Greek" as I have demonstrated, and yet he is an international filmmaker who has been influenced
by filmmakers from around the globe. He has observed: "I draw techniques from everything I've seen. . . . I continue to love . . . very much the
films of Murnau, Mizoguchi, Antonioni. More recently: Tarkovsky's
Stalker, Godard's *Every Man for Himself* and of course *Ordet*. . . . But
the only specific influences I acknowledge are Orson Welles, for his use of
plan-sequence and deep focus, and Mizoguchi, for his use of time and
off-camera space" (Wilmington 34). This chapter is dedicated to mapping
some of these influences, acknowledged and unacknowledged. For as
Michel Ciment has astutely observed, "Angelopoulos belongs to a generation for which the cinema could no longer be innocent" (Ciment and
Tierchant, *Theo Angelopoulos* 3). His cinema is born with an awareness
of many who have gone before and is thus consciously (and perhaps un-
consciously as well) a departure from this aesthetic legacy, as Ciment
concludes.

GREEK CINEMA, ANGELOPOULOS, AND
THE GREEK NEW WAVE

It is more than ironic that the first popular Greek feature film was a silent version of *Golpho*, the bucolic romantic stage melodrama that "history" keeps interrupting in *The Travelling Players*. Angelopoulos knew, of course, that in selecting this popular play for his film, he was simultaneously acknowledging the origins of Greek popular cinema.

Angelopoulos is, as we shall see, connected to Greek cinema, especially the "New Wave" of the late 1960s and early 1970s. Thus we need to understand something of the scope and development of Greek cinema. Yet on the other hand, he is unique among Greek directors in having succeeded during difficult times in securing funds to actually make his films—almost always as European coproductions—and in having seen those films win awards, critical acclaim, and foreign distribution. Local jealousies have therefore come into play, which, together with the collapse of any viably commercial Greek cinema (see below), means that since the early 1980s it is often easier to see his films abroad than in Greece.

Cinema in Greece has always been overshadowed by the other arts: literature, pictorial and plastic art, and music. Modern Greek poets, as we have discussed, such as Constantine Cavafy and George Seferis, together with others such as Odysseus Elytis and Yannis Ritsos have written some of the best poetry anywhere in the twentieth century. In fiction authors such as Nikos Kazantzakis, Antonis Samarakis, Spyros Myrivilis, Costas Taktsis, and others have explored many facets of Greek life to international recognition. And in music, composer-performers such as Mikis Theodorakis, the late Manos Hadjidakis, and Yannis Markopoulos have fused strong folk song elements with a contemporary flavor to form an authentic modern popular Greek musical tradition.

In contrast, Greek cinema remained basically an entertainment medium during its heyday of the 1950s and up through the mid-1960s with no artistic or intellectual pretensions, and few works were screened abroad. Of course the films of Michael Cacoyannis, Nikos Koundouros, and a very few others were exceptions to this rule.

As a pop entertainment medium, Greek cinema until the late 1960s had several important characteristics. First, as late as the mid-1960s, Athens alone had over six hundred active movie theaters and ticket prices were still cheap, so that one would have found many Greeks who went to the movies three to five times a week. In Athens, however, this more often than not meant going to American and European (French and Italian) films.

The Greek popular cinema developed its two major genres—melodrama and comedy—primarily for the villages and small towns where Greek-language films were preferred. And through such busy studios as Finos Films, movies starring comics like Thanassis Vengos and romantic dramas and comedies starring the Brigitte Bardot of Greece, Aliki Vouyouklaiki, poured onto the Greek screens at a rate of almost 150 a year, a number that, in a country of only eight million, almost equaled Hollywood's annual production rate at that period.

While none of these films made it to festivals or foreign distribution, they served an important cultural service for millions of Greeks. They were good entertainment. And as such, they grew out of the tradition of stage entertainment, particularly the epitheorisis (vaudeville-style) shows discussed in chapter 1. It is a significant footnote to this popular film tradition that a large segment of Greece's youth today loves to watch these old films *on television*. This is a generation tuned in to heavy metal music, trendy designer clothes, and, now, old Greek movies. This can be seen, as Angelopoulos himself has said, as part of a "retro" movement among Greek youth: "This is, of course, a desire for lost innocence and a kind of nostalgia. In Greece, the young see these past times as 'magic' and innocent. Life seems so simple and good in those old comedies and romantic melodramas" (interview, Athens, July 1993).

On the one hand it may seem quite understandable that cinema lagged behind the other arts in Greece. Aglae Mitropoulou has explained some of the reasons: political instability, shortages of money needed for quality productions, and the difficulties of competing with both Hollywood and quality European films. If one adds to this list the problems of censorship, the obstacles are clear. And yet it seems that perhaps the most important of the lot has simply been a lack of interest in cinema on the part of the leading intellectuals, artists, and writers, who have over the years chosen song, poetry, prose, and canvas to express their visions.

I say this for it should be clear that Greece is not unique in having experienced political upheavals and lack of funding for projects. Other countries, such as the former Yugoslavia, Spain, India, and Argentina, under similar circumstances have managed to produce unusually fine films despite (or perhaps because of) disadvantages.

But by the mid-1960s, a new generation of filmmakers was beginning to emerge in Greece. This group included Pantelis Voulgaris, Nikos Panayotopoulos, Takis Kanellopoulos, Alexis Damianos, Tonia Marketaki, and Costas Ferris, among others, who were raised on the French

New Wave, East European cinema, and new trends elsewhere. Thus they saw the potential for film to be an important cultural force in expressing and commenting on Greek realities and issues. All of these directors made debut films of great promise between 1965 and 1967.

But suddenly April 21, 1967, brought in the dictatorship of Yorgos Papadopoulos, and the Greek New Wave came to an abrupt halt. Strict censorship was imposed, and many filmmakers fled the country, particularly those with a left-wing political background. The Junta, as the dictatorship was known, made it impossible for many daring projects to be completed. Yet by 1970, the dictatorship had relaxed its censorship enough that a small group of talented directors again began to make films of sociocultural importance. Angelopoulos belongs to this group, for his *Reconstruction* (1970) was completed at this time, some three years into the Junta's rule.

All of this new generation of filmmakers shared a sense that cinema was a powerful medium to explore social issues in Greek culture (many, including Angelopoulos, shared a leftist viewpoint). Furthermore, this was a generation working outside the Greek "studio system," much like the French New Wave ten years earlier, making films on the cheap, with friends for the most part, and strongly aware of the cinema of other European, East European, and Asian countries—especially Japanese cinema—as well as the classics of Hollywood. In short, the works of this spirited and talented group demanded to be taken seriously along with poetry, art, music, and fiction as a part of a national ongoing dialogue.

There was an excitement in cinema circles during the Junta, for audiences knew that these young filmmakers were going beyond the borders of the safe to bring important issues onto the screen. The fact that they attempted to do so against the censors simply added to their attraction.

But two important changes occurred to deflate the movement. First, the fall of the Junta in 1974 meant the return of freedom, welcomed by all except die-hard fascists. Yet freedom also meant that it was more difficult to be "daring" since, suddenly, everything was permitted and no one wanted to listen—a situation we have seen repeated since then in the former communist countries as once prominent directors are now unable to find projects they are comfortable shooting.

And second, television, which ironically began in Greece on a mass scale in 1967, the year the Junta came to power, gradually led to the inevitable: the closing of movie theaters and the changing of viewing habits among Greeks. By 1980 there were fewer than three hundred movie theaters operating in Athens, and by 1994 that number had shrunk to some thirty-five as cable TV and private channels took over where there had once been only two state-run channels.

A DIRECTOR'S CINEMA: MICHAEL CACOYANNIS AND ANGELOPOULOS

Apart from the commercial Greek cinema outlined above, Michael Cacoyannis in particular managed from the 1950s on to make quality films for a world market. The differences between Cacoyannis, a Cypriot by birth, and Angelopoulos in their approaches to cinema are instructive.

Cacoyannis came to cinema with a strong theatrical background and with a special fondness for Greek tragedy. His understanding of tragedy, especially his enthusiasm for Euripides, infuses even his early neorealistic works such as *Stella* (1955), Melina Mercouri's debut film, and *The Girl in Black* (1956). In both of these films Cacoyannis established himself as a director capable of getting very strongly emotional performances—both comic and dramatic—from talented actresses. These well-crafted films have the character development and intense dialogue of quality stage dramas, but they also have an acerbic edge that suggests a critique of both Greek middle-class urban values and Greek village morality. Both films emerge as hymns of liberty to women who have been held back by patriarchal customs.

When Cacoyannis turned to the tragedies of Euripides, he was able to liberate them from "stuffy" performances and bring out the essence of the ancient dramas on-screen. In a remarkable series of films including *Electra* (1961), *Trojan Women* (1971), and *Iphigenia* (1977), Cacoyannis found a way to incorporate the spirit of Greek tragedy and the language of cinema to create powerful films set in ancient times but speaking to a wide modern audience. These tragedies are costume dramas, but Cacoyannis managed to open them up to cinema through the use of close-ups for personal moments and long shots for a sense of the epic and mythic scope of the dramas so that the tragedy comes alive.

Similarly, Cacoyannis proved adept at taking the Greek novel *Zorba the Greek* by Nikos Kazantzakis and working with Twentieth Century–Fox (which was founded by the Greek businessman Spyros Skouras) to produce a hit film in English starring Anthony Quinn and Alan Bates. The critical reaction to Cacoyannis's blending of art and commerce is perhaps best summed up by Pauline Kael's review of *Zorba*: "Responding to Michael Cacoyannis' *Zorba the Greek* is a little like taking a job with bad pay but marvelous fringe benefits. The central Life Force conception, banal and forced as it is, yet yields up something to us, something we want to believe in, and so it helps us enjoy the good things in the movie" (195). In short, Cacoyannis has been successful commercially and with qualified critical acclaim at adapting literary works—tragedies and novels—to the screen.

Angelopoulos's approach is almost the exact opposite. His dedrama-
tized films—none of which are adaptations of the work of others, and all
of which prove more static than active and more silent than argumenta-
tive—could not be further from the approach championed by Cacoyannis.
Greece's two best-known filmmakers, therefore, point to a very wide spectrum of possibilities for filmmaking.

THE GREEK FILM CENTRE

The establishment of a Greek Film Centre has been both a boon and a
thorn for Greek film. Television effectively ended the period of Greek studios, leaving a vacuum in terms of any organized way for Greek films to
be made. The Centre, established in 1981, was meant to help fill the gap.
From the beginning the Centre had the support of the late Melina Mercouri, the former actress who became minister of culture. In a preface to
a catalog of films supported by the Centre during the period 1981–1986,
she wrote: "The films listed here are intensely individual, full of contrasts
immensely varied—like freedom itself. In answer to the crisis now facing
the civilized world, in answer to the reductionist model which is being set
up before us, let cinema take a vigorous stand against schematization,
universalization, for the future will be what we make it: either a dream in
all its rich diversity, or a nightmare in its lethal uniformity" (*New Greek
Cinema* 6).

From the beginning, however, the Centre became a politicized arena
with charges and countercharges of favoritism leveled at Centre director
after Centre director. Nevertheless, the Centre has over the years been
able to point to a distinguished record of support for a variety of worthy
projects best exemplified in the special Greek cinema program, "Cine-
Mythology: A Retrospective of Greek Film," that traveled across the
United States in 1993.

Unquestionably a number of fine films have been made with the support of the Centre. However, as the critics note, instead of being a factor
in the advancement of the Greek film industry, it has virtually become the
industry, since there are no real ongoing film producers left in Greece.
Thus the danger of a monopoly that decides what is and is not to be
made, with many of the films produced never reaching the screens of even
the Greek cinemas after a one-time screening at the Greek Film Festival,
held in Salonika each September.

These difficulties aside, the Centre has been a supporter (but never the
sole funding source) of the following Angelopoulos films: *Voyage to
Cythera, The Beekeeper, Landscape in the Mist, The Suspended Step of
the Stork,* and *Ulysses' Gaze.*

ANGELOPOULOS AND EUROPEAN CINEMA

The great directors are first of all creators of form; if you wish, they are rhetoricians. This in no sense means that they supported the theory of "art for art's sake."

(André Bazin)

Angelopoulos is beginning to be discovered in the United States since winning the Grand Prix at Cannes in 1995. But he is best known in Europe where he has been celebrated for over twenty years. For despite the importance of his Greek heritage as I have outlined it, he is also very much a European director. Let us examine to what degree this is true. But let us do so realizing that in an overall sense, Angelopoulos belongs to a general tradition of European filmmakers on the Left that came of age in the 1960s and has, in its works, created both personal visions and sociopolitically conscious narratives. The similarities and also influences are many, as listed below. But let us mention yet another at this point: Wim Wenders. James Quandt has written that three of Angelopoulos's films—*Voyage to Cythera*, *The Beekeeper*, and *Landscape in the Mist*—form a loose road trilogy that bears more than a few similarities to Wim Wenders's road trilogy: *Alice in the Cities*, *Wrong Movement*, and *Kings of the Road*. "The Greek director's vision of his country," writes Quandt, "with its boarded-up cinemas, aimless youth and disillusioned old people, its faceless towns and expressways, coincides with Wenders' vision of Germany" (25).

The French Connection: "Increased Realism of the Image"

The French connection for Angelopoulos is a strong one. As noted, he studied and worked in Paris and speaks French fluently. I would suggest that the influences from France would include, first of all, the general ones shared by the French New Wave of taking film seriously (this includes the freedom to experiment with film language), of using film to express a personal vision, and of shaping political-social points of view as, for instance, Jean-Luc Godard did in the 1960s and 1970s.

But I also sense in Angelopoulos's work the influence of or at least a similarity to elements in the films of Jean Renoir and Robert Bresson, which, as André Bazin observed, practiced and explored "an increased realism of the image." The emphasis on the continuous image rather than a cinema of montage (swift editing) as championed by the Russians is particularly important for the understanding of Renoir's sense of realism. Bazin expressed it this way when he noted that Renoir first "uncovered the secret of a film form that would permit everything to be said without chopping the world up into little fragments, that would reveal the hidden meanings in people and things without disturbing the unity natural to them" (38).

Part of the power, for instance, of the closing shot of Renoir's *La Grande Illusion* is that we watch the two protagonists in one continuous shot walk into a wintry Alpine landscape, heading for the border, and becoming, as they get farther away from us, mere dots on the white horizon. A more Hollywood-style ending for this film about two French escapees from a German prison in World War I might have been to use an edited series of shots including close-ups of the men's faces, perhaps some closing dialogue, and strong music to guide our emotions. What Renoir does, however, by allowing us to watch the scene in the "natural" position of one witnessing two people walking away through a snowscape is to force us to contemplate their lives in relation to their present context— that of freedom and movement in nature—but also with a sense of nature as the force much larger than any personal destiny.

Compare the ending of Angelopoulos's *The Suspended Step of the Stork*. The reporter walks through the wintry landscape near the border as a dozen men in yellow raincoats climb telephone poles and begin to string wires between them, heading across the border. The effect is very much the same as that gained from *La Grande Illusion*. Because we are not subjected to a montage of short images, we are allowed the freedom to experience the realism of the image as it unfolds in real time and with a minimum of camera movement.

To what degree Angelopoulos feels he is directly influenced by French realism as described by Bazin is not the issue. What is important is that Angelopoulos's sense of realism is grounded in the same dynamics as those developed by Renoir and other French directors and, later, by the Italian neorealists.

Similarly, Angelopoulos shares with Robert Bresson the sense of building cinema through simplicity and minimalism. The quotation at the beginning of the chapter, "Build your film on white, on silence, and on stillness," best expresses his philosophy that less is definitely more when it comes to cinema. Furthermore, Bresson has written, "To create is not to deform or invent persons and things. It is to tie new relationships between persons and things which are, and as they are" (7). An example from Bresson's *Mouchette* (1967) is helpful.

The film follows the life of a young girl in a French village. The dramatic is downplayed, but many horrible things happen to her during the course of the story. At film's end we see her humming to herself on a hill by a lake. It appears to be a happy moment of solitude. Then she simply rolls down the hill into the lake and never comes up. It is clearly a suicide.

But there are no tears, no shouting, no memorable last words. There is only the simple act of quiet desperation done "naturally." The power of this unexpected ending is impossible to convey on paper. We are, quite simply, shocked, and forced to replay the film in our heads to grasp how absolutely correct this ending is.

Angelopoulos inhabits a similar muted cinematic landscape. He too could have spoken Bresson's words when the French director remarked, "Your imagination will aim less at events than at feelings while wanting these latter to be as documentary as possible" (8).

Italian Influences

That the cultures of Greece and Italy have, since ancient times, been interwoven is well known. On a cultural level, of course, we can point to the fact that Virgil's *Aeneid* builds on Homer's epics concerning the Trojan War, that for young Romans, to be educated meant either to have spent time in Athens or to have had Greek tutors and to have mastered Greek, and that Christianity developed in Italy at least partially on the foundation of Platonic philosophy. That the two peoples mixed in many locations, including Sicily, which had become a major Greek stronghold in ancient times, is also clear. And yet, as the Holy Roman Empire and the Byzantine Empire centered in Constantinople became distinct domains, differences have also developed.

The reverse influence—Angelopoulos's effect on Italian cinema—has already been alluded to in Bertolucci's praise of *The Travelling Players* as having had a strong impact on his own *1900*. Certainly other Italian directors have felt the influence, as have critics and audiences who have long been enthusiastic about Angelopoulos's attempt to build an authentic cinema beyond the realm of classical Hollywood structures.

But what of Angelopoulos's Italian connections? On a literal level, Angelopoulos has made use of Italian influences by working on all of his screenplays from *Voyage to Cythera* to the present with the Italian writer Tonino Guerra. Guerra had worked on a number of scripts for Antonioni, whose films Angelopoulos admires greatly. Similarly, he has used Marcello Mastroianni as the protagonist of *The Beekeeper* and *Suspended Step* and Omero Antonutti as the leading figure in *Megalexandros*. Why use these Italians? Certainly, of course, in the case of Mastroianni and Antonutti, the names and the faces have guaranteed a more visible profile for his films since almost no Greek actors are known abroad. But the Italian influence is also easily explained as one that allows Angelopoulos a "sympathetic" Mediterranean perspective which is, at the same time, different enough from his own and that of Greeks generally to create the distance he enjoys in portraying "the other Greece" he seeks. One can also say that part of the glory of Greece has always been the ability of Greeks to make use of the concepts and ideas of others to improve their own. Greeks developed their alphabet from the Phoenicians, they borrowed the wine god Dionysos from the Middle East, and many of their legends came from even farther away.

The lighthearted Oscar-winning *Mediterraneo* (1991, Gabriele Salvatores) was a joyful and comic underlining of "one face / one race" as the dictum applied to Greeks and Italians. And clearly on a more subtle and sober level, Angelopoulos has felt comfortable in working with an Italian writer and Italian actors because, on the one hand, they do share a lot in temperament, attitude, and outlook. And yet differences must also be important. Just as, stylistically, his long shots keep us at a distance considering the characters and stories in the context of their surroundings, so working with actors and a writer who are not Greek creates a similar "long shot": something similar to Greece but not exactly the same.

It would be natural to expect to see some influence in a Mediterranean filmmaker from the Italian neorealism movement of the late 1940s and early 1950s. But except for the documentary-like attributes of his first feature, *Reconstruction*, which bears some similarities to Luchino Visconti's *Ossessione* (1942) and Francesco Rosi's *Salvatore Giuliano* (1961), the influences appear minimal. Rather, the greatest Italian influence on Angelopoulos is Dante and Dante's version of the Ulysses story, as is detailed in chapter 8. Briefly, it is Dante who has Ulysses (Odysseus) leave Ithaca once he has settled scores because of his desire to wander. While Homer emphasizes Odysseus's wish to return home, Dante sees Ulysses's wanderings in search of "fresh knowledge" as representing the very essence of his character, as W. B. Stanford notes. This version of Ulysses/Odysseus's nature becomes, according to Stanford, "the master passion of his whole personality in the post-classical tradition, notably in Dante, Tennyson, Arturo Graf, and Nikos Kazantzakis" (75).

East European-Balkan Accents: The Beauty and the Ugliness

There is no doubt about the Balkan content of many of Angelopoulos's films, especially as noted in the previous chapter. But we can be more specific here about the East European and Balkan accents in his style and approach as well as in his subject matter. For Angelopoulos has gone beyond borders stylistically to forge his own "Balkan" Greek cinema. In speaking about the Balkans in general he has said: "One era is ending and another is about to be born. We are very much 'in between' all of us here. . . . I don't know what will happen now. But a new epoch is beginning. Borders, attitudes, relations, nations, all will change" (interview,

Athens, July 1993). There is no wonder, therefore, that he is influenced in various ways by those making films in this troubled area of the world.

More precisely, when asked why he so consciously makes films that are so completely "un-Hollywood," he answered that there are almost "no films that truly show all that is going on especially in this part of Europe." His aim, therefore, has been to show that each individual's life is "affected by these terrible problems we face that are larger than we are. I wish to capture something of the melancholy which we feel today, surrounded by murder here and there, and catastrophes in general" (interview, Athens, July 1993).

Even more so than in Western Europe, the East European, Balkan, and former Soviet filmmaker felt the need to be a spokesperson, critical of both The System and the outside forces working against individual freedom and fulfillment. As David W. Paul comments in his introduction to *Politics, Art and Commitment in the East European Cinema*, filmmakers under communism working in Eastern Europe and the former Soviet Union have always felt "the inseparability of arts and politics" (1). Angelopoulos's cinema reflects a similar bond connecting form, content, and purpose.

More specifically, several critics, including Penelope Houston (28), have noted the similarity between the long takes and exterior tracking shots in Angelopoulos's films and the directorial style of Hungarian director Miklós Jancsó. Like Jancsó in films such as *The Round Up* (1965) and *The Red and the White* (1967), Angelopoulos rejects montage in favor of the continuous take, but a continuous take often coupled with tracking and circling camera movement that calls attention to itself and thus to the changing perspectives the camera offers of the subjects before its gaze.

The similarities between Jancsó and Angelopoulos in terms of historical orientation and stylistic focus are even stronger than might first appear. The following description of Jancsó's cinema by Mira and Antonin J. Liehm could equally well be applied to Angelopoulos: "All political systems, all historical epochs, can be accommodated in this cinematic *ballet of violence and oppression*, evolved from the tension between the 'beauty' of artistic stylization and the 'ugliness' of testimony" (394, italics my own). What the Liehms emphasize is that the aesthetic form offers a counterpoint to the "violence" of authority/politics/power that manages to lift the moment beyond its historical context onto a more universal plane.

Jancsó's approach can further be described as an effort to avoid simple cause-and-effect psychology and Aristotelian motivation of internal character development. Again, we recognize that Angelopoulos has made a similar perspective his own. When the Liehms say of *The Red and the White* that "for the most part figures are filmed in deep focus against an unchanging, indifferent, and lyrically 'beautiful' landscape " (395), we realize that Angelopoulos's technique is completely in tune with this earlier East European filmmaker's goals.

JAPANESE SILENCE AND OFF-CAMERA SPACE

> *Angelopoulos watches things calmly through the lens. It is the weight of his calm and the sharpness of his unmoving regard that give his films their power.*
> (Akira Kurosawa)

Japanese cinema and culture might at first glance seem very far removed from Angelopoulos's work. But Angelopoulos is aware of their influence on him, as noted at the beginning of the chapter in his homage to Kenji Mizoguchi. Much of the violence and even what is normally considered dramatic or important to a narrative occurs off-camera in Angelopoulos's works. In the rape scene, for instance, in *Landscape in the Mist* we do not hear or see the rape. We only see the results as the camera tracks in for a look at Voula staring at her bloody hand. Of course Greek tragedy also kept much of the violence offstage so that audiences could similarly concentrate on the results and not the action. But Angelopoulos has said, "The same is true of Chinese and Japanese theater" (interview, Athens, July 1993).

Of the Japanese filmmakers, Kenji Mizoguchi's name is the one he mentions most often, and he invokes, among others, the film for which Mizoguchi is best known in the West, *Ugetsu Monogatari* (*Tales of the Pale and Silvery Moon after the Rain*, 1953). This film about several characters in sixteenth-century rural Japan is "full of beautiful images," as Georges Sadoul comments, "that have the mystical beauty of classical Japanese paintings and are even occasionally reminiscent of the paintings of the sixteenth-century Flemish painter, Breughel" (389). Many of the characteristics of his cinema are directly mirrored in aspects of Angelopoulos's films that I have described above. David Thomson formulates four premises concerning Mizoguch's work:

1. That Mizoguchi has an extraordinary capacity for relating Japanese legend and art to the twentieth-century medium.
2. That *Ugetsu*'s fusion of fantasy and reality—despite the classical setting—is as expressive of the dreamlike nature of filmgoing as, say, *Citizen Kane*, *Vertigo*, or *Pierre Le Fou*.

3. That Mizoguchi describes people under ordeal with a calm and resignation that is as encouraging as the way Renoir treats his characters.

4. That he sees a basic disparity between the hopes and preoccupations of men and women that can make for tragedy or comedy, and which is essentially mundane despite the exotic period and phantasmagoria of *Ugetsu*. (417)

Thomson goes on to note that in such a universe as Mizoguchi represents, it is often unclear whether characters are at the center or on the periphery of the "action" unfolding, a description that fits many of Angelopoulos's characters precisely. Electra, for instance, in *The Travelling Players* emerges as the main figure in the troupe, yet as such, she is often simply standing in the background as events unfold in the foreground. Thus, in both Mizoguchi and Angelopoulos, to be a protagonist may often mean to be simply a witness to what occurs rather than a prime mover.

Angelopoulos is also influenced by Ozu Yasujiro's cinema. In *Tokyo Story* (1953), for instance, the final shot is of the father sitting alone in his home. The silence and the continuousness of the shot are important. We focus on the protagonist all the more because of the silence. He is old and alone, and the simplicity of the shot coupled with the silence, except for the sound of a few boats on the river nearby, increases our feelings of sympathy for this man.

Clearly Ozu's cinema emerged from Japanese traditions of painting and art, as Noel Burch has observed: "Essential traits of Japanese painting and narrative arts, and of typically Japanese social behavior are always present in his films" (184). The evocation of "the floating world," of a bare minimalism of background and simplicity of line that characterize Japanese art and the cinema of Ozu clearly appealed to Angelopoulos in his effort to evoke "the other Greece" using "other" cinematic means than those employed by traditional commercial cinemas.

Orson Welles, John Ford, and the Hollywood Musical

Angelopoulos has an appreciation for American film despite his work's obvious differences from the typical Hollywood narrative film. His respect for Orson Welles is documented in more detail in chapter 8, with special consideration of the influence of *Citizen Kane*.

Deep focus, however, needs more commentary. Orson Welles did not invent the use of deep focus—an image in which foreground and background are simultaneously in focus, often so that the action in one plane can comment on that in another—but he did explore more fully than anyone before him the potential of this technique to reveal character, story, and thematic concerns. Similarly, Angelopoulos has gone even further to frame each shot so that depth of field becomes a significant "character" in and of itself, especially since so little dialogue occurs in his films. Thus the stark beauty of the wedding scene in *Suspended Step*, for instance, in which the bride and her followers are on the riverbank in the foreground and her groom and his followers on the opposite distant shore, is made even more powerful because we see everything in sharp, deep focus simultaneously.

The influence of American musicals might at first seem surprising. But Angelopoulos has said, "They stayed inside me subterraneously, the films of Minnelli and Stanley Donen" (Wilmington 33). And when we consider the importance of music as well as silence (the paucity of dialogue making the use of music seem all the more significant) in his films, a thread of influence is understood. For at the heart of the musical is the effort of people to express themselves not through dialogue but through song and dance. When we add that ancient Greek drama, both tragedy and comedy, began in song and dance, Angelopoulos's approach becomes all the more understandable. Angelopoulos clearly appreciates the stylized presentation of character and story through music in the American musical, combining, as in Minnelli (e.g., *Meet Me in St. Louis*, *An American in Paris*, *Kismet*) and Donen (e.g., *On the Town*, *Singin' in the Rain*, *Seven Brides for Seven Brothers*), both realism and expressionism. *Reconstruction*, for instance, begins and ends with the mountain folk tune; *The Travelling Players* begins and ends with the accordion player, while most of the "political" conflicts within the four-hour film are waged through opposing songs.

Finally, the John Ford influence is one of both vision and simplicity of presentation. Ford saw himself as a commercial filmmaker, especially of Westerns, but though it has never been the fashion of American directors, particularly of Ford's generation, to hold forth on thematic and philosophical dimensions of their films, critics and viewers alike are aware that Ford created his own vision of America's destiny and its past. His use of Monument Valley, Utah, for instance, became the "trademark" of his West, a place where lone individuals acted out their destinies against a magnificent landscape. And Ford's continual return to that landscape, as opposed to, say, a California desert near Hollywood, reminds us of Angelopoulos's fascination with his own beloved northern and isolated rural Greece (in Ford's case, the director apparently enjoyed his isolated locations as one bastion against nosy studio executives).

That Ford, like Angelopoulos, was concerned with history and culture beyond the realm of mere movie entertainment has been detailed by numerous film scholars. Joseph McBride and Michael Wilmington, for instance, observe that Ford was "an outsider in search of an allegiance, harkening back to a simpler, purer existence" and vision of America (17) and thus representing a contradiction between the individual and the community, between personal destiny and the law. What helped punctuate these contradictions, however, and also bridge them were rituals—funerals and weddings in particular—which we find throughout his films. Once again, Angelopoulos's sense of both the contradictions within history and a culture and the role of rituals—funerals and weddings included—as forms of communal and personal renewal and communication bears marked similarities to Ford's outlook.

SOVIET AND RUSSIAN KINSHIPS: CINEMAS OF DISTANCE AND COMPASSION

Angelopoulos was, before glasnost and the fall of the Berlin Wall, more ironically amused than bothered by the fact that his films received no distribution in the Soviet Union or in many of the Eastern Block countries. For as a filmmaker concerned with depicting the process of history from a predominantly "leftist" and even Marxist (especially in *The Travelling Players*) perspective on-screen, he received almost no attention from critics or audiences behind the Iron Curtain.

In the case of the Soviet Union, such neglect appears all the more peculiar, for there are influences from and parallels to both the silent Soviet cinema of Sergei Eisenstein in the 1920s and the work of Andrei Tarkovsky in the 1960s–1980s, as noted in chapter 1. The basic connection, it seems to me, between Angelopoulos and the best of the Soviet filmmakers is that they all have taken cinema quite seriously as an artistic medium but also, even more important, as a means of dialectically exploring history, culture, and politics.

Eisenstein is known, of course, as the filmmaker who most championed the technique of "montage" (swift editing of short shots to create a special impact) as seen in films such as *Potemkin* (1925) and *Strike* (1924). Thus on the surface level, no one could seem further removed from Angelopoulos, with his extended and deliberate static long shots and carefully calculated slow tracking shots. And yet the two men are united by their need and ability to experiment with film language to discover how best to present their dialectical visions. Each in his own way is reinventing cinema for his own ends. Furthermore, we should note that Eisenstein never limited his montage to swift short cuts dialectically contrasted to each other. He spoke, for instance, of "polyphonic montage," "through a simultaneous advance of a multiple series of lines, each maintaining an independent compositional course and each contributing to the total compositional course of the sequence" (75). By "lines," Eisenstein explains, he means voices, varying camera angles and distances, music, foreground and background, light and dark, and much more. In this expanded view of montage as a rich texturing of tensions, visual and sound related, within a frame, we can recognize much of the density of an Angelopoulos shot, scene, or sequence.

In *Ulysses' Gaze*, when Harvey Keitel and his old friend are toasting filmmakers they love, the friend asks about Eisenstein. Keitel, playing a Greek-American filmmaker, answers, "We loved him but he didn't love us." What did Angelopoulos mean to suggest? "I don't know," he has said. "It just came out when I wrote the script, but I do agree it is possible to consider that there is montage within each of my frames. I do consider him a great filmmaker" (interview, Athens, July 1995).

One final parallel and perhaps influence connecting Eisenstein and Angelopoulos. *Potemkin* is always mentioned as one of the great early Soviet films. And yet it represents a period before the Russian Revolution and focuses not so much on the pre-Revolutionary forces as on the suffering of the victims, those innocent civilians cut down on the Odessa Steps by czarist troops. Eisenstein captures the pain of simple people suffering unjustly because of forces that they cannot control. Similarly, Angelopoulos does not present the wars, revolutions, and dictatorships in Greece in a documentary or with a typical focus on important events and battles. Rather, he, like Eisenstein, captures the sufferings and confusions felt by common folk who are unable to control the historical forces they cross or belong to.

In this sense, I would say that Angelopoulos shares with Eisenstein a dialectical view of cinema and history that both distances and draws us in to feel compassion for the underdogs who have suffered greatly throughout history.

Part Two . . . . .

FIVE FILMS

Then the mind-traveled man leant on the wild pear's trunk:

the pilgrims still lay, wearied, on the ground about him,

and in the shedding petals of dawn's rose he saw

his whole life like a legend walk toward the bright sun.

He spread his hands and blessed his mind and all his life:

"May you be blessed, my life, the bitter laurel's brief

and scented garland still upon your snow-white hair."

(Odysseus in Nikos Kazantzakis's Odyssey: A Modern Sequel)

I have a soft spot for the ancient writings. There really is nothing new. We are all just revisiting and reconsidering ideas that the ancients first treated. (Theo Angelopoulos)

Chapter Four

Reconstruction: "Help Me, I'm Lost"

RECONSTRUCTION (1970), his first feature, offers a preview of Angelopoulos's films to follow. And yet it stands on its own as well, not only for its vivid black-and-white cinematography, but because it is his only film that places a woman at the center of the entire narrative (*Landscape in the Mist*, with its twelve-year-old Voula sharing the focus of our attention with her younger brother, would be a distant second in this category). In this film, a modern Clytemnestra murders her returning husband as in the ancient myth. And, through Angelopoulos's reconstructions, the film sketches a view of the larger "death" of Greek villages during the first half of the twentieth century.

"Help me, I'm lost," cries protagonist Eleni to her brother once she has confessed her crime near the film's end. It is a cry that, amplified through this award-winning debut film, speaks for a whole culture about "the other Greece" that Angelopoulos has dedicated himself to speaking for and about.

Opening Shots: Documentary Folk Songs

A bus arrives in a mountain village in the rain. The scene gives new meaning to the adjective "desolate," for the sound of the rain is quite loud and the stark black-and-white cinematography of Giorgos Arvanitis heightens the "monochrome" quality of the landscape and the village.

A thirtysomething man gets off and walks through the rain and mud up through the village. An old Greek mountain folk song is heard on the sound track, sung by a male singer in the high-pitched, "pinched" voice style of Epirus, the northern area of Greece that borders on Albania:

> Pretty lemon tree
> with so many lemons.
> I kissed you and got sick
> and didn't call the doctor.
>
> Bend down your twigs
> so I can cut a lemon.
> I kissed you and got sick
> and didn't call the doctor.

Angelopoulos's first feature was drawn from a newspaper story of a village woman and her lover who murdered her husband, a guest worker in Germany, upon his return to the village. On the surface, such a tawdry tale seems more the stuff of the new "true crime" shows on television than a basis for a serious filmmaker making his debut. But in opening up this back-page news item, Angelopoulos managed simultaneously to evoke a whole world of decaying Greek village life and to imply mythic elements that point toward the best-known Greek legend of a returning husband murdered, the Agamemnon cycle, as depicted by Aeschylus in his *Oresteia* trilogy. And he has, as well, tapped into an oral folk-culture tradition, as discussed in the first chapter.

But further tensions are created from the very beginning. As noted in the introduction, the actual beginning of the film features the male narrator (Angelopoulos himself), in voice-over, giving a "documentary" thrust to the film by quoting the falling population statistics for the village (1,250 in 1939, and 85 in 1965). Of course Hollywood (*Casablanca*, to mention a prominent example) makes use of the same technique of wrapping an individual drama within a much larger "true story" frame. *Casablanca* is not just another romance but a wartime romance taking place while World War II was still in progress. Similarly, *Reconstruction* cues us to consider the individual tale that follows on a larger cultural scale and with an almost anthropological focus.

The film thus fuses documentary, drama, tragedy, myth, and folk ballads (the lemon tree song). Yet the film is in structure and theme also, as the title suggests, a series of reconstructions. One is forensic: the district police have arrived in the village to re-create the crime as part of their investigation. Another is journalistic: the police are soon followed by the media trying to get a "hot" story for the press and for television. The film demands our close attention because the switches between the "real" events and the reconstructed ones are jumbled. We are not allowed to follow the simple chronological drive of a genre police film.

What results from all of these interweavings of narrative and cinematic technique is not a Greek version of neorealism but, as Nikos Kolovos observes, "meta-realism" (44): we understand that, taken together, all of these reconstructions point beyond the local murder to deeper crimes and clues, beyond individual situations to that of a dying Greek village and thus to Greek society itself, to modern history as well, and to that which goes before and beyond history, myth.

FILM NOIR IN GREECE: "SHE CAST A SPELL ON ME"

A synopsis of *Reconstruction* helps us reconstruct the fragments in their presented order so that we may begin to reassemble them as we ourselves wish.

5. Eleni under arrest in *Reconstruction*

Before beginning, however, we should recognize that in this, Angelo-poulos's first feature, he has followed a time-honored tradition of young directors starting out: that of nodding to the crime film genre, most espe-cially the "tough guy" film noir Hollywood works of the 1940s and 1950s, such as *The Maltese Falcon*, *The Big Sleep*, *Detour*, and many others, including Michael Curtiz's *Angels with Dirty Faces*, the first film Angelopoulos remembers seeing (Themelis 5). Directors who have made such a debut include Jean-Luc Godard, with his Bogart homage and par-ody in *Breathless* (1959), and the Coen brothers with *Blood Simple* (1984). He has, of course, made the genre completely his own by switch-ing the location from a city to a village and by making a "tough woman" the center of attention instead of a male detective or criminal.

Fade in:

A man in his early thirties arrives in a desolate mountain village in northern Greece and walks into one of the stone houses. A young girl is eating at the table. The man asks the girl's name, but she does not answer. Then she finally asks him, "What's your name?" Outside the home, the man's wife, Eleni, returns, and after a pause they embrace in the rain. Two other children, one girl and one boy, are present.

As the group sit around the table inside as a family for what is clearly the first time in many years, the image becomes a freeze-frame and we hear a harsh mountain instrumental folk tune (words given above). Credits roll.

When the credits are completed, the first "reconstruction" scene begins.

The police detective asks Eleni how her husband (Costas) looked. "I was in a daze," she comments, appearing to put the blame on her neighbor and lover, Christos Ghikas.

There is a cut back to the time of the crime: we see Christos and Eleni dragging Costas's body out into the night. We sense that Eleni is in clear control. She suggests they might cut Costas up in pieces. Christos immediately slaps her. What should they do with the body?

They bury it.

The next day Christos is heading down the mountain to a river.

Back at the house, Eleni plants onions in the freshly dug up ground in the garden. Later, inside, Eleni is doing dishes when her daughter arrives from school. "Your father left again," she says.

Reconstruction scene 2 now follows: The police ask Christos to explain what happened, and he suggests that it was Eleni who put a rope around Costas's neck. When she contradicts this version, Christos blurts out, "She's trying to get rid of me too." Four police officers and one detective are present.

Flashback again—the day after the murder. We see Eleni working part-time in a kafeneon. When Christos shows up, she says, "Come tonight." That night, as goat bells are ringing in the dark, Eleni and Christos escape the village and head by boat across a lake to Yannina, a small northern city and center for all surrounding villages, where they take a room in a hotel using the dead husband's identity card to check in with.

Christos leaves her alone in the hotel room, where she watches from the window as children play by the lake. Christos's wanderings through the town bring him to a coffeehouse, to the bus station to buy a ticket to Athens, and then onto the Athens bus. When the bus stops for all the men to relieve themselves by the roadside, Christos leaves the bus and doubles back to town.

Returning to the hotel room, he does not speak but rather drinks. Then, when she has partially undressed, he springs up saying, "I'm going for a walk." He wanders the town by night. She remains alone in bed, waiting. He finally returns, pounces on her, and they attempt crude sex fully clothed.

It is the dawn of the next day, and they walk along the muddy highway.

Reconstruction sequence 3 follows: Eleni has confessed. The press has arrived. We learn that the two younger children will be sent to an orphanage, and the older daughter will be taken by a wealthy businessman in Vienna as a kind of maid. Christos's assertion is, "She cast a spell on me."

In a chronological leap backwards to a time after the murder but before the police arrived, we see a journalist (played by Angelopoulos in a cameo role) arrive from Athens. It is market day: cattle are being herded around, and there is dancing in the village to the flute and lute. Suddenly there is an atmosphere of village life, a reminder of what it might have been like years ago. In the midst of all, there is gossip about Eleni.

Finally, an old woman tells a policeman on the road about the murder. We then see the detective approaching the stone house, goat bells sounding all around.

In the village kafeneon we hear men talking. One old man says, "If your wife is a whore, you either kill her or she kills you. There is no other way." The journalist (Angelopoulos) records this on a tape recorder.

Eleni sweeps the floor of the shop where she works as soldiers sing.

Police come to her home. Later Christos visits her. "You got me into this, bitch," he says. She tells him, "If anything goes wrong, I'll take all the blame."

Eleni next crushes her husband's suitcase with an ax and carries a sack of his belongings up the mountain where she burns them. What follows is a series of actual documentary interviews about the life of guest workers in Germany done in voice-over while the image of the village remains on-screen. The male interviewer asks why each individual goes to Germany. Answers include "Life is better there," "I will grow fat and pretty in Germany," and "We can go to cinemas there."

One old man speaks about the village in the old days: "It was good then, there was work and play. But we will die and the village will be empty. This will not be good for the cities either."

The police finally arrive.

For the first time we see the complete village and hear voices of the villagers. The police walk down the mountain as the camera slowly tracks in on them. Then Eleni's brother, Yorgis, shows up at her house. He speaks with the police.

Eleni is hanging clothes. Her brother begins to talk seriously with her as a haunting mountain tune begins on the sound track. We see goats as Eleni and her brother sit on a mountain and walk by a river. At home again, she makes bread as Yorgis questions her. "The police went to Yannina and they know you are lying."

Eleni is silent.

Yorgis: "Somebody saw Christos that night coming here."

She suddenly breaks and appeals to her brother, "Help me. I'm lost." He pauses and says, "What have you done, poor fool?" There is no music and no emotion shown. She answers, "It is nobody's fault." At dawn, Yorgis waits for the police.

Cut to reconstruction scene 4. Both Eleni and Christos are finally brought before the detective, who swears at them. Christos says, "It's not me, I swear by my children." Eleni lunges at the detective but is held back by the police. The detective asks her to show them what she did with the rope. She breathes heavily, holds the rope, and throws it down.

Outside reporters and a camera crew are shooting. It is time to take Eleni away.

Village women gather. After the camera does a complete circular pan, the women attack Eleni as the open Jeep begins to pull away. They try to pull her from the Jeep, screaming.

The final scene takes us back to the moment of the murder.

The husband, Costas, walks into the house after we see Christos go in, but Costas has not seen him. A dog howls. We watch the front of this simple stone house.

Silence. The three children come into the yard and play. Finally Christos leaves. Eleni watches the children play a game of tag. They all go inside. The door closes and the "Lemon Tree" folk song begins again.

The Death of the Greek Village

The old man's statement, two-thirds of the way through the film, that the death of the village "will not be good for the cities either" is an unexpected finger pointed from within the film at those, mostly in cities, watching the film (ironically, no film could be shown in the village represented in *Reconstruction* since no cinema existed there).

Greeks used to joke that Athens was not a city but simply the largest village—with over four and a half million inhabitants—in Greece. Because contemporary Greece has grown so rapidly, especially since the end of the Greek civil war in 1950, one could truthfully say that almost everybody in Athens either came from a village originally or is a second-generation Athenian. And certainly it takes no sociologist to remind us that those who move from a village to a city often go to extremes in attempting to erase their rural backgrounds.

Thus one can sense, particularly for 1970 when *Reconstruction* appeared, how many questions Angelopoulos's debut film created about the changes that Greece—particularly rural Greece—had undergone since the end of the war. Consider the following three points. By 1970 the Greek film industry, as mentioned in the previous chapter, had made hundreds of light comedies and equally light romances and cheap melodramas, almost all of which hinged on the simple formula of the village girl or fellow moving to Athens. Until television began to take serious hold on the Greek population in the mid-1970s, ticket sales for Greek films were primarily in the towns and villages. By beginning his feature film career with a film that excludes the city and focuses entirely on a village, and a clearly dying one at that, Angelopoulos was announcing himself not only as a strong leftist politically but as a filmmaker willing to fly in the face of traditional narrative and commercial success.

Second, note that by 1970 the "export" stereotype of Greece as a land of sunshine, comedy, passion, and lively music (especially by Mikis Theodorakis and Manos Hadzidzakis) had been set by films such as Cacoyannis's *Zorba the Greek* and Jules Dassin's *Never on Sunday* (1960). From the very beginning of his career, therefore, Angelopoulos forced audiences to acknowledge, consider, and deal with "the other Greece," the one not enjoying urban development, a tourist boom, and a steady rise in the standard of living. We should add, too, that this rural Greece of villages near the Albanian border is a Greece that few Greeks have ever seen. The film was, therefore, something of a cultural electroshock for Athenians in particular at the time of its release.

Finally, by 1970, the Greek Junta led by George Papadapoulos and several other army colonels had been in power for three years and had imposed a very strong censorship on the arts. Even many productions of Aristophanes and Euripides were banned during the first two years of the Junta when their level of insecurity ran particularly high. Given this seemingly ominous totalitarian context, 1970 would appear to be the worst of times for a new filmmaker to make a debut with a film involving politically challenging dimensions.

Irony has always been a strong suit in Greek history, and Angelopoulos's *Reconstruction* fits in this tradition well. For the Junta leaders were all villagers themselves who took over the country in large part because they felt the moral fabric of contemporary Greece was wearing thin. Their hope was to restore village morality and "Greek Christian values." *Reconstruction* could be seen as a document of the sad condition of the country in which so many villagers had abandoned their homes; it could also be argued that the film is a kind of backhanded parable on what happens to unfaithful wives in rural patriarchal cultures.

Let us be clearer about Angelopoulos's interest in the death of traditional Greek villages. He has said that the village in Greece was a complete world in miniature: "The old Greek villages had a spirit, a life, full of work and play and festivity. Of course Greek villages began to lose population by the turn of the century, but it was really World War II and the subsequent civil war in Greece that completely destroyed the reality and concept of the Greek village. Our whole way of life was changed by these two catastrophes (interview, Athens, July 1993).

Would Greece still be a village-centered nation without the two world wars? Angelopoulos replies that change would have come anyway. But not so swiftly and not so drastically. He notes: "The changes would have been made in a much more gradual and gentle way. You have to understand that part of the result of these wars was that in the 1950s over 500,000 village men went to Germany, but also to America and Australia and other places to become guest workers. That meant a big shift in village life. Suddenly the men were gone and the women remained. With all these changes, the *spirit* of the villages began to die." *Reconstruction*, set in the early 1960s, captures this death well. But is Angelopoulos a romantic from Athens who dreams of a flight to the villages? "No," he says emphatically, "I have no such desires or hopes!" He comments, rather, that he was marking the passing of something beautiful that has died. Angelopoulos finishes by stating: "It is like the death of a strong love affair—you want to remember it, think about it, examine it. It is hard to let go of! What do I want to happen? I simply want our life here to become more human. We need to return to those places to find much of what is still important and authentic to our lives (interview, Athens, July 1993).

Put all together, *Reconstruction* "announced" clearly that a new voice had entered Greek cinema. The message was not lost on European critics and festival audiences either. The film swept the 1970 Greek Film Festival awards in Salonika (best director, best cinematographer, best film, best actress, plus the overall critics' prize) and, among international awards, won the coveted Georges Sadoul Award in France as the best film shown in France in 1971.

THE UNITY OF PLACE AND DISUNITY OF TIME

Angelopoulos maintains a clear unity of place in *Reconstruction*: the northern mountain village. His reconstruction of events, however, leads him to deconstruct time. The place is known, and the action is not only simple—a returning husband murdered—but, as we shall discuss, mythic. But how those events are presented, re-presented, and reconsidered is anything but simple.

What are we to make of Angelopoulos's scrambling of time? Of course on one level this approach cues us that he will not employ the conventions of the dominant Hollywood narrative cinema. Such a move toward a more active demand for the audience to participate in the telling of a story also means that Angelopoulos wants us to consider the validity of any reconstruction of reality, including, finally, cinema itself. For we become aware that it is the filmmaker himself—unidentified—who has shuffled the time sequences we watch. Certainly the film could be reedited chro-

nologically and might, by the way, have done much better at the box office in such a traditional form. This is not, however, what Angelopoulos
was after in his first feature.

For Angelopoulos, the disunity in time quite simply mirrors the breakdown of the village and thus of Greek culture itself. The reconstruction
occurs from outside the village (district police and Athenian reporters)
and never leads to a solving of the crime: we are left looking at the outside
of the simple stone house and we are never privy to what really happens
or why.

ELENI'S STORY

Reconstruction does not slavishly repeat or reconstruct the Agamemnon
legend in modern village clothing. Rather, Angelopoulos boldly began his
feature career choosing to focus on the woman, Eleni, who is simultaneously Clytemnestra, a modern village guest worker's widow, a mother,
an adulteress, and, finally, a murderer. Since women were the ones who
usually remained at home in these dying Greek villages, we recognize the
significance of Angelopoulos's narrative and choice of protagonist. We
are viewing Eleni's story.

But what we see is disturbing, for insofar as we are denied a traditional
(even by the standards of Greek tragedy, as we have noted in earlier chapters) psychologically based sense of character, narrative, and motivation,
we find ourselves *watching* this silent woman, but not coming to know
her in any of the usual ways in which we get to know screen characters.
Yes, we see her drag the body out, and we see her planting spring onions
and working in the kafeneon and interacting with the police. But we
never hear her express her reasons for the act or for taking Christos as a
lover, or for trying so ineptly to lay down a "cover" in her trip with Christos to Yannina. We thus have no way to know how she feels or what she
thinks. Clearly, Angelopoulos's conscious approach to narrative presentation in his first feature was a brave leap.

Yet we begin to *feel* through the accumulation of details, of shots, and
of moments the oppressive weight of this male-centered society in which
she lives. She serves men in the kafeneon; she is investigated by male police and followed by male correspondents and TV crews. And in her brief
trip to the city, she must remain alone in the room while Christos wanders
through what Angelopoulos reveals as very much a city of men in tavernas and kafeneons, of male soldiers marching and male civilians roaming
through the streets. Finally, in "documentary" style, it is an old man in
the kafeneon who tells the camera that a woman who cheats on her husband is a "whore."

Angelopoulos carefully avoids the melodrama that would result if Eleni did express herself fully or give a "tragic" monologue in the tradition of ancient drama. Rather, her silence speaks for itself. Furthermore, because, as in all of his later films, "repressed history" is being represented by the film, the brief moment of expression—when she simply appeals to her brother, "Help me, I'm lost"—we glimpse her anguish with even greater force than that of a conventional dramatic film.

In terms of Aeschylus's trilogy, Angelopoulos has condensed the three separate tragedies into one work. And, as we have discussed, if the classical *Oresteia* finally offers a victorious vision of Athenian society under law, *Reconstruction* shows the Furies of the village attacking Clytemnestra, offering no hope for a better tomorrow. Reading the film through the lens of contemporary Greek history, we see that the destruction of Greek village culture through the men's emigration to Germany in the 1950s and 1960s particularly led to an inversion of the ancient myth. The guardians of mothers and women, the Furies, have actually turned on a mother. Unlike the ancient drama, the film portrays no Aeschylean Athena or court of Athenian law that can or will set things right again through compromise and open discussion.

The end of Eleni's story is that she, ironically, finally gets to leave the village, but not on any terms she would ever have desired. Angelopoulos's first feature furthermore captures Eleni as extremely durable and focused. As we shall explore in subsequent chapters, Angelopoulos opens up the possibilities of a "new humanity" in later films such as *The Suspended Step of the Stork*. But in his first film, he closes with the bleakest of possible endings: we have experienced life in a dying village, and we have witnessed one story as Eleni loses her children, her lover, her home, and, of course, the husband she has murdered. She has also been spared death at the hands of angry village women only to meet, later, the workings of "justice" in courts far away from home. The ending is tragic. Yet Angelopoulos allows not an ounce of sentimentality or melodrama. There is only the plaintive sound of the Greek folk song reminding us that this is not an isolated story even if it occurs in an isolated, dying village.

What, finally, do we make of the "film noir" approach to this first feature? *Reconstruction* fits the genre in its general shape of a story in which the criminal does not get away with his or her crime—a story like that told in the first film Angelopoulos remembers seeing as a child, Michael Curtiz's *Angels with Dirty Faces*. As that film ends, James Cagney, as a once good streetwise kid turned punk gangster, is walking to the gas chamber, and he shouts out, "I don't want to *die*!" We learn earlier in this classic of the genre that Cagney is not actually expressing cowardice but is shouting these words to send a warning to the younger streetwise kids in his old neighborhood. As *Reconstruction* ends, Eleni is heading to her day of reckoning (although there is no death penalty in Greece). But she does not shout or, for that matter, show emotion. Except for the unique breakdown with her brother in which she confesses, she is resigned by film's end to face what she must face.

Such a spirit is, of course, in tune with film noir. So also is a general feeling that society is largely to blame for the protagonist's downfall. Angelopoulos shades this observation in that he does not portray society as evil but rather reflects the changing nature and economic structure of rural Greece over the years. And the grainy black-and-white cinematography of Giorgos Arvanitis also calls to mind the classics of the genre from *Double Indemnity* to *Kiss Me Deadly*.

There are, however, no gangs, no mob, no flashy violent scenes, no jazzy sound track; nor is there, as in Godard's *Breathless*, a postmodern parody of film noir. Instead, Angelopoulos used a true story and some shades of the genre to fashion a film that clearly announced to the world that he was a new filmmaker to be reckoned with.

Chapter Five

The Travelling Players: Figures in the
Landscape of Myth and History

> *Clytemnestra: You are the snake I gave birth to,*
> *and gave the breast.*
> *Orestes: Indeed, the terror of your dreams saw things to come*
> *clearly. You killed, and it was wrong. Now suffer wrong.*
> (Aeschylus, *The Libation Bearers*)

Two Scenes

SHAKESPEARE'S lines delivered in *As You Like It* have perhaps too often been quoted carelessly, but they have fresh currency when considered in relation to *The Travelling Players* and Angelopoulos's films in general:

> All the world's a stage,
> And all the men and women merely players.
> They have their exits and their entrances,
> And one man in his time plays many parts.

> (II, vii)

But *The Travelling Players* adds a line to Shakespeare, "Yet history may at any moment invade the play and change the text." This film is an almost four-hour epic journey into Greek history from 1939 to 1952, tracing the wanderings of a small acting company throughout rural Greece.

For within this Shakespearean context even the title, *The Travelling Players*, has profound resonances. Angelopoulos's concern in this, Greece's most ambitious, most experimental, and most expensive film made until 1975, is with a journey into "the other Greece," historically and culturally, through time. His concern is also with the presentation and reconstruction of that history and culture. More accurately, he is at pains to make the viewer aware to what degree history and culture are figments of presentation and enactments of "scripts" written and unwritten, remembered and forgotten, which continually reappear in reconstructions that echo the past yet point toward a future, uncertain as it may be.

Despite his recognition at home and abroad for his first two features, Angelopoulos's leap into *The Travelling Players* was unexpected and certainly unprecedented in Greece or, for that matter, abroad. It was all the more so because the film was made during the reign of the Colonels, the ruling military Junta of 1967–1975. In fact, the film may well have been made because the Junta came to power. Angelopoulos has credited the Junta as the troubling political event that forced him and many other young Greeks in the 1960s to rethink Greek history and culture. He has said: "I and many others sought the roots of the Junta through history, attitudes, social and political change. In a way, the dictatorship was my source of inspiration. Had it not existed, I may have done very different films. It was the same as so many fine films produced in America during the McCarthy years" (Weaver 14).

Consider two scenes I have alluded to in chapter 1. In the first, a young man in a uniform walks onto a stage during a performance and shoots an older woman and man to death. The two actually die onstage. The audience applauds wildly. The curtain closes. The moment takes place more than halfway through *The Travelling Players*, and in one swift tightening of the narrative strands of this seemingly loose and disparate odyssey, drama, history, myth, and personal destinies suddenly cross and become clear.

For the young man is Orestes. He is an actor and young communist *andartis* (communist mountain warrior). And the woman and man murdered are Clytemnestra, his mother, and Aegisthus, his uncle, who together betrayed Agamemnon, his father, to the Germans who executed him. The scene unfolds during World War II while the traveling players, the central focus of the film, are performing the popular Greek nineteenth-century folk melodrama, *Golpho, the Lover of the Shepherdess*.

The moment is much more ironic than dramatic, for the murders are actually so casually carried out that any sense of suspense or "drama" is missing. In contrast, this murder scene of Clytemnestra and Aegisthus was interpreted in various ways by Aeschylus, Sophocles, and Euripides, but in all cases, the intensity of the buildup, the tension of the moment itself (only Aeschylus depicts an onstage murder), and the passion of the aftermath are at the heart of these stage tragedies fashioned from the myth of the doomed house of Atreus.

Not so in Angelopoulos's "undramatic" version. The audience's strong applause, of course, further heightens the irony, since Angelopoulos has set us up to believe that the audience in the theater cannot tell the difference between the melodrama and the actual murders. The ironies extend through time to the ancient legend of the Agamemnon cycle. These modern Greeks carry out what appear to be similar acts of betrayal and revenge. But the differences between these moderns and their ancient namesakes seem far more significant than their similarities, as we shall discuss (note that only Orestes is actually named in the film: we do not hear anyone say "Agamemnon" or "Clytemnestra" or "Aegisthus"; they simply are those figures by extension and assumption, given "Orestes," although the names do appear in the published screenplay).

The second scene opens on a lake in northern Greece at dawn. Winter, slate gray, calm. A boat carrying "twenty handcuffed men" (Angelopoulos's description in the published Greek screenplay) glides across the lake. Silently. The boat reaches the shore and the police push several new prisoners, including Pylades, Orestes's friend in the ancient legend and one of the traveling players, into the boat. It takes off again. Orestes, Electra, and the Poet (another traveling player) watch, etched against the gray of the lake. They do not move. No music, no sound except the gentle purr of the boat's engine.

There is a chilling beauty to the scene. We experience both the darkness and also the distilling clarity of the winter landscape that becomes the "theater" for what seems so untheatrical: a boat full of silent men picking up a few more men and moving on, in silence. Yet we feel this moment has a large emotional and politically significant impact.

The importance of this exile scene taking place by a lake must also be noted. For as the following chapters demonstrate, rivers, lakes, and the open sea become for Angelopoulos a means of separation as well as of "baptism" and spiritual renewal. And the silence speaks volumes here and throughout the film. The year of this scene is 1939, and Pylades, a friend to Orestes, has been betrayed by Aegisthus, a fellow traveling player and a fascist collaborator. But there are no passionate speeches as in ancient tragedy, and no faith in verbal combat and dialogue as in traditional films. Only the sound, from time to time, of the wind, and then silence.

Furthermore, we are struck by the absolute simplicity of this "documentary" moment, which becomes, as we have noted in chapter 3 about many of Angelopoulos's scenes, something with the quintessential significance, calm, and beauty of Japanese and Chinese painting. Or it can be seen as similar to the silent Byzantine-style icons staring out from the walls of countless chapels and churches throughout Greece and the Orthodox Balkans.

The Travelling Players flows between such bipolar extremes.

It is both highly stylized and also natural, often simultaneously. On one hand, there is the world of theater interrupted by history—personal and political. On the other hand, there is the world of nature and human history framed so as to suggest, if not the "theatrical" (for what is usually thought of as dramatic has been drained from the image and the scene), at least the artistic world of representation found in Byzantine icons or Japanese pen-and-ink paintings.

So much is presentation and representation, and it takes many forms. There is history as spectacle: marches, gatherings, battles. There is violence disguised as "play," as in the rape of Electra by fascists wearing clown masks. There is direct camera address in long monologues to us, the viewers, by Agamemnon, Electra, and Pylades, a technique that alienates and thus distances us from the narrative while simultaneously allowing us to glimpse another vision of these characters. There is the presentation of history and life as a "musical": folk songs, Greek blues (rebetika), political hymns—from the Left and Right—show tunes, American jazz, and British melodies as well as Nazi marches become, instead of direct dialogue between characters, a primary form of communication and means of "fighting" in *The Travelling Players*. And there is the constant double vision of events and characters that the viewer must experience because the characters echo the ancient myth and tragedy of the house of Atreus.

Angelopoulos has called *The Travelling Players* his most Marxist film (Pappas 36). He is, of course, speaking most particularly of his dialectical view of history, which leads him to create a truly "historical film" in the sense that we become more aware of the historical flow of conflicting forces, ideas, and events than of the "dramatic" re-creation of history through individual destinies. But "dialectical" should not, we must emphasize, be understood to be a simple division of opposites. Rather, as this chapter explores, Angelopoulos's dialectical vision is one of a multiplicity of realities existing within each single image, moment, and character.

THE SHOW MUST GO ON: "ALL THIS ATE UP MY LIFE"

The divisions noted below are those Angelopoulos supplied in the published script (in Greek). They do not, however, appear on the screen.

Not only is Angelopoulos's approach to filmmaking quite at odds with classical Hollywood narrative, but his scripts themselves also bear no resemblance to traditional screenplay format or conventions. Rather, like many other European directors, including Ingmar Bergman, he simply tells his story with dialogue added in. Phrases given in quotation marks that are not identified as dialogue below are taken from the published screenplay to illuminate the intention Angelopoulos had for particular moments.

A final note on the published version: Fotis Lambrinos has edited the published script and added footnotes to particular lines to suggest which author or figure Angelopoulos is quoting or alluding to. In this sense Angelopoulos is clearly providing the screenplay not just as a record of what appears on the screen but as a work in and of itself that can be savored for its cultural, political, and intellectual implications.

1

Credits play as we see a theater curtain and hear the three thumps on the floor that announce the beginning of a performance. An old man walks out in front of the curtain wearing an accordion, announces that the play *Golpho* is about to begin, plays the accordion, and goes back behind the curtain. We hear him sing, "The actors are great and famous and also young."

2

NOVEMBER 1952

Cut to a gray morning in winter as the traveling players stand, with suitcases, at a train station. "We are tired, there are few performances," we hear one say in voice-over.

Cut again, this time to a banner in a small town announcing LONG LIVE THE ARMY. It is still 1952, and in a slow track backwards, the camera follows the troupe through the town as a megaphone in the background broadcasts political information.

3

AUTUMN 1939

The troupe continues walking past the town square, but it is now 1939, the troupe is now fifteen years younger, and there are clearly more members as they walk up to a local taverna. Blaring speakers make it apparent that Metaxas, the dictator-general, is ruling Greece.

The group is in the darkened taverna, their coats and hats still on. One begins singing a romantic tune ("One Evening"). Through the taverna windows we can see Metaxas's young "black shirt" military units jogging into the square, then goose-stepping and saluting. As the camera comes back to the group, Aegisthus (Vangelis Kazan) stands on the table and begins to sing an old patriotic song. This draws a stony silence from the rest of the troupe.

The troupe checks into rooms in a small hotel around a courtyard. One of the women, Clytemnestra (Aliki Georgouli), acts out a scene from the play they perform around northern Greece, *Golpho*. Then she says, "Nobody wants to see us."

It is night. Electra (Eva Kotamanidou) walks along the balcony of the hotel as we hear a fellow singing a love song. She opens a door and closes it. We hear the sound of heavy lovemaking. She listens at the door and becomes upset. She sits on the balcony and cries. Later. We see Clytemnestra leave the room her daughter listened to. She goes along the corridor of the balcony as Electra watches.

We next see Clytemnestra in bed with her husband, Agamemnon (Stratos Pachis), both asleep. Orestes (Petros Zarkadis), in an army uniform, enters the room, kisses his mother, and speaks briefly. She begins a monologue without sitting up, as if asleep, about a memory of a summer day in a garden when Orestes was three or four and she heard a fellow playing a violin. Orestes then leaves the room and sees Electra outside. He runs to his sister and embraces her as she cries.

Later Agamemnon, carrying the young son of his daughter Chrysothemis (Electra's sister, played by Maria Vasileiou) on his shoulders, speaks with Orestes as they walk along. An accordion plays the song "Margarita." When they reach the hotel steps, Agamemnon turns and, with "words full of death" (a foreshadowing of his own), speaks about seeing angels descending from the skies into a large hall crying out, "The great Babylonians have fallen, have fallen."

Orestes and two other young fellows, Pylades (Kiriakos Katrivanos) and the Poet (Grigoris Evangelatos), walk along railroad tracks. "We will have war here soon," says Pylades, who, as in the ancient myth, is Orestes' faithful friend. Soldiers will be leaving for the border. Pylades begins whistling and the others join in: clearly they are "in tune" with each other (whistling will be picked up as a "language of friendship and communication" later in *Voyage to Cythera*).

Beside some bare trees by a riverbank, Pylades reads from a newspaper about the conditions necessary for a true Marxist revolution to take place. The three young soldiers chant in unison "like a chorus," continuing this Marxist revolutionary speech taken from the writings of Lenin. "It is coming," Pylades says. The camera pans to the old man, and they greet him. The "white-haired man" holds Orestes' hand.

As these three friends leave and climb up a steep staircase, a group of "black-shirt" Metaxas followers come by, one carrying an ancient bust of what appears to be Alexander the Great (a similar bust will appear at the conclusion of *Megalexandros*), while another is dressed in an ancient Greek soldier's costume. The three friends begin to laugh.

A stage is set up in a kafeneon. The actors are all at last in their *Golpho* costumes, Greek mountain costumes of small kilts and tight white leggings for men and long white dresses with embroidered tops for women. The troupe stands at the window with backlighting and sings an "advertisement" to the "street": that is, to potential customers. They look, at this moment, like characters in a Karaghiozis Greek shadow-puppet show, which always begins with such a "preview" song. The music is provided by "the accordionist."

We now see the same scene from outside the kafeneon. The players do a little dip-and-rise dance as they stand in line, singing. We feel them as a "team" and, as such, as a group of individuals with the spark and energy that must have united them originally.

They are traveling players. There is a sense of purpose, unity, joy in this dance. This is the happiest moment for the group in the whole film. Agamemnon leads the troupe, but each character takes his or her turn at leading the group in their "preview" song.

They then come into the street and do what looks like a variation of a square dance. A crowd begins to gather.

A costumed performance of *Golpho* actually begins on a stage.

Late that night behind the kafeneon, we see agents of Metaxas's secret police in plain suits chase Pylades down the street as he wears his theatrical *evzone* (northern Greek white kilt) costume. Orestes escapes but the police grab and beat Pylades, throwing him into a car as they drive off.

We next have the winter morning lake scene described above, in which Pylades is taken by boat away toward exile and prison.

Back at the kafeneon, the traveling players are packing up. But their silence and the actions of Electra and the Poet lead Aegisthus to realize they know he betrayed Pylades. He nervously leaves the room after a confrontation with the Poet.

4

LATE THE EVENING OF OCTOBER 28TH, ALMOST THE 29TH, 1940

The players are on a train in the third-class section. Agamemnon faces us and begins to speak the first of three long monologues in the film. He came to Greece in 1922 from Asia Minor, Ionia, when the Turks and Greeks exchanged populations (roughly two million Greeks living in Turkey came to Greece). He speaks of the boat ride, of falling into the water, like sheep, and being saved, of reaching Piraeus and seeking work, and finding work for two drachmas a day. "All of this ate up my life," he says. This Agamemnon is not a king returning victorious from Troy but rather a simple, honest man who has been forced to become a refugee and a traveling player without a home. Thus has Angelopoulos reclaimed Greek myth from the past by making it present, and from the conservative guardians of "high culture," Greek and foreign, by making his Agamemnon a working-class refugee.

Morning. The players get off at another country town station, carrying their suitcases and other prop baggage. As they walk, the sea is on one side of them. They again walk through a town, but this time there are political banners everywhere and they run into a marching group of soldiers coming the other way. There is, Angelopoulos writes, with all of this confusion of actors, bands, marching soldiers, and townspeople, a sense of "a religious holiday festivity."

Golpho begins again, this time in a "small theater." As in the beginning of the film, we hear the three taps on the floor before the curtain rises. But the production is interrupted by an announcement that the Italians invaded Greece at 5:30 that morning. Then the play continues. It is full of innocent romance between the country girl, Golpho, and her shepherd love, Tasos. Suddenly there is real bombing in the distance. Panic erupts in the theater. World War II has begun.

The point of this "theater of interruption" throughout the film is in part that *Golpho* is an idyllic folk play about a Greece full of happy peasants that never existed. This in large part explains its popularity throughout Greece since its opening at the turn of the century, for it is a form of escapism into an imaginary folk Greece. But as critic Peter Pappas has suggested, with the bombs falling and interrupting the production, Angelopoulos "is doing more than interrupting a performance: his is, to put it simply, exploding a myth" (37).

Exterior, early morning. Agamemnon, in uniform, says good-bye to Electra and Chrysothemis.

Agamemnon is in uniform in his bedroom with Clytemnestra. She laughs at him, and he slaps her. The war is breaking up the troupe. When he leaves, the traitor, Aegisthus, enters Clytemnestra's room. He finds her crying, takes off his coat, and closes the door.

5

JANUARY 1ST, 1941

Rain, exterior, day. A crippled Greek from the Albanian front in the town square. An accordion plays. Electra in the street, followed by a fascist Italian soldier. They enter a hotel room and she asks him to strip. He does, slowly, shyly at first and then apparently with male pride. He stands, fully naked, before her (and us): full frontal male nudity. We thus experience her gaze at this naked fascist. We watch him for a full half minute until he feels at last shy, "used," and covers himself as she stands up, walks out, and closes the door. This is, of course, a remarkable scene in a number of ways, but especially because it reverses the dominant "gaze" of cinema, which has been so clearly described in feminist film studies, notably by Laura Mulvey, as "the male gaze." Given Hollywood's patriarchal structure and orientation toward "gazing" at women as objects, it is significant that the first nude we see is a male fascist who has stripped before a woman's gaze. The political implications of the scene are as far-reaching as the gender-oriented issues. The *New York Times* critic wrote, "It is a scene of merciless justness" (Eder).

6

APRIL 27TH, 1941

A neoclassical hall with fascist architecture. The Nazi flag being flown. The German Occupation has begun. It is the first day the Germans entered Athens.

AUTUMN 1952

Electra is dressed in black. Pylades comes up to her in their bedroom. "Let's go," he says.

The traveling players walk by the sea in autumn. A young eighteen-year-old sings, "Give me sweet kisses." And then we begin to hear a megaphone blaring political announcements about upcoming elections. The group is now by the railroad tracks again.

WINTER 1942

Same location ten years before, during the Occupation, with German signs up. German troops marching.

A dark kafeneon. The traveling players and some German soldiers listen as Aegisthus asks who is hiding a British soldier, thus making it clear who he is working for. Then a performance begins, with one difference. The Germans arrest Agamemnon during the show.

Agamemnon stands during a cold winter dawn against a whitewashed stone wall with faded red letters scrawled on it, E.A.M., which stand for the Greek Liberation Army, a united resistance group in Greece organized by the Greek Communist Party (KKE). He faces us and says, "I come from near the sea. In Ionia. Where are you from?" We pull back to a long shot behind the ten Germans who obviously know no Greek. There is the firing, and Agamemnon slumps to the ground. We track in to the dead actor.

Note the importance of this setup. Angelopoulos gives us Agamemnon speaking to us, establishing his own identity and then asking ours in the ancient tradition of greeting a stranger that is found in Homer and surely goes back even further. The personal, ancient, humanizing contact is established first before Angelopoulos gives us the long shot that includes the Germans, who have missed what he said and would not understand it anyway. Then his death, in long view, made even more significant by the seeming insignificance it is given. A shot and a body slumps. But the point is, we know that person now and the cruelty of the moment is all the more amplified by the silent efficiency of his murder.

The remaining troupe members walk down a street in town led by Clytemnestra in black walking with Aegisthus.

Clytemnestra and Aegisthus are in an old hotel. Aegisthus paces nervously.

7

1943

Scores of townsfolk in line to receive some kind of rations.

Electra is led by her sister into a hotel room, and there is Pylades in his EAM uniform. They embrace in this secret brief meeting.

Chrysothemis carries a bottle for oil and walks down streets with EAM signs painted everywhere. She enters a merchant's shop and is led by an overweight middle-aged man down into the cellar. He taps one of his oil kegs and, in the darkness with one light on her, she begins to enact what is clearly a ritual payment. She stands, removes her dress, and, covering her breasts with her hands, begins to sing, clearly without a talent or a will for it, the lyric "In your eyes there is a calm sea" as he sits with his back to the camera, masturbating. This scene is a "mirror" to that in which the young soldier is humiliated, only this time the woman (Chrysothemis) is not fully abased since she acts voluntarily in a specific trade-off. She has thus, in effect, prostituted herself with a middle-class merchant.

She leaves the shop as two men come past her, walking in the other direction. As she rounds the corner, the shop owner comes out to lock his door and is gunned down by the two men. It is clear to Greek audiences that they are EAM members who may or may not have been tipped off by Chrysothemis about his wartime profiteering. But it is exactly this kind of point that may easily be missed by those not familiar with Greek history since no traditional "setup" is given. We can easily imagine an earlier scene in which we would hear the two EAM men speaking about the merchant as a profiteer who must die, but agreeing that they should wait until after she leaves to execute him. Once again, Angelopoulos denies us such conventional narrative links.

Chrysothemis enters the old hotel where the troupe is staying, parts the simple curtains decorated with paintings of sheep on a Greek mountain, and places the oil on the table at which the group is seated. They stare in

6. *The Travelling Players*: Chrysothemis strips for the collaborator oil merchant

awe at the bottle, obviously not having seen olive oil in a long time. The camera pulls back through the drapery so that their moment becomes a "behind the curtains" drama.

8

THE BEGINNING OF 1944

The traveling players are shuffling down a snowy mountain road singing the same "preview" song we heard them sing earlier. There is a lightness, a pure pleasure in the moment that they are acting out only for themselves, for as they dance through slush, there is no one else around. Once more, they are like a line of shadow-puppet figures against the white sheet of a Karaghiozis show. Not only that, they are shot so that our view of them is at times obscured by trees and telephone poles. Somehow the cheerfulness of their singing warms the bleak landscape as they sing and dance along, followed by two mules carrying their prop cases.

They suddenly stop singing and look horrified. Then we see them approach a large plane tree (most Greek villages have a plane tree in the village square for shade and as a traditional meeting place) by a well with two men hanging from a large branch. These would be EAM members hanged by Germans, but again, no one says a word of explanation. We simply experience the moment of discovery of these deaths. The sound of the wind is all we hear.

Later on a snow-covered mountain slope, the group (seven members left) spot a lone chicken. Their look is once again, as with the bottle of oil, one of awe. They slowly circle the doomed animal and close in on it through the snow. With no dialogue or close-ups at all, Angelopoulos captures "hunger": seven people attacking a lone chicken in winter.

9

SPRING 1944

Rain and thunder in a mountain village as a bus leaves.

Then we are by the seaside. The bus is stopped by German soldiers. The whole group gets out, along with the other Greek passengers. German soldiers all around. They are herded into an abandoned and crumbling Byzantine fortress where tents are set up for prisoners.

Evening. They are lined up against the wall, obviously for execution. Aegisthus steps forward to pitifully plead for his life but collapses. Soldiers drag him back in line and he tries to hide behind Clytemnestra, as if that would help. Then the sound of shooting begins and they all hit the ground. But they are not shot. The shooting continues. And we realize that the Nazis are being attacked. We watch a blank wall as the battle rages, off-camera.

It is dawn, and we see scores of Greeks rushing back into the old castle carrying the Nazi banner. They climb to the top of the walls and toss it into the sea. Church bells ring off-camera as everyone shouts joyously. The Germans have been defeated.

Cut to the shore outside the castle as we see dozens of Partisan EAM soldiers on horseback shouting as they ride toward the castle. Cries of "Freedom to the People!" This is a heroic and historic moment. But again, Angelopoulos denies us the traditional heroic shot—the shot that would place the camera so as to show us the scores of horsemen galloping toward us and to make us feel their intensity even more strongly. Angelopoulos's shot is powerful as well. Yet the emphasis has been placed on the group rather than on individuals in the group, the latter being Hollywood's traditional way of presenting battle scenes.

10

SEPTEMBER–DECEMBER 1944

A town square is packed with people, backs to the camera, waving Greek, American, and red communist flags. Celebration, singing an old andartis (EAM warrior) song. Then shots ring out and the crowd runs, leaving five dead. We now hear a Scottish bagpiper and then see him cross the square playing a tune.

A communist march through town with lots of banners and pictures of Lenin. Evening. The traveling players are packed and trying to get out of town. They carry their baggage, but then the sound of communist songs, followed by gunfire, is heard. We see a wide street with a cross street at the end; the players hurry around one corner to hide. This becomes a kind of "stage" as first government troops and then communist troops enter and push each other back, firing. Most of the time, however, the street is empty as we hear shooting from both sides. When the coast is finally clear, the troupe continues its effort to get out of town.

Seaside at dawn. The traveling players walk along a beach. Suddenly British soldiers appear and search them. They find the costumes and then ask them to perform for them. A makeshift stage with curtain is set up on the beach and a performance given. Then this turns into a dance as the accordion player provides the music and the British soldiers dance with each other.

11

JANUARY 1945

Night in a town. Electra walks down a dark street as we hear all kinds of music from the distance, including French and Latin-American rumba tunes. She is wearing her *Golpho* costume. A wall she passes has "Long Live EAM" (in Greek) written on it. She meets Pylades, Orestes, and the Poet in communist uniforms.

Inside a large building on a staircase, we hear *Golpho* being performed. What unfolds is the murder scene described at the beginning of the chapter as Orestes, true to the ancient myth, avenges the death of his father by murdering Aegisthus and his mother, Clytemnestra. But he does so onstage and there is loud applause as they die. The curtain closes and Electra comes onstage to share the moment.

Later we see Electra enter her mother's hotel room; she puts a tango on the record player, takes off her jacket, dons her mother's coat, and stretches out on the bed.

Men in long coats and hats in the hallway enter her room. We see only the hallway as we listen to them dragging her out.

In a dark taverna, four of these men wearing carnival clown masks with bulb-shaped noses hold Electra down on the floor while the fifth, also in a bulb-nosed mask, slaps her and begins to rape her. Few scenes on the screen have seemed so violent. Yet the violence does not come from graphic detail. Rather, it is the darkness of the room, the framing of the rape so that we do not really see Electra at all but simply five male backs, cloaked and hatted, hunched over her. These are right-wing government henchmen looking for information about Orestes. The rape lasts more than a minute of screen time, which feels like an eternity and becomes an interrogation. But Electra tells them nothing except that he has gone "into the mountains." In effect, this is telling them nothing, for the mountain country is where the communist troops lived.

Dawn. By a riverbank, Electra wakes up. She has obviously been dumped there by the fascists. She stands up, brushes the dirt from her mother's coat, faces the camera, and begins to talk to us, quietly, calmly, her arms folded. What follows is a description of how the civil war began once the Germans left. It is a long speech taking up over five minutes, describing the "battle of Athens" in December of 1944, which lasted 33 days and left 28 dead and 200 wounded as the government troops clashed with the communist Partisans.

The juxtaposition of the rape and the speech is important. The contrast is complete: from victim to a woman historian, and from a person denied individuality to a complete human being before us who, in the way she recounts her history of events, demonstrates that she is strong enough to survive it all. This is her finest performance, and it is not onstage but in the open, by a river, for us, the viewers, and it concerns history.

12

FEBRUARY 1945

A town square surrounded by American, British, and French troops. The communists (ELAS: Greek National Liberation Army) arrive one by one on horseback and surrender their weapons as part of the agreement at the end of the Occupation. The scene takes its time so that we feel the importance of this moment.

A Jeep carrying drunken British soldiers and Chrysothemis drives down a street and stops at an old apartment building. She laughs, gets out, and says, in English, "See you later."

Electra is in her room as we hear Chrysothemis's son reading about a battle from a book. She goes to the hallway and sees Chrysothemis, ready to leave, carrying a suitcase. They stare at each other without saying a word as we hear the boy reading. Then Chrysothemis leaves.

Three men enter the building and come into Electra's room. They search and sit on her couch without speaking, staring at her. "What do you want?" she asks. They stare, throw down three photos, and leave. Electra picks one up. It is a picture of Orestes in his andartis uniform.

Night in this small northern town. Political right-wing slogans are being blasted on speakers. Electra walks past small shops. We see a kafeneon and several right-wing henchmen dragging out a few new victims. Then we hear a communist slogan, "Long live EAM."

13

JANUARY 1ST, 1946

Electra walks to a simple taverna-nightclub at night, as we hear music. A wall sign tells us it is a special "First of January, 1946" celebration with a "large orchestra." Electra enters and simply stands in the doorway, as we see and hear dancing to the music of a woman singing backed up by the orchestra. Then a "duel" begins between a table of right-wing government supporters (all male and wearing cheap suits and hats) and a group of couples (male and female, with no hats) representing the Left and the communists. As in the early kafeneon scene in the beginning of the film, the political duel is waged musically as each group sings different songs with their own political slant, ending with the orchestra—a jazzy group including sax, trumpet, drums, guitar, and accordion—backing them both up.

Nothing is ever said about why Electra has arrived, but we can easily surmise that it is because she sees the men who brought her Orestes' photos, and she wishes to find out what has happened to him.

She never asks, however, for she stands, statuelike in the doorway, seemingly entranced by the spectacle before her. The young couples now get the orchestra to play Glenn Miller's theme song, "In the Mood," and they begin to swing. Then one right-winger pulls a pistol on a young leftist who opens his jacket to show he is carrying no weapons. All the other young men do likewise. There is a silent moment and then the young couples file out, leaving the whole hall to the right-wingers. Alone together, except for Electra in the far doorway, they strike up an old Greek song, and the men pair off and begin to waltz with each other in a bizarre dance of men without women, a clear parody of what a New Year's celebration should be (half the population excluded!). Electra says nothing but, after taking it all in, turns and leaves.

There can be no doubt that this association of right-wing politics and a hint of male bonding bordering on homosexuality was influential for Bertolucci when he made his historical epic *1900*, in which he openly develops the theme of homosexuality as being tied to fascism. Angelopoulos does not go that far. That is, he is not saying that all supporters of the 1946 government were gays. The visual composition of the scene, however, does clearly suggest that the nationalism the Right supported at that time, in Angelopoulos's view, was so extreme that it excluded a "normal" participation of the public.

In the corridor outside the dance hall, Electra meets the old accordion player of the traveling players, who has been playing with the orchestra. He says the war will continue and she explains that Orestes has not returned.

FIRST OF THE YEAR, 1946–NOVEMBER 1952

Dawn. The group of right-wing men wander down the empty streets singing. They finally reach the square where a royalist government rally is taking place. It is now 1952 and political speeches are being made. In the crowd we see what Angelopoulos describes as "the traveling players of 1952," including Electra, who walks through the crowd and out the other end.

14

1949

Coming down a side street is a Jeep full of soldiers with a mountain band in front playing the traditional clarinet and tambour. As they draw closer, we see that one soldier is standing, holding the head of a bearded communist in each hand—a common practice during the civil war was to behead the communists who were captured.

We now see soldiers leading a group of twenty or so communist prisoners with hands over their heads. Electra follows as they are led into an open area and lined up. The camera goes down the line and returns to focus, as Electra comes closer, on Orestes, bearded, tired, but smiling to Electra.

15

1950

Seaside, dawn: a boat, as earlier in the film, arrives on a slate-gray sea bringing released prisoners. Electra waits around a corner. Pylades is let off the boat as an ex-prisoner, carrying a suitcase. They stare at each other, then walk off together.

Inside an old kafeneon, Pylades, smoking, watches as soldiers march by. He then begins his monologue, which he delivers in a very low-key, clipped speech, without making any eye contact with us. He explains that he was captured in 1947 and thrown in prison and that prisons all across Greece were full of political prisoners like himself. He speaks of the tortures he suffered and the efforts of the guards to get him to sign a confession renouncing his beliefs. He did not sign.

Next we have a lengthy wedding scene in which Chrysothemis marries an American soldier. The wedding feast takes place on a beach. A table is set up, the couple arrives in a Jeep, and all sit down to a feast. Chrysothemis introduces her husband to Electra, who says nothing, and to her son, who says nothing. There is music, and everyone dances to Nat King Cole singing "Mona Lisa." Then there is an old Greek tune, and the couple do a Greek dance by the sea; the dance turns into a fast swing number. When they get around to toasting, the son, now in his late teens, stands up, grabs hold of the tablecloth, and begins to walk off, dragging everything off the table, crashing onto the beach as he continues to walk, and the camera tracks him across the beach and, finally, out of the frame.

An old hotel. Electra and Pylades enter and climb the stairs. Inside Electra's room, the Poet sits. He begins to speak about revolutions, including the Spanish civil war of 1936. He speaks poetically, movingly, painfully about Freedom's becoming "crippled."

16

1951

A prison yard near the sea. Electra enters as we hear a rebetika song in the background. Inside the prison she is led, finally, to the morgue. Orestes is laid out on the table. She stops in the doorway and stares. When she finally approaches her dead brother, she utters a line from *Golpho*, "Good morning, Tasos."

A dark muddy road as the traveling players follow a car bearing Orestes' body. They reach a burial place by the sea. The traveling players are in a line behind the burial site. The body is lowered into the hole and two men begin to shovel in the dirt. Electra begins to clap. Then the others join in. The camera draws back so that we see one large cypress tree in the background (the traditional graveyard tree of Greece, which suggests, in its height, that it is reaching toward "heaven") with the group continuing to clap, as if for the liberated soul of Orestes.

NOVEMBER 1952

Outside an old theater at night. People entering with umbrellas through the rain. Inside, the traveling players are preparing yet another performance. Only this time Chrysothemis's son is dressed in an evzone outfit of a Greek shepherd, taking on Orestes' role as Tasos. Electra sees to his makeup. "Are you afraid?" she asks. "No," he says. As he climbs onto the stage, she whispers, "Orestes." Pylades bangs the hammer on the floor three times, the accordionist begins, and the curtain is ready to be raised yet again.

AUTUMN 1939

The final shot is of the whole group, all of the traveling players as they once were, suitcases in hand, at the same train station where we have seen them before, the town of Aigion. And in voice-over, we hear the accordionist, "It was autumn 1939, and we had reached Aigion. We were tired. We had two days to rest."

THE CREATION OF *THE TRAVELLING PLAYERS*: PORTRAIT OF AN ARTIST AS A TRAVELING DIRECTOR

The story of the writing, planning, and filming of *The Travelling Players* is an odyssey unto itself and helpful for our appreciation of the film as a whole. Let us backtrack a moment to the making of his first feature, *Reconstruction* (all notes on this production are taken from Constantine A. Themelis's interview). Angelopoulos has said that he actually had the idea for *The Travelling Players* even before making *Reconstruction*. But he decided, finally, on *Reconstruction* because it was clearly a cheaper film to make. Where did the story for this first feature come from? Angelopoulos read about a real village murder in a newspaper and went to the island of Corfu where the murder had taken place. In the actual story, a village woman did strangle her husband and bury him in the front garden, planting spring onions over him. "Those little onions had impressed me terribly," Angelopoulos has said about why he decided on this story for his first film.

What followed was an odyssey of discovery for Angelopoulos about "the other Greece," a Greece he did not know and, in fact, had not visited. He explored Corfu, followed the women's trial and had it transcribed for his study, and then moved over to the mainland to explore the mountain villages of Epirus, the northern Greek territory bordering on Albania. He chose to go there since it was clearly impossible to make the film on the actual island of Corfu: feelings ran too high against outsiders' delving into a crime the village and the island were trying to forget. After traveling all over this area, which at the time was difficult to do because of poor roads, he settled on two villages that were finally used: Vitsa and Monodendri.

He needed to write the script, however. This he did initially with the help of the well-known Greek playwright Stratis Karras. But we need to note that Angelopoulos's method of writing screenplays is also very different from traditional screenwriting methods. "Most times [my] scripts are not written by scriptwriters, of course," comments Angelopoulos. "They serve as catalysts in order for things to surface or like devil's advocates, I would say. They oppose a suggestion for a scene and you are forced to think it over and so on" (Themelis 5).

Angelopoulos had actually begun this project with another writer, Thanasis Valtinos, who held many discussions with Angelopoulos about how to structure the story and then withdrew from the project. The young director held further discussions with Karras about fine-tuning the story and the characters. But then Angelopoulos did all of the writing, listing the script credit as his own, "with the participation of" Karras and Valtinos.

From the beginning of his career, Angelopoulos has been fortunate to work with Giorgos Arvanitis, his DP (director of photography). Not only did Arvanitis give this film (and all of Angelopoulos's subsequent films) its distinctive look, but he was also responsible, indirectly, for the casting of *Reconstruction*. It was in the home of Arvanitis's mother-in-law that Angelopoulos by chance met a local woman who had never acted, Toula Stathopoulou, who became the "perfect" figure for what he wished to capture. In all subsequent films he has blended real actors with nonprofessionals, but at the time he chose nonprofessionals because of his realization that most Greek actors "are spoiled in a certain way: if they cannot be melodramatic, they think that they simply are not acting" (interview, Athens, April 1976).

The shooting was done in twenty-seven days on location in those isolated northern villages with a crew of five, an extremely small group for a feature film. I do not need to suggest how difficult it is to shoot in such a remote location. It is important to understand that Angelopoulos not only managed it but thoroughly enjoyed the challenges location shooting in remote areas created. For it would be one thing if Angelopoulos wished to make films about "the other Greece" in content but not in location. After all, that is the way most films are made. Jules Dassin's *Phaedra*, for instance, intercuts shots of the island of Hydra, the highway along the coast south of Athens, and several other locations to make one sequence appear as if it were all happening on Phaedra's island. The Greece in Dassin's film thus becomes, as in almost all Hollywood films, the Greece that Dassin needs to create for his story. Not so with Angelopoulos. His films are about "the other Greece," filmed in "the other Greece" with the location becoming almost an equal partner with the story and the characters. If he does, in style, create a "metarealism," the location provides a realistic, "documentary" basis.

The whole experience of shooting this first film changed him. He came face to face with "the other Greece." As he has commented: "It was the discovery of another Greece which I did not know. I came across an interior space—what can be called an inside Greece—which was unknown to me and to most people of my generation. I am referring to people who were born and raised in the city and ignored and even underestimated this other reality. It was a true discovery for me" (Themelis 4). From that moment on, Angelopoulos has continued to explore that "interior space," and *The Travelling Players* has of course been part of that exploration.

He had been making notes about that film for years when, finally, in September of 1973 he "finished" the script in two weeks on "a Greek mountain by myself" (all information on the filming of *The Travelling Players* is from my interview with Angelopoulos in Athens, October 1975). As he wrote, he was very conscious of the music for the film: "I was only nine years old in December 1944, but I still have vivid memories of the melodies the soldiers used to sing. Naturally there are songs that my friends and collaborators also reminded me of, and then also the composer and musical director for the film, Loukianos Kilaidonis, was helpful."

Once he completed this first draft of the script, he began location hunting throughout Greece, once more seeking out remote and "unchanged" Greek sites that would fit the various period requirements of the film. He visited almost every village and town in Greece, taking more than two thousand photos. He then made two more trips around Greece with Arvanitis, his cinematographer. Finally they chose locations, though some places had to be slightly altered: "The beach at Aigion, for instance, had lampposts that were too modern, which we changed, and in the square of Kardista we had to spend a day taking down all the television antennae that appeared in the shots we wished to make."

But a more serious issue concerns the difficulties he ran into with the dictatorship in shooting such a political film. After his trip around Greece he became directly involved in some of the tragic events of the time. He participated, for instance, in anti-Junta protests at the Polytechnic University next to the National Museum; these led eventually to a police and military attack on the protesters that left roughly three hundred dead and many more wounded. Because of his involvement in this and other protests, he left for Paris suddenly and came back only when it seemed safe to do so.

He then, in 1974, began to talk with his producer about shooting the film. The producer was worried about the Junta's reaction, but Angelopoulos notes:

> I finally convinced him, saying that to make the film was somehow a way to survive in those terrible times. So we got the license and started in February of 1974. Nobody knew exactly what we were making, including the producer! Not even the actors knew. The script was known only to me, and I did not want the others to know in advance so that word would get out about the film and thus endanger it. Of course people had an idea about it, but they only got the script day by day as we shot.

The police sometimes came around, but Angelopoulos told them he was making a film about the myth of Orestes, adapted to the time of the German Occupation, and that satisfied them, for Greece, like Yugoslavia and other countries that had suffered under the Germans, used to make a lot of World War II "Resistance" films.

Most of the shooting was done around Greece from February to May of 1974. Because Angelopoulos prefers an autumn or winter look in his images, he then stopped production until November 1974, finishing in January 1975.

Angelopoulos was very careful in his casting because he did feel, as we have noted, that Greek actors tend to be too melodramatic. But he was very pleased with those he chose and said that the only difficult moments came in the shooting of the monologues: "We had to rehearse the monologues many times. Every part of the monologue had to be worked out carefully and prepared ahead of time. The actors were not allowed to improvise."

He hastens to add that he has had no training or experience in theater or television directing and thus that his handling of actors has been his own development based on his understanding of cinema and the images he has wished to create. Crowd scenes—moments depicting either the entire troupe of traveling players, or soldiers, or other large groups—occur throughout the film. But he states that the orchestration of these ensembles was never a problem for him. That goes for the integration of the music in a scene as well. Instead of simply shooting such scenes silently and dubbing music in later, as Hollywood often does and as Italian filmmakers, for instance, always do, Angelopoulos provided the music on location so that the cast felt the moment: "All the music was taped at the time we were shooting. We worked with a stereo tape recorder and two microphones. One microphone was for the action and the other for the music. Nothing was added later."

Most American films are shot on roughly a five- to six-week shooting schedule (with several months afterwards, of course, for editing and postproduction). But Angelopoulos needed much longer because of the "look" he was (and continues to be) after:

> We wanted to shoot the whole film in cloudy weather, which, of course, is difficult to do in Greece! So often the compromise was to shoot late in the evening or very early in the morning, which among other things creates another problem. Evening light is a bit reddish because of the sunset, and a bit later it is blue as night falls, while morning light is violet. Naturally not having much time to shoot at any of these times, we would have to wait all day or till the next day to shoot another scene!

But despite such long periods of inactivity, once he set up a scene, he seldom needed many takes. Angelopoulos has said that Jules Dassin came on location at one point and asked how long a particular scene had taken to shoot. When Angelopoulos explained that he had done it in two hours, Dassin was incredulous. "He said that he would have needed at least two days with twenty-five takes to do the same shot!" Angelopoulos commented with obvious pride.

The final budget was about $250,000, which might have been what Hollywood was spending on advertising for a modest film in 1975. This budget reveals an amazing economy in all senses for a film involving so many people, on-camera and off, plus so many time periods and locations, often difficult remote areas.

THE CRITICAL RESPONSE

With this single film, Angelopoulos suddenly became recognized everywhere as a unique voice in world cinema. Greek-American critic Peter Pappas, aware of both the Greek and European as well as American critical traditions, was able to write in 1976 that from then on, Greek cinema should be divided into pre-*Travelling Players* and post-*Travelling Players*: "It is an important film not only for Greeks, but for everyone who is interested in the future of cinema" (36). Michael Wilmington reflects a similar position when he writes that *The Travelling Players* can be seen as "Brecht crossed with Aeschylus and Mizoguchi," adding that, "It is Angelopoulos' view which, like Ozu's of Japan, Ford's of America, may change radically the way we perceive his country, its past, its dreams" (32).

Furthermore, the British Film Institute offers its own best-film "Oscar" each year. In the past, films by Antonioni, Satyajit Ray, Alain Resnais, Jean-Luc Godard, Yasujiro Ozu, and Bernardo Bertolucci had won. But in 1975 the honor was awarded to *The Travelling Players* by Theo Angelopoulos. And, as mentioned in the introduction, the Italian critics voted it the best film of the decade in the world. The award read in part, "The most original and important film of the year"; given a twenty-year perspective since then, we can clearly state that Angelopoulos's epic journey through Greek history from 1939 to 1952 was one of the most original and important films in the second half of the twentieth century.

Reviews were not universally kind, however. The *New York Times* represents an early American response to Angelopoulos's epic in calling it "a film of startling beauty and originality" but finally "a bloated, spoiled masterpiece" that exhibits a "monstrous lack of restraint" (Eder). Some Greek left-wing and communist reviewers charged that the depiction of the civil war was not graphic or complete enough (Pappas 39). And even those who championed the film admit the demanding basis from which one must begin. In this sense, Peter Pappas is once again accurate: "*The*

Travelling Players is an intellectually difficult work. It requires extraordinary concentration from the audience" (39).

But, as I have argued, the demands on the audience are necessary, given his subject matter—a bringing to light of "the other Greece's" history and culture—and the films are more than worthy of the need for "extraordinary concentration."

ORESTES LIVES

No single reading of this complex film can hope to unravel Angelopoulos's text fully. That is not my effort. Rather, my attempt in both the synopsis and the analysis is to point some signposts as to how Angelopoulos has traveled through history and culture cinematically to offer a vision of survival and, perhaps, of replenishment. For this epic and tragic journey, like Homer's in the *Odyssey* and Aeschylus's in the *Oresteia*, ends in hope in a triple sense.

Such hope is not perhaps immediately apparent. By film's end Orestes has been executed in prison and the communist cause has been defeated by the conservative royalist Greek forces together with foreign (American and British) support. The second half of the film has a strongly tragic feel to it, not just because of what has happened to the individual traveling players, which is a modern reenactment of the ancient myth as presented by Aeschylus, but also because of the tragedy of civil war, the worst fate any nation can face.

And yet there is a sense of muted triumph and thus a sense that Orestes, his beliefs, and his faith in the "revolution" still live. There is the triumphant applause led by Electra at his funeral as if in honor of his spirit, which suggests a kind of resurrection in the Greek death-ritual tradition we discussed earlier. Then there is the protest of Chrysothemis's son at his mother's wedding to an American soldier, a protest that can be felt to be a continuation of the "revolution" against the ruling conservative middle-class and foreign powers. Later, Chrysothemis's son follows in his uncle's footsteps in two important ways: he takes on the name "Orestes" and he takes on the role of Tasos, the lead in *Golpho*, with the penultimate scene of the film's being his first performance onstage. He has finally come of age and become a traveling player himself.

The show does go on. The troupe will continue, and the dead will be remembered and replaced. In chapter 1 we discussed how Aeschylus's *Oresteia* ends with a "comic" vision—in the largest sense of comedy as triumph, as in Dante's *Divine Comedy*—for Athena and the laws of Athens triumph over the blood curses of the past. Angelopoulos has no such sweeping ending, for history is still in flux, and there has been no clear-cut "victory" such as in Aeschylus. But that Chrysothemis's son carries on Orestes' tradition, thus preserving the troupe, is indeed a victory, small and limited to the immediate group as it may be. Orestes lives, and thus the community is renewed.

Yes, all of this is challenged and altered by the scenes of the aging players in *Landscape in the Mist*, but that involves another place and another time, as we shall discuss.

ELECTRA'S TALE

The second half of *The Travelling Players* becomes Electra's tale even more than Orestes'. Although Electra's brother's presence is felt even in his absence, it is Electra's presence that carries us through this half of the film when so many of the troupe are dead or imprisoned or, as in her sister's case, "selling out" through her liaisons with foreigners and Greek profiteers (the oil merchant). The traveling players would not have continued without Electra's quiet strength, her strong integrity and refusal to buckle under to fascism in any form or in any way, her dedication to her brother, her ability to take the worst that could be thrown at her, including the rape, and survive.

It is, after all, Electra who prepares the new "Orestes" to go onstage at the end. She is, granted, generously supported by Pylades, who becomes her husband. But it is Electra who exhibits leadership ability. The "resurrection" of Orestes at the grave site, as she initiates the applause that the others then take up, is a powerful case in point.

A brief comparison of Electra with Eleni in *Reconstruction* is helpful, revealing both a contrast in character and life situations and a similarity of traits that might not at first seem apparent. Eleni becomes the Clytemnestra figure in Angelopoulos's first feature. She too has her strength, and in *Reconstruction* we feel that the men around her are not as strong or long-suffering as she is. But as a provincial woman who has never had a chance to travel, to see the world, to gain any other perspective, Eleni is, we sense, an embodiment of the death of the Greek village. For while we apprehend her strength, we are also aware that her restrictive environment has greatly limited her opportunities and freedoms.

We immediately see Electra as different because, as a traveling actress, she has built-in freedoms and chances that Eleni could only dream of. Electra can be seen as representing the survival of "the other Greece" that refuses to settle down, that refuses to compromise with those forces that have subverted much in Greek life (she does not marry a foreigner, does not confess to the fascists, does not sell her body for material goods, and so forth)—and that offers a nurturing, helping hand to the next generation, as seen in her loving aid to the younger Orestes.

The Travelling Players, in fact, turns on the point of her rape and the monologue that follows. The rape is the single most horrific event in the film. And her calm, steady, measured monologue to us afterwards in cold daylight is more than her "finest performance," as we have noted earlier. It is the point in the film when we realize that nothing can destroy or subvert such an individual except death itself. That Angelopoulos has chosen to center his text so clearly on Electra, with a sterling performance by Eva Kotamanidou, says much for how we finally leave this odyssey through more than a dozen critical years of Greek history. Because she is so much a part of the scenes of the second half, we are, in effect, drawn into experiencing history from her perspective.

And what is her viewpoint? She is surrounded by many borders, traveling between and beyond them all, as an actress, a participant, a sister, a daughter, a victim, and a survivor. She is a woman and a wife, but not a mother. She refuses to cooperate with fascist forces, Greek and foreign, but she is not a communist or party member of any group, a point made stunningly clear in the New Year's Eve "dance" and singing sequence between fascists and leftists. And she is a professional who has denied herself the position of "housewife" in any traditional sense. Unlike Eleni, who is anchored in her stone home in her stone village, Electra is a female Odysseus who never finds an Ithaca.

No simple dichotomies exist in *The Travelling Players*. While the film is interwoven with threads of triumph in which Orestes and his spirit survive and in which Electra becomes a focus of strength and integrity, we must note that Angelopoulos presents no simple Marxist dialectic of good and evil, Left and Right, conservative and radical realities with the "workers" winning out against the ruling class. Greek history and culture caution against such reductionism. Rather, as Charles Segal has said about the global rediscovery and popularity of Greek tragedy since World War II, it has "filled a need for a vision in modern life, a need for an alternative to the Judeo-Christian view of a world order based on divine benignity and love" (23). Angelopoulos's vision as presented in *The Travelling Players* suggests a similar complex, troubling, yet finally replenishing view of reality in the twentieth century.

Chapter Six

Voyage to Cythera: "One . . . Two . . . Oh, My God. I'm Out of Step"

THE FILM DIRECTOR AS TELEMACHUS: IN SEARCH OF
A NARRATIVE POSITION

> *The older distinction between fiction and history, in which fiction is*
> *conceived as the representation of the imaginable and history as the*
> *representation of the actual, must give place to the recognition that*
> *we can only know the actual* by contrasting it with or
> likening it to the *imaginable*.
> (Hayden White)

VOYAGE TO CYTHERA could be called Angelopoulos's version
of Fellini's *8½*, that is, a director's self-reflexive meditation on the
difficulties and joys of creating a film. Yet if we follow through on
this parallel, we must begin with an awareness that Angelopoulos's film
involves a filmmaker as Telemachus in search not only of an Odysseus
father figure but of a way in which to narrate such a story on film as it
intersects with the history of Greece from 1949 to the present.

Late in the film, the chain-smoking, middle-aged film director protagonist, Alexander (the Telemachus figure), who resembles a younger
Angelopoulos, listens to police testing their walkie-talkies in a kafeneon.
From a distance he hears: "One . . . two . . . testing . . . one . . . two . . .
testing." Suddenly we hear him whisper to himself: "One . . . two . . . Oh,
my God. I'm out of step." It is the only time in *Voyage to Cythera* that we
hear the film director speak to himself. For his characteristic "action" is
one of cigarette-in-hand silence.

The moment is a charged one, for in the film-within-the-film being
made, Alexander, starring as a director of a film, meets his old father,
Spyros, who has returned to Greece from the Soviet Union under the amnesty of the late 1970s, which allowed Greek communists to return home.
But ironically Spyros is being sent away again by Greek authorities for
"causing trouble" in his home village. The being "out of step" can thus be
seen as a son's evaluation of his own life and, by implication, that of his
generation, as he is finally confronted with a "father" who represents a

past—the Greek civil war—that most Greeks have felt uncomfortable even mentioning. *Voyage to Cythera* is a troubled Greek filmmaker's voyage in search of a narrative position or authority from which to film another difficult page in Greek history that has not been told: the return of the communist exiles to contemporary Greece.

As we have observed, all of Angelopoulos's films are "reconstructions" to one degree or another, but what differs is the means and motive of those doing the reconstructing. The reenactments in *Reconstruction* were ordered by the police in an effort to discover what actually happened during the murder in an isolated village. *The Travelling Players* uses the world of provincial theater to "act out" and interact with Greek history. In *Voyage to Cythera* the self-reflexivity concerns cinema and the making of a movie as these activities intertwine with the realities of how the return of an old communist (the Odysseus figure) influences Greek culture of the 1980s. Alexander, a middle-aged Telemachus, lives through his own version of Fellini's $8\frac{1}{2}$, as the making of a film not only opens up the world of imagination and cinema, but also becomes Angelopoulos's reflection on the historical wounds that have not healed since the end of the Greek civil war in 1949.

The synopsis that follows is of particular importance for this film. As a film about a filmmaker with shifts between the film being shot within the film and life itself, *Voyage* foregrounds how shaky the boundary between "on-screen" and "off-screen" life can become. The film-within-the-film seems quite "real," and what is clearly real seems quite fictional. Despite such confusion, we do learn, however, that at no time in the film does anyone reach Cythera, an island at the southernmost tip of the Peloponnese in Greece. Cythera is also the mythical birthplace of Aphrodite and thus the subject of poems, paintings, and allusions ever since, as Yvette Biro notes: "the isle of dreams where one can dedicate oneself to happiness or the search for it" (50). Quite simply, as Greek critic Vasilis Rafalidis has written, "*The Voyage to Cythera* is a journey that never takes place" (19). For instead of Cythera, we watch the film move to a village in Greek Macedonia, the home of the old communist.

More important than comprehending the line between imagination and reality in this film, however, is the need to grasp, as Hayden White notes in this chapter's epigraph, that history and fiction (and thus narrative film) necessarily must share territory in order to begin to claim distinguishable identities. Angelopoulos makes us aware of the actual in the imaginary and, in White's terms, the imaginary in the actual. Once more myth crosses paths with history, as in Angelopoulos's previous films.

Here we learn that in this version of the *Odyssey* by Angelopoulos, Telemachus (Alexander) is middle-aged, not a youth as in Homer's epic, and a filmmaker who must confront his "father" before completing his film and thus before getting on with his life and career. But his name also links him to that familar history and myth—the story of Alexander the Great—which took center stage in *Megalexandros* and echoes through so many of Angelopoulos's films. Instead of attempting to conquer the entire known world, however, this modern Alexander wishes to explore the possibilities of conquering cinema for his own purposes.

CYTHERA IN THE MIST: "IT'S ME"

It is dark. The music is orchestrated, full, and serious. It is night. We see a galaxy swirling in the heavens. As we shall see in the next chapter, *Landscape in the Mist* begins with the telling of a creation myth. *Voyage* starts similarly by presenting the entire universe. This opening shot therefore frames the tale that unfolds within, of course, a much more limited universe in Greece.

Cut: Marching music from World War II. From a window a woman calls, "Alexander." We see a boy running through old Greek streets, then by Hadrian's Arch (Roman ruins) in Athens. German soldiers are chasing him.

Cut to contemporary Athens and the very modern apartment of a film director, Alexander. (Alexander is played by Italian actor Julio Brogi, who appeared in Bertolucci's *Before the Revolution*, among other films, and is dubbed with Angelopoulos's own voice throughout the film—this adds yet another autobiographical level to this film about a filmmaker.) He is seen waking up from his dream of his past, turning on the serious, fully orchestrated music we heard earlier on his stereo system.

Now we are in a film studio where a group of thirty or forty old men stand in line for a casting call. They stand out against a blank background like so many figures in Karaghiozis, the Greek shadow-puppet theater. Each one steps forward to a desk and says, "*Ego eimai*" ("It's me"). Alexander walks through this scene smoking. The expression—"It's me"—is a very common one in Greek, used a hundred times a day in a dozen different circumstances. It is also a classic distillation of individuality: We, in English, have borrowed our term "ego" directly from εγω meaning "self." And the verb "I am" combined with it gives the expression a double sense of selfhood: literally, "I am myself." This repetition is compounded into the kind of accumulative effect Angelopoulos's scenes can have because of simplicity and repetition.

Cut to a break in the casting call with all of the men standing outside the studio in the street. Alexander comes through doing a little shuffle and jump, as if he is concentrating on something, remembering something, or lost in some private narrative (an action that mirrors the "suspended step of the stork" echoed by the television journalist in the later film of that title).

Inside a kafeneon, Alexander's mistress, an actress, complains to him that they never see each other anymore. He does not answer. The music swells with a strong evocation of romance and nostalgia as an old man (Manos Katrakis) walks in with a wicker basket selling lavender. Alexander is immediately captivated by him. In the background outside on the studio street, workmen carry "ancient" statues (clearly they are props: balsa wood copies).

Alexander follows the old man with complete absorption: He has seemed totally distracted till now. Alexander shadows the man through a gray and unappealing cityscape. They approach the harbor. Now we do not see the old man. But we see a large, imposing ship, the *Ukraina*, arriving from the Soviet Union. We see a *reflection of the old man in the water*.

This moment, without further embellishment, becomes the transitional point, etched in water, between the reality of a filmmaker trying to make a film and the actual narrative of a son and daughter awaiting a long-exiled father's arrival. Without announcement, the film-within-the-film has begun.

With Alexander, now a major protagonist within his own film, is his sister, Voula (Mary Chronopoulou). "After thirty-two years, why are you still running after a shadow?" she asks. (Note: the very young brother and sister in *Landscape in the Mist* are also Alexander and Voula.)

"Ego eimai" ("It's me"), the familiar line we have heard at the studio, now echoes from the old man. We see him, suitcase and violin case in hand, standing by the ship in high angle (we are looking down at him). This is not the audition or the rehearsal. This is the film the roomful of old men wished to be in. Now the "father" who has been absent for thirty-two years has come home.

Alexander and Voula approach him. "Mother is waiting at home." Their old "father" says, "Aren't we going to kiss each other?" Voula kisses him, then Alexander. What is clear immediately, of course, is the emotional *distance* maintained between father and son, a distance that is heightened for us because Angelopoulos keeps us guessing as to how much what is unfolding is "actual," how much "imaginary" (the film-within-the-film). Realize, furthermore, that unlike many movies about films being made, here Angelopoulos blurs the distinctions by *not* showing a movie crew filming what we see. This simple choice keeps us suspending disbelief and thus entering the "story" as if it were real, just as a typical film commands us to do.

The father, son, and daughter walk, against a lead-gray sky, through a poor section of the city. "I'm afraid," he says to them, referring to his homecoming with his wife. This line, coming from an older character, a returning father figure, contrasts sharply with the line "I'm not afraid" spoken by the young children in *Landscape in the Mist*. Of course, with this contrast, Angelopoulos is suggesting the difference between innocence and experience and youth and old age. But the implications, I suggest, run even deeper, embracing, for instance, a contrast between a complete world-weariness (Spyros) and an incorruptible courage and innocence (the children in *Landscape in the Mist*).

Inside the house he meets his wife, Katerina (Dora Volanaki). She asks, "Have you had anything to eat?" Again, we are surprised that there is no tearful reunion, no tender embrace. Instead Angelopoulos presents a very reserved reception. But for those familiar with Homer, such a homecoming should not be startling, for in the *Odyssey* there is no immediate embrace either, as Penelope continually "tests" Odysseus as to his identity before she can fully accept him as her returned husband. It is a process that reveals, once more, her wisdom and faithfulness.

There is street noise outside. Many relatives have gathered in this old house. Spyros now turns and walks out of the house. He stands alone with his suitcase. Alexander follows him through the city.

They go to an old hotel. Alexander tries to explain how his mother feels. Spyros says that this was the hotel he used to come to with Katerina when they were dating. Alexander says that they will leave for "the village" the next day.

Cut to a car driving on a mountain road through mist.

At a certain point the car stops, and Spyros whistles in a complicated way, half tune, half speech. After a pause, a whistling message returns. Katerina explains that this is an "old outlaw" (communist mountain troops') secret code. Voula and Alexander ask what has been said. "He has told an old friend, Panyiotis, that he has returned."

It is a barren winter landscape in Macedonia, Greece's northern region, with light snow still on the ground. On a frozen hillside, Spyros meets his old dog, which he calls by name, Argos, the name of Odysseus's dog who greeted him in the *Odyssey* when he returned to Ithaca. Then his old friend Panyiotis appears. They embrace. And they walk through the cemetery as Spyros calls out the names of friends whose tombstones he passes: "Ahhh, Dimitri," and others (the power of this scene is explored below).

Sitting in the cemetery, Panyiotis explains that the village is not the same as it used to be when Spyros left some thirty-two years ago.

We see in the distance, suddenly, what looks like an army of villagers

7. *Voyage to Cythera*: Spyros enters the old family home in his Macedonian village

on foot, in cars, Jeeps, motorcycles, all moving across the landscape. "The whole village is selling everything. Life is easier down below in the valley." "They are coming," Spyros says. Is he speaking of his departed friends? Or of Death itself? Panyiotis then begins to sing an old folk song, "Forty Red Apples," and Spyros joins in. Finally, Panyiotis explains that he wants to tell Spyros that he has always loved Katerina since they were children. Thus, in the *Odyssey* parallel, he would be a "suitor."

Spyros says nothing. But he stands and lifts his arms and begins to dance a "Pontiko" dance, singing "Forty Red Apples." Panyiotis claps time and the sound track carries the eerie, nervous beat of a Ponti dance tune. We see the dance in medium close-up, as described in chapter 1. Then from a distance, etched almost in the style of Ingmar Bergman's figures in *The Seventh Seal*, we see them against the sky. Finally, in extreme long shot, we see them as dots on a landscape.

Alexander arrives, calls out, "Father," and says it is time to open the house. They walk toward the village. Spyros approaches the old family home, a two-storied large village home, painted light blue and in the northern Greek style (a lot of wood and plaster). Spyros approaches the door with a large key handed to him by Katerina. He enters the house repeating, "Forty Red Apples," a ballad about lost love and old age.

Once inside, they begin to take the newspapers off the windows. It is a splendid old house with everything left as it was. We experience the place, the space, the past as it is affecting them now, in the present.

A winter day. A mountainside. The "group signing" of the contract with a winter resort company is to take place. Hundreds of villagers on one side and a table set up with officials holding bullhorns on the other. (How strange the human voice sounds through these instruments and how often Angelopoulos has officials speak through them!) The officials tell the villagers to come forward in "alphabetical order to sign." We understand that this calling forth, one by one, to the table, looks and sounds a lot like the casting call in the studio at the beginning of the film.

Spyros walks through the scene, followed by Alexander in a trench coat he wears throughout the film. The music is full of nervous violins and is a variation of the Ponti music we heard in the cemetery. Spyros starts tearing down boundary markers and goes into a dilapidated barn where he takes out a shovel and begins to dig.

"All must sign or the deal is off," says the bullhorn-bearing official, nervously. Panyiotis comes over and tries to stop Spyros.

A flap is occurring at the signing table, we assume, because Spyros has not signed, and the whole scene breaks up with everyone leaving and making a terrific amount of noise.

Spyros is left alone at last, on the mountainside.

It is night. Cut to inside the house. There is a large, round dining room table. A meal is prepared and all are seated. There is the noise of a crowd outside, as Voula slices a loaf of bread, identifying each piece for each person there and not there ("the stranger who is in need," and so forth). We gather that this is a family ritual being repeated once more. Voula says to Spyros: "Why don't you let your wife sign? She raised us and never smiled." The meal is interrupted as villagers call from outside for "Katerina" since they do not want to deal with "him." What they want is for Katerina to sign the contract. It is an all-or-nothing deal. If Katerina does not sign, the deal with the resort group is off. Voula also expresses her reservations about Spyros: "You took to the mountains, leaving us alone."

Spyros goes outside and confronts Panyiotis, who is with the other villagers ("suitors"). "Spyros, you're dead. A ghost. You don't exist. You were condemned to death in Larissa four times," Panyiotis says. He takes out faded newspaper articles he has carried all these years and throws them down. Spyros picks them up and pockets them. "You can't play havoc with us again," says Panyiotis, in tears.

I have been at pains to suggest that Angelopoulos offers no slavish working out of any of the Greek myths he alludes to in his films. But let me suggest in this one scene how much he has "rewritten" the original myth as it has come down to us in Homer. Certainly Panyiotis is almost literally cast in the role of a suitor because of his lifelong interest in Katerina. But therein lies the contrast with Homer as well, for Panyiotis has also been a close friend to Spyros, a situation that never occurs in Homer, and furthermore he has never expressed his love to Katerina; thus he is blameless in comparison to the hundred suitors in Homer, who not only badgered Penelope constantly but almost ate her out of estate and home. The scene is an emotional one by itself as an honest sharing of difficult expressions between two old friends long separated. But the scene gains still more power when the viewer recognizes the Odysseus theme once more, both as the film invokes the legendary story and as it diverges from it.

Back inside, Spyros speaks to his violin, and we think he is alone. "At first you think of Greece and what you left behind." He is clearly talking about his exile. "I've got three other children over there." We then see that Katerina is in the room and that he is speaking to her. Katerina listens and simply asks, "What is she like? The other?"

Note that this scene also both echoes and inverts Homer's version of Odysseus's tale. First we should remember that a major characteristic of Odysseus in Homer is that he is a teller of tales—and not only tales but clear fabrications as well. In fact, he is so fond of role playing that it is very difficult for him to express simple honest truths.

Spyros is the exact opposite. Panyiotis has been very blunt and honest in telling him the truth. Spyros has been the same in revealing his other life in Tashkent, Uzbekistan. And Katerina, who is cast in the role of Penelope, engages in none of the feisty verbal jealousy and give-and-take that appears in the *Odyssey*. We are disarmed by her simple "What is she like? The other?" and left to wonder whether this is coming from weakness of character or a complete selflessness that understands and accepts the hardships her husband has endured.

Cut to day. Panyiotis comes to the house. Spyros tells him, "I'm staying."

Spyros is on the country road. Panyiotis comes up: "They made us fight each other." He speaks of the Greek civil war. "Man against man, wolf against wolf, now everything is destroyed." They share cigarettes. Panyiotis begins to sing an old war song. Spyros sings "Forty Red Apples."

A dark gray sky. The mountainside. A single bare tree. And Spyros. Old, frail, like the tree. He is near the old barn. It bursts into flames and quickly is destroyed. We sense that Spyros set the fire.

Cut to a Mobil sign on the highway at a gas station where Voula and Alexander have pulled up for gas. Bland jazz playing on the car radio. As they refuel, Voula says, "I don't plan to spend my life running after ghosts." Alexander replies, "It's never too late." She agrees and simply walks off into the dark.

The police arrive in the village. Alexander comes too. Nervous violin music in the Ponti style plays once more. The police start running off to different parts of the village. Katerina goes to the ruins of the burned barn.

Then, Katerina, Alexander, Panyiotis, and the police go to the house. Panyiotis whistles. Pause. Spyros whistles back. They all stand in front of the house. "What did he say?" the police ask. "He's not moving," is Panyiotis's answer.

Katerina approaches the house and says, "Ego eimai" ("It's me," the same phrase that punctuates the beginning of the film). He opens the door. She says, without anger or judgment, "You haven't changed. You always go off on your own when you are afraid." She leads him out. They stand alone in front of their home. He says, in Russian, "Rotten apple."

The police explain that Spyros is a "displaced person" and, as such, is without nationality. The police ask Alexander, "Are you sure he is your father?" Alexander does not answer (he does not even repeat the line Homer gives Telemachus, "People say I am his son, but what son knows his father?"). The police, however, then say, "All right, you convince me he is, but we can withdraw his permit to be here at any moment."

Katerina announces, "I am staying with him."

Cut to interior of a theater. Alexander is backstage listening to the end of the play (gunshots, killing). There is applause and a curtain call. We see his mistress on stage. The theater empties and he and his mistress make love in the empty theater (a scene that is very similar to the lovemaking scene in *The Beekeeper*, which takes place in an empty cinema).

It is evening in a city. Alexander is alone.

He is in his office. He listens to the answering machine. One of his staff talks about the boat to Cythera and lists all the stops the boat makes. We assume this is for a location for his new film. Alexander does the little self-absorbed shuffle and hop he has done at the beginning of the film. He then looks at a page of his script. The lines there are from the film-within-the-film we are watching. Thus we assume that this scene is "real" and a time-out from the internal movie, as was the lovemaking scene above.

But we do not know. It could be, once more, a scene from the film he is making, which is then about a filmmaker who wishes to make a film on Cythera.

A winter mountain landscape. Spyros and Katerina are in the back of a truck. We hear a bugle playing Taps on the sound track.

Spyros and Katerina arrive in some dreary small town. They are in an old empty waiting room, as for a train or boat. Spyros says, "I hear you." Then he begins a monologue in Katerina's presence. "I fooled you five times. Five wars, prison, the firing squad." The camera circles him slowly, moving in on him, and then finally moving away from him as he says, again, "I hear you." Boat sirens and horns are heard in the background. Is he speaking of Death? Katerina remains silent. It is a very powerful scene, all the more so for its utter simplicity.

Cut: Alexander is smoking by the sea at night in front of a cantina truck serving coffee and sandwiches. Panyiotis is there drinking coffee. The sound track is typical Greek bland pop bouzouki music. Panyiotis again says that Spyros has brought all his troubles upon himself by not signing papers, but we perceive that he is using Spyros as the scapegoat. Alexander does not speak.

While Alexander stands there, a police Jeep goes by, having taken Spyros away.

Cut to a small Coast Guard launch. Sad bouzouki music playing. The police take Spyros out on the boat. They approach a Russian ship, and in English the harbor police talk back and forth with the Russian officials (off-camera), who ask to speak to Spyros. But the police report to them in English that Spyros says only "Rotten apple." The Russian officials (through bullhorns!) say that they do not understand and thus cannot take him.

The Greek officials bring him back to shore and leave him alone.

We hear another bullhorn announcing an upcoming "festival" of the dock workers, "with many artists." Inside the kafeneon, Katerina is lying down. and she speaks, half asleep. It is about how she met Spyros; it is about young love. "It was the Feast of the Assumption. We were on the oxcart twelve days, working stripping tobacco leaves. I saw him." And she adds her father's question about who he was. "He is a refugee from Ionia, Father," she replies. Thus we know that Spyros, like other Angelopoulos characters including Agamemnon in *The Travelling Players*, is from Asia Minor (Turkey) and came to Greece in the 1920s. And just as the three key monologues in *The Travelling Players* sharply illuminate the characters of their speakers, so Katerina's speech here reveals her to us in a quite different light. We see her as a much more complete person, as one who is articulate and concerned, long-suffering and even-tempered.

The police come in to take Spyros to "international waters until further notice." They put him on the raft, with an umbrella, in the rain. Alexander watches but does not run to help.

Inside the kafeneon, rebetika music from Asia Minor plays. Journalists come up to Alexander and ask, "What is your relationship to him?" meaning Spyros. Alexander walks away without speaking.

Outside an announcement is heard: "Jugglers and musicians and magicians will perform." There is the sense that a dark carnival is unfolding. Alexander walks up into a studio, and we realize that the music we hear is on a tape in the studio and that, once again, it is a film-within-a-film we are watching.

Musicians arrive outside in the rain. In the midst of all of this muted carnival, a magician shows Alexander a trick. Alexander stands with Katerina, his mother, by the sea and puts his arm around her, looking out to sea. Back inside, the musicians begin to play "As Time Goes By," which seems both familiar and totally out of place in this context. Then there is an old Tom Jones song, followed by an accordion piece.

Alexander goes into another room to make a call, and we see the back of a set, which once again alerts us to the "movie-within-the-movie." And yet we still have no means of judging whether this is outside the film, and thus "reality," or not.

There is a splendid shot of Alexander with a cigarette standing as the "carnival" goes on, observed in the mirror, while Glenn Miller's "In the Mood" plays; we recall the New Year's Eve scene observed by Electra in *The Travelling Players*. His mistress is beside him repeating lines we heard at the beginning of the film about how she believes "only in my body."

Outside on the dock we hear "Alexander's Ragtime Band" playing. The police arrive. The music ends. It is at this point that Alexander says to himself, "One . . . two . . . Oh, my God. I'm out of step." Then the stage is set up for the performers outside as the stage crew setting up the festivities call out, "One, two." An announcement follows: "The weather has not been kind, but we have been asked to have our festival anyway in honor of the old man who is out at sea."

Katerina is asked to step onstage. She comes forward and speaks: "I want to go to him." We hear a lone violin. It is Spyros's violin. The camera pulls back and the police agree that if she wishes to go, it is her business. She repeats, "I want to be with him"; again the violin, and the camera holds on Alexander's face watching all of this.

Cut to Katerina and Spyros embracing as we hear gulls. They are on the raft, out at sea. "Daybreak," he says. "I'm ready," she says. They both stand, backs to us, looking ahead at the sea. They stand separately but together.

They become dots on the watery horizon. Fade out.

8. *Voyage to Cythera*: Spyros and Katerina, as Odysseus and Penelope, float away, alone, from Greece

ODYSSEUS RETURNS: THE EMBRACE IN THE CEMETERY

It is difficult for those outside Greece to realize how absolutely topical *Voyage* was for Greeks when it appeared in 1984. Thousands of exiled Greek communists had begun to return from Eastern Europe and the far reaches of the Soviet Union, especially from Kazakstan and Uzbekistan, after a general amnesty in the 1970s permitted them back. It is also a fact that many of these exiles returned to the Soviet Union once they confronted a Greece they could no longer recognize or adapt to. I have personally interviewed Greeks in Tashkent who felt that the quality of their lives in the now defunct Soviet Union was better than that in their isolated Greek villages today, or in the pollution and confusion of contemporary Athens.

In *The Travelling Players* Angelopoulos gave voice to the Greek civil war on the screen, and in *The Hunters* he explored how the "corpse" of the civil war influenced Greece in the 1970s. *Voyage* updates *The Hunters* and broadens the spectrum by telling the story from the viewpoint of a living communist "corpse" who has returned from a thirty-two-year exile to Greece in the 1980s. Once again, Angelopoulos's suggestion is that Greece is not ready to come to grips with its past. In *The Hunters* the corpse is returned to the snowy landscape in which it was discovered, while in *Voyage* Spyros is set adrift on a raft headed away from Greece into international waters, with no home to steer toward.

But there is a touching twist on the legends and myths surrounding Odysseus. In Angelopoulos's ending, Odysseus is not alone. Katerina— his Penelope—has joined him. Whatever happens, they are together. She can embrace and accept what Greece cannot.

Spyros is played by Manos Katrakis, one of the best-loved Greek actors for several generations. Casting meant a lot in this case, for Angelopoulos chose not only an actor who had played everything from *Hamlet* to *Oedipus Rex* but a man who was very ill with cancer at the time he agreed to be in the film, and who died shortly after shooting ended. Angelopoulos explains that he hesitated about asking a sick man to take on such a demanding role, but that Katrakis told him from his hospital bed, "I want to do it even if I die. If you take the risk, I take the risk" (Themelis 8).

Angelopoulos accepted the challenge, and *Voyage* became a better film for this agreement. For there is a haunting dignity to Katrakis's gaunt face and hollow-eyed stare that even a great actor could not will into being. Katrakis, wearing old clothes on his emaciated frame, standing still in a room or in a landscape, draws us to him. It is indeed a rare performance.

Nowhere is this more evident than in the cemetery scene when Spyros returns to his Macedonian village and embraces his old friend, Panyiotis. I have described the poetic realism of this desolate landscape and the emotion of Spyros's embrace, of his calling out to his dead friends buried in the cemetery, together with his singing and dancing to a swift "Ponti" tune.

But to read a description of this is not enough. One must imagine this grand old emaciated actor performing all of these actions, and at that point the term "screen acting" takes on new meaning. Even those who do not know what a Ponti dance is understand the intensity of the moment as Spyros's past floods back to him, and he expresses it as Greeks have always expressed themselves through history: in dance and song.

Furthermore, Angelopoulos builds this scene on a realism that is almost completely documentary. He explains that he was asked to shoot a television documentary about a village, like the one he finally used in Macedonia, that had only one inhabitant. Angelopoulos, working as usual with Giorgos Arvanitis, his cinematographer, did so. During the one-day shoot, he notes, the villager took them to the cemetery, where he danced a Ponti dance for them since he was from the Ponti region. Angelopoulos was impressed, and thus the scene wound up, as described, in *Voyage*.

Despite the difficulties that follow in the film, this embrace between old friends is significant. For that brief moment, the past and the divisions are set aside, and the two men are what they wanted to be: friends. Modern Greek history has passed them by, however, and the village Spyros thought he was returning to no longer exists. That Greece is gone. Instead, Angelopoulos shows that there is a large corporation ready to buy out the village for a resort complex to be imposed on the land from whichever city the home office happens to be located in. This time Odysseus is not helped by his son (Alexander, the filmmaker) to slay the suitors. And there is no Athena to step in, as in the conclusion of Homer's *Odyssey*, to make peace. In Angelopoulos's Greece of the 1980s the embrace of old friends is undercut by the greedy villagers who sell their "Ithaca" to the highest bidder.

PENELOPE SETS SAIL: "I WANT TO GO TO HIM"

Katerina, Spyros's wife and thus the Penelope figure in this narrative, continues in Angelopoulos's line of strong-willed and long-suffering female characters. We have noted that *Reconstruction* is centered on Eleni, and that the second half of *The Travelling Players* belongs to Electra and the quiet endurance and resolve she embodies. Katerina is no less a person of integrity, sympathy, and innate endurance.

The Homeric echoes resound. Katerina has been patient and faithful over the years. But there is a deep pathos that Angelopoulos evokes in his film's contemporary allusion to the myth that goes beyond Homer's joyful conclusion to the *Odyssey*. Homer glosses over the matter of age, for instance, giving no importance to the fact that Odysseus has been away for twenty years. Penelope apparently has lost none of her beauty or youth over the years. Furthermore, Homer, after the initial hesitation and testing that goes on between Penelope and Odysseus, finally lets them enjoy a glorious night in bed together.

Angelopoulos has pulled back from such fairy-tale material, which seems perhaps closer to *The Arabian Nights* than to the coming together of an actual man and a wife separated by so many years and so much grief. In the silences and glances and the shadows of the scenes in *Voyage*, Angelopoulos allows us to experience the difficulty of this homecoming.

They have, for instance, so little time to themselves alone. People are constantly coming and going in the city, in the village owing to the land sale, and then at the dockyard as the festivities are being planned in the midst of Spyros's own drama. Thus her final decision to go to him becomes what it should not have to be: a performance announced onstage. She is not a traveling player by trade. But in Angelopoulos's rendering of this woman from a small Macedonian village, modern life has forced her into taking center stage and then going offstage into the sea, drifting toward the horizon with her husband.

Spyros's fate, expelled by his own country, is a sad one. But there is a feeling of inevitability about it, given that he will not accept the sale of his family home to the new capitalists. Katerina's decision to leave, however, is a surprisingly brave and selfless one. She is, after all, giving up everything at this point to follow a man who is more stranger than husband after so many years, and who has, as he confesses, three children "over there" and thus another life and wife.

The pathos that Angelopoulos builds in these scenes springs also from the contrast of this Penelope with the clever beauty found in Homer. Katerina is old. She has lost her looks and remains more in the background of scenes than as a center of attention. And certainly sexuality and sensuality are not prominent factors in this reuniting of two souls so long separated.

Her decision, rather, grows out of deeper urges and feelings that she does not articulate and perhaps cannot. Whatever the results—and the prospects are surely dim—she wishes to share the rest of her life with him. She has, therefore, accepted him and all of his past, his sorrow, his politics, and his failed dreams.

THE RELUCTANT SON AND THE HESITANT DIRECTOR

The fate of Spyros and Katerina is resolved in the closing shot even if it is not attained. But what of Alexander? Angelopoulos purposely leaves his film director protagonist as the most unresolved of all of the figures in the film.

Alexander is, after all, the one who wished to sail to Cythera on a film project, but who never begins this voyage. Instead of the island of mythical hedonism and sensuality far to the south, he journeys, in his film-within-the-film, to the north and toward his roots. But since he is author, director, and star, much remains ambiguous in this tale about a returning father. For as director, Alexander has, in the first place, chosen the unknown old man in the coffee shop selling lavender to be Spyros. Thus we have the ambiguous situation in which the "son" creates the "father."

It is on his role as a son to the returning Spyros in the film-within-the-film that we must focus. Yvette Biro has commented that Spyros and Alexander—father and son—resemble each other in surprising ways: "The marginal character of the exile," she writes, "makes Alexander see what is marginal in himself" (52). At the heart of the seeming contradiction in Alexander, of course, is the need as director to be in control and to orchestrate all. And yet Alexander the character and son is hesitant to act, to interact, to speak, to do more than remain as a reluctant son. He is unable or unwilling to help his father in his struggles as he returns to his crumbling Ithaca.

Spyros is a man of few words. Yet he does have his moments when we glimpse the inner man: during the cemetery dance and song, as discussed, and during his brief talk with Death in the empty station. In contrast, Alexander allows himself no such communication. Only when he says, "One . . . two . . . Oh, my God. I'm out of step," do we sense his inner preoccupations, and then only inconclusively. Angelopoulos makes no effort to create in Alexander a character we are easily attracted to or sympathetic with.

Consider, for instance, how many films about making films we have had in recent years. Of these self-reflexive works, perhaps François Truffaut's *Day for Night* (1973) is the most memorable. Truffaut takes us through the whole filmmaking process and exposes all the humor and pathos connected to the creation of a film. But certainly a large degree of our pleasure is due to Truffaut himself in the role of the director, infusing that role with all of the quiet charm that made him attractive both as a person and as a director.

Angelopoulos's Alexander offers us no such access to either a filmmaker's thoughts or his personality. But there are, as we shall explore in chapter 8, similarities between Alexander's search for Spyros as a "father" and the quest of the protagonist in *The Suspended Step of the Stork* for the Greek politician turned refugee. And certainly one of the strongest parallels is that of the middle-aged man's need to follow the older tragic and enigmatic "father" figure, but without the courage or will to take on or totally accept the odyssey these older men have embarked upon.

Katerina shows the strength of acceptance in her desire to follow her husband. Yet as a son, Alexander makes no real effort to help his father or, finally, to intervene on his behalf with the officials. Nor does Alexander show any desire to urge him and his mother not to leave. Instead, he remains frozen, watching them fade away on the horizon.

Finally, however, Alexander is not simply a reluctant son, but a hesitant film director as well. We cannot really tell where the film-within-the-film begins and ends. Yet we assume, even though we do not hear the customary "Cut!" or see the camera shooting the raft disappearing into the distant sea, that we have ended with a final scene from the film-within-the-film. In fact, it is possible that the whole film is a dream inside the filmmaker's head. Fellini in *8½*, and Truffaut in *Day for Night* enjoy suggesting how film and real life often cross paths, but we are never in doubt as to which is which. With *Voyage* we just may have a Greek cinematic parallel to James Joyce's tour de force, *Finnegans Wake*, which takes place entirely within the sleeping and alcohol-soaked mind of a Dublin pub owner. But the nonstop flow of real and invented words clues us that this is not a waking reality. "That is absolutely correct," says Angelopoulos. "In a real sense the whole film takes place in Alexander's head" (interview, Athens, July 1995).

Chapter Seven

Landscape in the Mist: A Documentary Fairy Tale

The Light Was Divided from the Darkness

L ANDSCAPE *in the Mist,* which won the European "Oscar" (Felix) as Best Film of 1989, could be subtitled *Children in a Documentary Fairy Tale.* Quite simply, it is Angelopoulos's most accessible film. It forms the third part of what Angelopoulos has called a trilogy of silence, which can be identified loosely as a voyaging trilogy also comprising *Voyage* and *The Beekeeper.* History and, for that matter, the world of adults are left behind in this tale, Angelopoulos's only film centered on children.

The frame he creates weaves together elements of myths and fairy tales, but he also includes documentary-like realism. Thus we are continually aware of the five-year-old boy, Alexander, and his eleven-year-old sister, Voula, who are the focus of this narrative, both as children in their own worlds and as children being forced by the reality of their surroundings to lose much of their innocence far too early. As Stephen Holden wrote in his *New York Times* review, "exceptional beauty" becomes "an elegiac allegory of initiation into a forbidding modern world" (12).

Near the opening of *Landscape* the screen is completely dark as the young girl tells her younger brother a story she has told many times. It is a creation myth, and it is obviously meant as a comforting tale, for it is the young boy who asks to hear it again. The myth, as we hear it in voice-over from the sister, begins: "In the beginning there was darkness and then there was light and the light was divided from the darkness and the earth from the sea, and the rivers, the lakes, and the mountains were made, and then the flowers and the trees, and animals and birds." We then hear a door opening and closing and footsteps. But we see nothing. "It's Mummy," the girl says and adds, "This story will never finish."

At that point the door opens slightly, letting in light, as if illustrating the myth just told. As the door opens farther, light washes over the brother and sister, who pretend to be asleep in the same bed. The door closes and the mother's footsteps recede.

Much is established in this simple scene played out literally in the dark. On a cinematic level, of course, Angelopoulos encapsulates the medium of film itself, which is, after all, a play of light and darkness and the various shades in between. Furthermore, that he presents the scene almost entirely in the dark suggests how he as filmmaker can create a narrative out of "nothing." While *The Travelling Players* concerns theater, and *Voyage*, filmmaking, *Landscape* presents the importance of the most elemental narrative form of all: the *spoken* myth, story, fairy tale.

But the scene suggests more. We already know from an earlier opening scene at a train station that the children are longingly seeking their absent father, who they claim is in Germany. On the other hand, all we learn of their mother is from this creation myth scene: the footsteps and the opening and closing of two doors. We never hear her speak, and we never see her. She is thus, for all practical purposes, just as absent as the missing father or perhaps more so: the fact that they live with her but that she is physically and emotionally withdrawn from them is even more harmful to the children's development than the father's literal absence.

History is not Angelopoulos's focus in this film. Rather, *Landscape* is grounded in myth and fairy tales. And, beyond the usual *Odyssey* allusions, it is centered in the most basic myth of all to any culture, that of the creation of the universe. Clearly the creation myth doubles back as an individual one too, for the two children set out in search of their own origins. Their odyssey is yet another variation on the Homeric epic. But in this example we have two children rather than one in search of a father they do not remember and have never seen. Instead of a faithful Penelope for a mother, they have an unidentified and unseen woman who lacks in maternal emotions and actions. This one scene suggests that she has frequently left them alone at night in their apartment. Even her return brings no kiss or greeting.

Furthermore, in this variation of the *Odyssey* theme, no Odysseus ever appears. Indeed, as we shall see, his very existence is called into question. Yet the ending, like a fairy tale's, does suggest, as we shall see, a triumph and fulfillment unusual in Angelopoulos's work, for the film that begins in darkness does close in light, even if that light is seen through the mist.

One further parallel must be noted. Though the *Odyssey* is the dominant echo in *Landscape*, a fainter but nevertheless distinct myth reflected in the film is, once more, that of the Agamemnon cycle. Once again, Angelopoulos does not lean heavily on such an echo. The traces of the myth do not reduce or lock in the actions of his characters, but rather just the opposite. For those familiar with Angelopoulos's films, the parallels are there. As brother and sister, these two young travelers at odds with the world are similar to Electra and Orestes in their alienation from their mother and their adoration of the absent father. In this parallel the variations on the mythical theme are quite ironic, for the mother's crime is not a literal murder of the father, as in the *Oresteia*, but a figurative one since, as the children's uncle suggests early on, she has slept with so many men that she cannot know who the father actually is (and, of course, this suggests that Voula and Alexander may even have different fathers).

The myth is directly suggested as well since the two wanderers do meet up with Orestes from the troupe we encountered in *The Travelling Players*. Thus there comes to be something of a doubling effect for the ancient pattern. Finally, however, all is wrapped in the mystery of the creation myth once more. But that mystery is in turn infused with the irony that Voula and Alexander will never be able to completely separate the "light" from the "darkness" even while they succeed in transcending all in the end, as they reach the luminous tree in a misty landscape in reality (documentary) or in their imagination as they die (fairy tale). Angelopoulos's ending can be read either way, as we shall discuss.

"WORDS AND GESTURES WE DON'T UNDERSTAND"

A girl of about eleven, wearing a dress and coat with a small book bag on her back, and a boy of about five in a dark jacket and shorts, with a green scarf around his neck to protect him from the winter weather, run toward the camera. It is night. The girl asks, "Are you afraid?" "No," answers the boy. We then see them approach a train station as we hear announcements about a train for Germany arriving and the departure of another for Germany soon to take place.

As the train continues to roll by, we hear the boy say, "I dreamed about him again last night. He seemed bigger than other times." They then rush the train as if they are going to get on, but they do not. They now fill the screen as they stand alone while the train disappears beyond them. The credits and a slow and richly melancholy musical score begin.

We will learn that she is Voula (Tania Palaiologou) and the boy (Michalis Zeke) is Alexander: the same names used in *Voyage*, as we have seen, for the film director and his sister; as mentioned in the introduction, Voula was also the name of Angelopoulos's sister who died as a child.

Cut to the creation myth scene described above, as Voula retells the story that has obviously been told many times before.

Then there appears an ugly landscape of rocks and rubble with cheap high-rise apartment buildings in the background. Voula and Alexander race along an embankment to what we come to realize is a barbed-wire enclosed prison compound where men stand motionless or wander aimlessly. Alexander seeks out one prisoner called "Seagull" who stands on a ledge flapping his arms up and down. Alexander explains that they are going to Germany to see their father.

We have a repeat of the train station scene: they stand watching the train come in as the camera slowly tracks in on them. This time, however, they board the train. Once aboard, Alexander says, "We made it!" and a long and happy hug follows. We sense the closeness of this brother-sister relationship in what we will later come to realize is the happiest moment in the film for them. Their odyssey has begun. As they sleep in the corridor of the train, we hear Voula's voice-over letter that she "dreams" to her father: "Dear Father, we are writing to you because we are coming to find you. We have never seen you, but we miss you. We talk about you all the time. Mummy will be upset when she discovers we are gone. Deep down inside we love her, don't think we don't. But she doesn't understand anything." She continues and concludes with: "We don't want to burden you. We just want to get to know you and then we'll go away again. If you send a reply, send it by the sound of the train. Tatan . . . tatan . . . tatan . . . (the sound of the train). Here I am. I am waiting for you." This voice-over dreamed letter thus establishes that no actual letter has been or will be sent, and neither do they expect a real answer. That Voula asks for an answer through the sound of the train clearly invokes the fairy-tale nature of the film. This "letter," the first of a series, becomes, of course, a simple and effective means of allowing us access to Voula's thoughts and feelings, since she has nobody else to express herself to except her brother, who is too young to understand. But there is one other dimension to these imagined letters. They serve a function for this film similar to that of the direct camera monologues in *The Travelling Players*. As in Angelopoulos's earlier film, these moments help both to punctuate the narrative and to establish a direct contact with the audience.

Cut to the conductor, who approaches them and asks for a ticket. They have none. They are taken off the train at the next stop, and the stationmaster tries to find out who they are and where they are going. Voula finally volunteers that they are off to see their uncle.

The exterior of what appears to be some kind of industrial complex. We see a middle-aged man standing and watching as Voula runs and embraces him. Alexander follows. The stationmaster appears to have brought the children here. The uncle takes him aside to explain that he cannot take any responsibility for them since he and his sister, their mother, have not spoken for years. Then when the uncle thinks that the children are safely out of hearing range, he offers the stationmaster a cigarette and explains, "There is no father. There is no Germany. It's all a lie. She didn't want to tell them that they are illegitimate." At that point Voula and Alexander rush out, for clearly she has heard him. She shouts, "You're lying."

Next we are in a police station corridor where the stationmaster has taken them. It is very dark, but we hear someone shout, "It is snowing."

Soon everyone is shouting, "It is snowing," and rushing out of the police station. The hallway is empty except for Voula and Alexander, who stand on one side of the door, and a man on the other who keeps saying, "He slipped the rope around his neck." The documentary fairy-tale quality is made manifest once more. On one hand the snow appears as some kind of miracle, while on the other we are hearing of a suicide. Outside the station, the police stand transfixed like statues watching the snow fall all around them. As the police are distracted by the "miracle" of snow, Voula and Alexander run off, captured for us in slow motion.

They ride on another train, and as they sleep, Voula dreams another letter to her father: "We are traveling, blown like a leaf in the wind. What a strange world. Words and gestures we don't understand. And the night, which scares us, but we are happy and we are moving on." As the conductor approaches them, we guess they will be thrown off again.

It is night in a northern Greek town. Voula and Alexander walk across a snow-covered town square as we hear mixed fragments of songs coming from a wedding celebration. A bride rushes out in the snow, crying. The groom runs to her and coaxes her back inside. Another pattern is becoming clear: while *Voyage* concerned the director's effort to figure out a narrative position in presenting a tale about a returning father, *Landscape* asks us to consider two innocent children who are constantly thrown into the middle of different people's "stories" and asked to try to understand their words and gestures, which they, of course, cannot "read" or understand.

What is the bride's problem? Why is she crying at her wedding? The children (and we the viewers) never learn.

Another "story" immediately follows as a tractor drags a dying horse into the square and leaves it there. Alexander starts crying as Voula stands watching the horse. As they watch, the wedding group wanders through the square singing and dancing. Then the horse dies. Alexander cries uncontrollably.

It is daylight on a mountain highway as Voula and Alexander walk along. They happen upon a young man with an old bus he has converted into a traveling home. He turns out to be Orestes (Stratos Tzortzoglou), the young boy who takes on the original Orestes' role in the traveling players' production of *Golpho*. He is now twentysomething, in blue jeans and tennis shoes, with a mop of hair and features not unlike those of a young Tom Cruise. He invites them to ride with him and they finally accept. As Orestes drives, he talks to them about theater and how difficult it is to make people laugh and cry. We see the costumes that were so familiar in *The Travelling Players*, and we hear the accordion music when Orestes begins to tell Voula and Alexander how their play begins each time. He then explains to them that the troupe is having trouble finding a theater to use because "times have changed." Voula falls asleep.

Later they reach a town. While Voula sleeps, Alexander watches Orestes take his motorcycle out of the back of the bus. They then see the traveling players themselves, walking by in a strong wind. Orestes explains that, "ravaged by time, they wander stubbornly all over Greece always performing the same play." He drives off on an errand as Alexander stands alone.

Finally Alexander wanders off, leaving his sleeping sister. He walks into a taverna and is asked to work clearing the tables in exchange for food since he has no money. But he can barely reach the tables. An old man playing the violin comes in and plays what we recognize as the theme song of the film. The restaurant owner chases the musician away.

Soldiers march around outside in the town square. Voula finds her brother and hugs him as if he had been lost for a long time.

It is evening in a town. Orestes speaks to them: "You are funny kids, you know that? It's as if you are going nowhere, but you are going somewhere." Alexander answers, telling Orestes that he too looks strange. Orestes laughs and explains that he will soon do his military service.

As they walk along, Orestes picks up a small piece of thirty-five-millimeter movie film. He holds it to the light and describes to Alexander what he sees, a landscape in the mist with a tree. Alexander sees it and asks to keep the film. Orestes gives it to him.

Voula wakes up in Orestes' bus and asks where she is. She looks out and sees Orestes waking up on the beach next to the sea. He is surrounded by the traveling players. As Voula and Alexander follow Orestes down the beach, the camera tracks past each of the players, quoting lines from *The Travelling Players*—not from *Golpho*, but from their monologues about the political history and events of World War II and the civil war. What those who have seen *The Travelling Players* realize is that in *Landscape*, thirteen years later, history itself has become a half-forgotten "reconstruction" repeated to no audience, with each line layered on top of the lines of the others so that instead of an arresting performance, we have an absurdist postmodern cacophony. Literally no one is listening, and, even if we have not seen *The Travelling Players*, we understand that these young children certainly do not comprehend the muddle of historical facts being tossed at them.

The character given the most play is an old fellow who speaks lines as if he is the "Spirit of Revolution" itself: His lines are broken, unfinished, half forgotten. As a Spirit of Revolution, he suggests that revolutions no longer have vigor or purpose.

The players gather loosely and the accordion player begins a performance of *Golpho*, once more, but this time with no audience. Then a man runs from a parked car in the distance across the field to announce that they cannot perform this evening in the auditorium because a group that paid more money is having a pop dance.

At this point Orestes' now middle-aged mother, Chrysothemis, checks her makeup in her compact mirror and asks Orestes to give her a ride into town on his motorcycle, suggesting, as throughout *The Travelling Players*, that she is looking for a good time, away from the rest of the troupe.

Audiences that have not seen *The Travelling Players* would fail to understand this level of the scene. Thus once more, as in William Faulkner's works or those of Gabriel Garcia Marquez, Angelopoulos's films can be appreciated individually, but taken together, with their multiple cross-references and allusions, they gain an echo effect that becomes a significant part of the pleasure of the text for those acquainted with the entire opus.

Once Orestes leaves, the rest of the troupe wander to the sea and stand there, not unified as in the opening and closing train station scenes of *The Travelling Players*, but as dispirited lone figures in a desolate landscape.

Voula and Alexander watch. And then Alexander says, once more, "I dreamed about him again last night." Now the words, in juxtaposition with the worn-out lines uttered by the aging players, have a completely different meaning for us. Alexander's line returns us to the reality of these two young children and their shared dreams and fantasies, a level of communication quite different from that of the players around them. On the other hand, however, we realize that their lines are also "reconstructions" and performances they and we have heard before, lines that become rituals which may or may not retain a level of potency and relevance.

Cut to a very rainy landscape on a highway as Voula and Alexander run toward us. Alexander stops and cries out, "I can't any more." There is thunder in the background. Voula bends over, in the downpour, and comforts, cradles her brother. She then starts her effort to flag down a vehicle and they are soon picked up by a truck driver.

At an all-night truck stop café, the driver takes them in for something to eat. He is unshaven and crude, drinking wine, smoking, and flirting with the new waitress. Something of an argument develops with a man at another table over the waitress.

On a dull highway, early morning, we see the driver pull his large B.A.F. truck off the road into the mud, get out, and walk around the truck. He comes back to the passenger side and tells Voula to get out. She hesitates, but he reaches in and pulls her out, telling her to come when he calls. She tries to run away and he catches her, dragging her to the back of the truck. There is no music in any of these last few scenes.

He climbs in behind her, into the dark space of the back of the truck, and the rape begins. We hear nothing except the passing traffic on the highway beside the truck. Time passes and Alexander jumps out of the cabin shouting for his sister. He runs past the truck, along the highway, shouting for her.

Later the driver climbs out of the back and goes up front. Slowly Voula sits up, her legs, with their stockings now pushed down, hanging over the back of the truck. Her head leans into the light, and she slowly raises her right hand to her eyes and examines the blood on it. There is no expression on her face.

There have been many rapes represented on the screen, but I can think of no more bloodcurdling example of the violation of innocence than this scene, which Angelopoulos stages, as usual, without emphasizing the graphic details of the event. Instead, the fact that we can neither see nor hear anything makes it even worse. Angelopoulos has explained that not only was he committed to such a way of shooting the rape, but he felt even more obligated since he was using a young actress.

The rape must, of course, be compared to Electra's rape in *The Travelling Players*. That one was depicted as grotesque, as the fascists, wearing carnival clown masks and their hats as well as their coats, pinned her down while the leader had his way and as carnival music played outside. The rape of Voula is even more shocking both because of her age and because of the "absence" in which it is shot so that the actual rape must, like violence in a Greek tragedy, play itself out offstage in our imagination.

And in both films, the rape forms a clear dividing line between "before" and "after" in terms of its effect on the women. Electra gives the longest and most moving speech of *The Travelling Players*, facing us, speaking directly to us. From that moment on, we sense how much a center to the world of the traveling players she becomes. Likewise, Voula is not the same person after the rape, and, like Electra in Angelopoulos's earlier film, Voula has a "speech" soon after the violation.

But before she begins another letter to her father, we find them in another train station, waiting. As the scene opens, a white chicken is standing in the waiting room and everyone is frozen in anticipation, as in the snow scene in front of the police station. Here a man slowly creeps toward the chicken and then pounces, grabbing it, and heading off, bringing the room back into "real life" animation, complete with the noise of a busy station. This documentary fairy-tale moment echoes back to *The Travelling Players* and the troupe's attack on the isolated chicken on a snowy mountainside, though the implications are different. The troupe's attack is a visualization of extreme hunger, while this train station scene seems to reflect some less clear power that causes the world immediately around the chicken to become transfixed.

Voula misses the scene, for she is asleep, dreaming another letter to her father. And while she "speaks," we see that Alexander is holding the scrap of movie film up to the light of the window, looking at the luminous tree in a misty landscape. Voula's letter begins: "Dear Father: How far away you are. Alexander says that in his dream you seemed very close. If he stretched out his hand, he would have touched you. We are traveling continually. Everything goes by so fast. Cities, people. But sometimes we get so tired that we forget you and we don't even know if we're going to find you or not. Then we get lost. Alexander has grown a lot. He has become very serious. He gets dressed by himself. He says things you wouldn't expect." We sense the element of doubt creeping into her mind, of course. But we are also listening for signs of what the rape has done to her, and this now follows as she continues: "I have been very ill the past few days. I was burning up. Now I'm starting to get better. But it's such a long way to Germany." A long pause follows, and then she speaks again: "Yesterday I even thought we should give it up. What is the use of carrying on? That we should never get there. Then Alexander got mad. The way grown-ups get mad and he told me I was betraying him. I was ashamed." She wakes up and Alexander is sitting beside her. "Do you miss Mummy?" she asks him. He does not answer. She stands in the doorway, back to the camera as usual, looking out at the railroad tracks as the camera slowly tracks in on her, as usual. But there is a difference now. For the first time in the film, she continues the letter while awake: "We each write to you the same thoughts. And we both fall silent before each other. Looking at the same world, the light and the darkness . . . and you." A large shift has occurred in Voula. Her unconscious dreaming has now been pulled into her waking life. The two are becoming one. This letter also brings together the creation myth that began the film and their personal odyssey when she adds, following "the light and the darkness," the words "and you."

As she finishes, we see a railway handcar go by from right to left carrying a group of men, in bright yellow rain gear, who stand motionless. The effect is "magical" on several levels: visually they draw attention to themselves as literally brightening up the frame, which is, as usual, composed of muted and dull colors. But we should also remember that in an earlier letter to her father, Voula asks that he reply through the sound of the train going down the track. Thus she has attuned herself to "reading" the landscape for messages from afar.

We do not understand what significance she gives to the moment. But we as viewers feel the double vision Angelopoulos so often provides us: is this indeed a message or another example of chance? Furthermore, as we shall see in the next chapter, these men in yellow reappear in *Suspended Step*, especially in the final scene, as agents of positive action: they are telephone line repairmen helping to reestablish communication.

Voula and Alexander are on yet another train.

As they pull into a station, the rich theme music for the film begins again. They get off, and we see in the distance an ugly plant that looks something like a nuclear power plant. They run down a dirt road bordered only by dirt. There is not a scrap of vegetation within the frame. Then they stop as the road ends with a huge earth-gouging black machine, which looks like some science fiction contraption. But it is clearly there to gouge the earth, filling up an endless line of trucks.

They turn and head back to the station where they are, by chance, reunited with Orestes. Cut to the seashore. They pull up on his motorcycle, and Orestes calls out, "We got away!" with a joyful expression. They stand staring at the sea in a line composed of, from left to right, Voula, Alexander, the cycle, and Orestes. The theme music continues as Orestes says, "Didn't I say you were funny kids?"

They take off again across a grassy hill but without a road. "I don't want this ever to end," says Alexander as he enjoys the carefree feeling of riding with Orestes. They come down to a beach area that has a mobile canteen with tables and chairs scattered on the beach. In the background is an old familiar-style Greek metal circular staircase rising from the beach to nowhere and looking very much out of place, of course.

Rock music is playing in English. Orestes orders a beer and soft drinks. He then approaches Voula, who is seated, and asks her to dance. This is the first indication that he now sees her as more than just a child. "I don't know how to dance," she says. "I'll show you," he retorts. When they come close to dance, however, they do not. They stand there, transfixed, staring at each other, as in similar moments I have described. She then turns and runs away down the beach.

When Alexander starts after her, Orestes stops him. "Leave her alone. Today she discovered something very important. We must leave her alone." Thus the unspoken, intuitive form of communication that we have often witnessed in Angelopoulos's films has again taken place. Orestes understands Voula without a word's having been exchanged. The camera closes in on Voula on the beach at the water's edge, kneeling as the water licks her legs.

We are now in a large train station with a huge photo of the Acropolis on the back wall. Orestes is holding hands with both Voula and Alexander as he leads them toward their train. But Voula breaks away and says, "Don't let's go yet." She stands, back to Orestes, head lowered. He stares at her. Then, laughing but serious, he says, "What have you done to me? I've lost my mind!" And he leads them away.

Another shoreline. This time the trio pulls up to the traveling players with Orestes' bus by the sea. They have all of their costumes on a clothesline, for sale. "Why are you selling the costumes?" asks Orestes, as he rushes over to them. "I don't like funerals," he says and leaves. The six remaining traveling players remain motionless, staring at the sea, no longer traveling. This is Angelopoulos's farewell to them. They now have nothing to say. It is, indeed, a kind of funeral.

Night in a hotel room. Voula and Alexander are asleep, but Voula

9. Voula, Orestes (center), and Alexander watching the "hand" rising from the sea in *Landscape in the Mist*

wakes up. The music begins. We hear a boat in the distance. She goes to Orestes' room but it is empty. In close-up, we see Orestes outside looking out past the camera, but we do not see what he is looking at. He stands up and backs off as if amazed at something. We now see a large white object beginning to emerge from the sea. At first it is indistinguishable; it might be a whale or large fish. Then we see a huge broken finger rise, and finally we understand: this is an enormous ancient hand. We hear a helicopter and the music. Then a shot of the helicopter.

Cut to the street in front of the hotel: Voula and Alexander come out of the hotel and walk past two men in yellow rain gear standing by their bicycles. They too are watching. The children run to Orestes, and then all three stand watching the hand rise. As it ascends, it turns, pointing at us and then off into the distance. We now see the waterfront skyline of Thessaloniki, and even though we can see cars going by, the city seems strangely quiet and, somehow, empty.

There is to this scene in particular what so many of the scenes in the film share: a stunning visual quality. As James Quandt has written, "The plangent beauty of *Landscape*'s imagery is untranscribable" (25). Before

10. *Landscape in the Mist*: the broken classical hand rising from the sea, raised by a helicopter

we begin to grapple with the question of what this image means, we experience its power and what can only be described as both a dislocating effect and a sense of transport as the image carries us beyond our everyday reality.

Voula and Orestes now look at each other as Orestes gets back on his motorcycle. "If I were to shout, who would hear me out of the armies of angels?" says Orestes, as he lowers his head to the handlebars. Alexander comes up and pats him on the back, comforting him.

On a bare earth soccer field between high-rise apartment buildings we see Orestes sell his motorcycle. That night at a disco bar frequented by many gays, Voula goes in search of Orestes as a Van Morrison–like rock song in English plays. She sees Orestes go off into the darkness of the club with a young man, obviously a pickup.

It is a brightly lit highway at night, and Voula and Alexander are walking down the road, their backs to us. Orestes drives up on his cycle: "You forgot your bag." Voula is clearly hurt. Orestes says, "I wouldn't like us to part like this." He gets off his motorcycle and goes over to her as she breaks into deep sobs. He embraces her, caressing her hair gently as she cries. Alexander stands watching them as the theme music plays. The camera circles Voula and Orestes in close-up. "Little Loner," Orestes comforts her. "That's the way it is the first time. Your heart beats so you think it will break. You feel terrible. You want to die."

Her sobs decrease, yet we feel her pain. Orestes has been her first love. But there is no kiss and no passion. There is simply compassion and, finally, separation. She pulls back and looks down to the ground. The camera pulls back as she comes to Alexander and they walk off, toward the camera. Orestes is left alone, waving, as we rise into the air. Is the camera, like the ancient hand, ascending? Our last view of Orestes is an aerial shot.

It is another train station, and Voula is inquiring about the cost of tickets to the border. "What's a border?" asks Alexander. Voula does not answer. Outside the station, in close-up, we see that Voula looks older, remarkably older since the opening shots of the film. She approaches a soldier and asks if he will give her 385 drachmas. There is an awkward exchange, which ends with the soldier's leaving money and running off. She picks up the money and runs away. Voula and Alexander are on a train again. This time they smile at each other until they hear an announcement that all passengers going to Germany must have their passports ready for inspection. Of course they do not have any.

Cut to a dark riverbank. We hear the water rushing by. Voula explains, "Beyond the river is Germany." There is no music. They find a boat. "Are you afraid?" asks Voula, repeating the opening question of the film. And the answer is once again, "No. I am not afraid." It is very dark now. We see a guard tower lit up on the border and then we hear "Halt," followed by a single shot.

Cut to bright light. Alexander says, "Wake up, it's light. We're in Germany." A deep dense mist. Voula says, "I'm afraid." Alexander then says, "Don't be afraid. I'll tell you the story." In close-up the camera is on Alexander's face as he says, "In the beginning was the darkness," and then repeats the line. He raises his hand as if either waving or wiping a window to see more clearly. "And then there was light." The theme music begins again. We now see a tree through the mist in the distance as Alexander takes Voula's hand, and they begin to walk through the mist toward the tree.

Then they start to run. When they reach the tree, they embrace it. This is our final image. Voula, Alexander, and the richly textured tree they have embraced. What has happened in this final frame? We cannot be sure, for Angelopoulos has left the ending open.

Did they survive the shooting in the dark (we heard only one shot, but we assume there could have been more) and reach "Germany"? But they have no passports, and Germany does not border on Greece, so how could they actually have reached the border in the first place? Or, if they did succeed in reaching the border, were they killed by the border guards? Is the ending thus only a dying dream of triumph? We do not know. What is clear is that they have reached, either way, a tree and not a father. But trees, as we know from myth and fairy tales, have their powers, their meanings, and their relationships to magic.

A final possibility exists: they have entered the strip of film that Orestes gave Alexander; thus their "Germany," their "happy ending," is merely a cinematic fantasy triumph. All three possibilities coexist in the final image, which, however, in all three cases, is, precisely, an image—that is, like the Byzantine icon, a "likeness" of transcendence.

FAREWELL TO THE TRAVELING PLAYERS

Landscape contains Angelopoulos's farewell to his traveling players. Despite its basic differences in orientation, *Landscape* needs to be considered closely in conjunction with *The Travelling Players*. Of course this is necessary on a literal level since the traveling players become a part of the young protagonists' "documentary fairy tale." Orestes, the youngest member of the players, is linked with Voula and Alexander in their own quest in a Faulknerian echoing effect, which, as I have pointed out before, can only be fully savored if one is familiar with both films.

What is the effect of seeing the traveling players wander into the town square as Orestes and Alexander look on? It is, after all, thirteen years since we saw them in *The Travelling Players*. Alexander sees them with the clear eyes of a child: "They look sad." And they do. But they also look ghostly, as if they are images on a Karaghiozis shadow-puppet screen.

Yet Angelopoulos's statement about these used-up actors is apparent. As James Quandt has written, in the demise of the traveling players and the Greek history they have traversed, we come to feel that "culture and history seem irrelevant in the new Greece. The past, once a suppurating wound on the body politic, now seems to have surceased. Those who remember are spent, paralyzed, redundant—exiles in their own country" (25). Angelopoulos's farewell to his traveling players is also a warning: contemporary Greece appears to have no awareness whatsoever of what went before.

Thus the striking power of the "hand from the sea" sequence. This scene, which is stunning in and of itself for its visual construction, casts its pointing finger on the whole text. It is, of course, a detached hand, separated for whatever reason from a gigantic statue lost in the sea. But the image becomes metaphor as we realize that the farewell to the traveling players appears as a depiction of an ahistorical Greek present which has captivated even Orestes. Remember that he had, at the end of *The Travelling Players*, taken on his uncle's role and, one supposed, politics. Orestes' farewell to the troupe undermines the past as he takes off on his motorcycle for other gay bars and a life of his own on the road.

The traveling players, those who have survived, that is, have not gone down in battle or in defeat. They have, rather, simply become irrelevant.

The Tree in the Landscape

As I wrote this chapter during the summer of 1995, Attica, the county that includes Athens, underwent its worst recorded ecological disaster. Forest fires raged out of control on July 21st, all beginning simultaneously throughout the area and all claimed to have been set on purpose by radical right-wing groups trying to make a point for their own political agenda. Whatever message these groups thought they were conveying, the point is that Athens and its surrounding suburbs have been robbed of much of the forest that had covered the mountains surrounding Athens since long before the Parthenon was built.

This actual ecological loss highlights an even stronger appropriateness to the ending vision that Angelopoulos presents in *Landscape*. In one sense *Landscape* can be viewed as a hymn to one tree. It is the tree that Orestes finds in the film fragment he picks up in a street (how did it get there? from which film did it come? where is the rest of the film?—these are just some of the questions that arise). And it is the same tree that

Voula and Alexander reach at the end of the film, when it appears as if in a vision or from a miracle. We cannot help but assume some mysterious identity between the tree in the film fragment and the one they finally reach. For this radiant tree is almost the only tree we see in the whole film. During the rest of the film we gaze at denuded landscapes, almost entirely devoid of vegetation.

Again, Angelopoulos creates a memorable moment through his own form of poetic minimalism. It would not be the same to end the film in the Black Forest, with the children surrounded by innumerable trees. Rather, the lone tree becomes an emblem with traditional associations, including that of the Tree of Life, but we are left to take the image further. If this tree is not their actual father—and it is not, of course—their embrace at the end suggests a fulfillment as if they have reached "a father," which in this case is nature itself. And it is a flourishing and thus nourishing tree, splendid in its foliage and brilliant in its hue.

More than anything in any of Angelopoulos's films, this lone tree, embraced by two children in the mist, becomes an image of hope and therefore replenishment for them and for us. Their odyssey is not over, and yet they have arrived somewhere.

THE HORSE IN THE SQUARE

Consider one final image. Alexander sobs as he embraces the dying horse in a dark and snow-covered town square, as Voula, his sister, stands beside him trying to comfort him early on in their journey. In many ways, it is the most emotional moment of the whole film, all the more so because it is so unexpected. We know that Voula and Alexander are on an odyssey, like Telemachus in Homer, to find their father whom they never do find and who may well not exist.

But suddenly appears this image of the boy, his uncontrollable grief, and the dying horse. It is powerful in and of itself as a self-contained moment. Yet how does it link to the rest of the film?

The moment, Angelopoulos has explained, came to him personally as an expression of the utter and complete grief that overwhelmed him as a child when his younger sister, named Voula, died (interview, Athens, July 1995). Thus his link is a very personal one, an autobiographical note. It expresses a wound that has never healed, a sorrow that could not be explained away.

And yet as expressed in *Landscape*, it becomes something much more than personal grief. But what it suggests ultimately is up to us not only to decide but to work through emotionally. Of course, it is easy to say that this young boy, who has been denied a father and a father's love and who has experienced an unloving mother, is expressing, desperately, his loneliness and need for affection. And we could point to similar scenes in Dostoyevsky and others in which the mistreatment of animals becomes a cathartic mirror for a character's own sufferings. But there are many other echoes as well, including Odysseus's grief at the death of his dog Argos, and even Odysseus's tears as he sat by the sea on Calypso's island longing for home. Dominating all of these echoes, there is the sheer, stark reality of two children alone in a bleak and cold world, searching and wandering, wandering and searching.

Angelopoulos's title alone signals us to be aware of that which is beyond human nature. These three powerful images—Alexander and the horse, the classical hand rising from the sea, and the final luminous tree in a bright landscape—become a triptych that embraces a wide spectrum of experience. From the absolute grief that the dying horse expresses, to the almost melancholy and disorienting wonder of watching a detached "classical" hand appear and disappear seemingly without context, to the tree that offers hope and replenishment, this documentary fairy tale takes us into realms of childhood that most films about children never dare to enter.

Chapter Eight

The Suspended Step of the Stork: "If I Take One More Step, I Will Be Somewhere Else"

DESPAIR AT THE END OF THE CENTURY

A YOUNG bearded journalist and a Greek army colonel stand on a bridge over a river that is the border between Greece and Albania. They wear coats to protect themselves against the gray dawn of a northern Greek winter day. The colonel points to a blue line and says that it is the end of Greece. In the distance we see Albanian guards, watching. The colonel lifts one leg and says, "If I take one more step, I will be somewhere else. Or die." The Albanian guards appear nervous. The colonel remains with one foot suspended and then slowly lowers it again . . . in Greece. He and the journalist walk away.

In *Suspended Step*, Angelopoulos touches the "metareality" in the troubled history of the Balkans during the end of the century. Angelopoulos, like the journalist, goes after a story, dares to lift one leg in an exercise of "what if," and returns with images such as the one described above that force us to meditate, in a clearer light, on the concept of borders and the territories—geographical, cultural, political, and personal—they lock in and out. As the colonel accompanying the journalist says soon afterwards, all of the hundreds of refugees we see waiting in this border town have come to see their condition as, in his word, "mythical."

Ironically, if an army officer, who, in this film, becomes something of a Greek choric figure, suggests such a dimension, then we should take him seriously, as the journalist does, as we observe Angelopoulos's suspended cinematic step. In this light *Suspended Step* is a search, a journey, a love story, a Christ myth, and a kind of homecoming all projected, finally, into the very end of the twentieth century—December 31, 1999—and beyond.

Despair at the End of the Century is the book, we discover in the film, that the central figure, a Greek politician played by Marcello Mastroianni, has written before he takes a step to "somewhere else," thus becoming the Odysseus/Ulysses figure of this narrative. In this sense the film becomes for Angelopoulos not only a complex and deeply affecting meditation on contemporary history as tied to refugees from everywhere who are trapped in the Balkans; simultaneously it emerges as an opening study of what hopes may emerge for a new order beyond the chaos of the present.

11. The television journalist takes a "suspended step" at the Greek-Albanian border: *The Suspended Step of the Stork*

PRELUDE TO THE GREAT MIGRATION: "I HAVE NEVER FELT LIKE THIS BEFORE"

Angelopoulos once more draws on a combined Homeric and Dantesque use of Odysseus and his travels as structuring and thematic elements for his film. Telemachus in this case is a young television documentary journalist in search of a "story" about a famous Greek politician who went off on a journey and was never heard of again. Odysseus in this film is an aging Greek politician who has either changed identities or is actually another person. He is not a hero winning the Trojan War for the Greeks as in Homer, but something of a holy fool who, in a Christlike manner, has given up everything to live among the most unfortunate of contemporary humans: the international refugees in search of a home, real or imagined.

We begin with credits on a dark screen and composer Eleni Karaindrou's slow yet somehow nourishing music, which in this score features the piercing saxophone work of the Norwegian jazz master Jan Garbarek. If music sets a mood and tone, and this full orchestra music does, it is one based on a simple melody, full of feeling and rich in possibilities.

Fade in on helicopters circling over a sea on a gray morning as the music continues. The serenity and yet strangeness of this ballet of aircraft over water echoes the "ancient hand" scene in *Landscape in the Mist*.

As in *Landscape*, Angelopoulos begins the film with a voice-over "preamble" from the main character. Here, the television journalist (Gregory Karr) tells us that on his way to the border to do a story, he thought about "that incident in Piraeus" (the port of Athens) in which Asian stowaways on a Greek ship, who had been denied asylum by Greek officials, cast themselves into the sea rather than be returned. This turning away of political refugees, of course, echoes the ending of *Voyage* as Spyros and his wife are sent off into "international waters."

At this point in *Suspended Step*, we are no longer focused on the helicopters, but rather on bloated bodies floating in the sea and being rounded up by two small boats. If it is the past that emerges from the sea near the end of *Landscape*, it is the painful present that is harvested from the sea in this opening moment of *Suspended Step*. There is no music as we watch the bodies.

The voice-over of the young male journalist then clues us that his story is more than a news piece. "I began to think about *them* [the bodies of the refugees] and to wonder how does one decide to leave? Why? And to where? And I thought about that ancient verse, 'Don't forget that the time for a voyage has come again. The wind blows your eyes far away'" (he is alluding to a line in Dante's *Inferno*).

The second scene is a long tracking shot: we watch a Jeep approach the border with Albania, and the journalist and the colonel accompanying him get out. The colonel must inspect a line of troops standing in single file, clearly etched against the winter river landscape behind them. It is a routine roll call except for one point: several times besides giving their names, these young soldiers add a comment that seems totally out of place for the scene. One young recruit says, after his name is called, "I am only afraid of the roar of the river at night." The colonel does not comment on these remarks, and no one seems to be upset or to even notice anything unusual in these statements. But it is the kind of intrusion into what appears to be a realistic scene that signals Angelopoulos's metarealistic approach to scenes, characters, history, and cinematic narrative. The moment is not surreal. We do not have, as we do in Luis Buñuel, for instance, a razor blade slicing a woman's eye (*Un Chien Andalou*) or dinner guests formally dressed sitting around a dining room table on toilets (*The Phantom of Liberty*). Rather, the moment has a solid "reality" to it that on the surface offers no jarringly strange juxtaposition such as is provided in Buñuel's films. But within this realistic frame, Angelopoulos stretches the limits of the real by having a young recruit utter a line such as "I am only afraid of the roar of the river at night."

At that exact intersection of the realistic image and the improbable line, Angelopoulos's metarealism begins. What makes the exchange improbable, of course, is that it may well express the soldier's unconscious or actual fears, but the line is inappropriate for a military roll call. That Angelopoulos mutes the response and passes on quickly to the next recruit without fanfare signals once more that such a metarealism should be taken as real within the frame of the film that unfolds before us. He sets up a "metareal" opening image—bodies floating in the sea—that has become too frightingly common in news reports on television especially. But an army roll call seems to be completely normal. And yet the final effect of such a personal fear expressed in such poetic language by a young recruit is to draw attention, for an instant, to the soldier's individuality within the military group to which he belongs. After all, the moment would have been both different and more "realistic" if the recruit had spoken in the usual half jargon, half swearing lingo of soldiers everywhere. But "I am only afraid of the roar of the river at night," coming from an unidentified character seen only briefly in a long narrative, clearly becomes one way in which Angelopoulos expands our concept of the real to include what we might usually call the poetic.

We now have the "If I take one more step" scene, on the bridge, described above.

When they leave the bridge on the border, we see the colonel lead the journalist down through the bushes to the river. There, as the gray river flows by, we hear very Balkanic music rather faintly coming across the water. In one of the few playful moments of the film, we discover that the music is literally coming across the water on a tiny raft, inside a cheap cassette tape recorder. A middle-aged Greek peasant receives it, pulling on a wire strung across the river. He takes out the tape, puts in another, and the raft is on its way again, back across the river to the "other country" but this time playing a mournful Greek pop song:

> Love is a full moon
> I drive my body mad
> And I dream of you.

This is as close as Angelopoulos comes to what at first feels like pure humor. And yet the appealing absurdity of this "traveling player" is undercut by the colonel's intrusion.

After taking the journalist up a watchtower to see a village across the river called "The Waiting Room," the colonel drives him into town, explaining in voice-over that thousands of illegal refugees—"Kurds, Turks, Albanians, Poles, Romanians, Iranians"—have wound up in camps there waiting for the Greek government to allow them to go "elsewhere." It is

at this point that he tells the journalist that their plight is "mythical."
Voyage ends with two people on a raft, displaced, with nowhere to go.
Suspended Step presents thousands of parallel cases, implying the other
millions around the world in similar "mythical" circumstances.

The journalist, tall, thin, bearded, and wearing glasses, then wanders
the riverfront market area of this old northern Greek town full of traditional Turkish-influenced architecture. In a slow zoom across the river we
see, for the first time, "him," the object of the journalist's search (Marcello Mastroianni), shopping and wearing a hunter's cap, shabby coat
pulled up against the cold, and boots.

Cut. At the hotel in town, the journalist is now joined by his team of
four: a camera-and-sound crew of three fellows and one female assistant.
As they check in, the clerk says to the journalist, "I've seen you on TV,
haven't I?" And as the crew choose their rooms, they conduct a little
horseplay, suggesting the good-natured teamwork they are used to without the need for comment. They are, we feel, their own happy professional carnival.

From his balcony, the journalist looks out again at the market and sees
"him" again. Slow zoom onto him.

We cut to the journalist and the crew walking to the railway yard
where many of the refugees are living in boxcars. The journalist points his
camera crew toward the stationary train of refugees, and the camera begins to roll.

What follows is one of the most haunting scenes in any of Angelopoulos's films. It is a long tracking shot along this train to nowhere. The line
of boxcars is stationary, but the left-to-right tracking (viewer's perspective) of the TV camera crew gives the illusion of movement as we slowly
track past six boxcars, each with a refugee family at its open door, each
with its distinct ethnic costume visible, each with its similar silent staring
of people displaced, waiting, waiting, waiting. The music is predominantly a lone accordion, reflective of the nostalgic but comforting tune we
have heard since the opening.

In this one tracking shot we have both the subject of the journalist's
opening question—refugees and what makes them leave and for where—
and a comment as well: because the journalist is a journalist, we are waiting for the voice-over "news." But the silence (together with the music)
allows us to go beyond the news, beyond the borders of explanations for
a moment to experience the existence of these refugees. The scene reminds
us of Walker Evans's photographs of the Depression "come to life" in
muted colors, in a slow-tracking frieze, which represents all those who
have nothing, at the end of the twentieth century.

Beyond the visual images of refugees, however, Angelopoulos adds
voice-overs of bits and pieces of speech in all of the languages represented,

each explaining how they escaped torture, death, hardship in their own lands. All of this "documentary" material as a truck arrives dumping used clothing for the refugees and a group of refugee children push and shove to gather them all up. We see the television crew filming the event. Then the image becomes one on a screen in a television studio screening room as our young reporter watches the screen. He next goes through a file of photos in an archive of the office, returning to the screen to look at a freeze-frame image of Mastroianni.

Cut to a fancy cocktail party at which the reporter begins speaking in English to the foreign wife of the politician who disappeared (played by French actress Jeanne Moreau). She explains that he walked out of his job, his marriage, and his life after writing a book, *Despair at the End of the Century*, and that this departure was an earlier one from which he did return after forty days but "like a stranger." We see a copy of the book with a younger Mastroianni on the cover.

We find the reporter at his all-white apartment surrounded by books he is using for his research. Also present is his sullen young girlfriend in a black miniskirt. He quotes to her from the politician's conclusion at the end of his book, "*And what are the key words we could use in order to make a new collective dream come true?*" As the politician's wife then arrives, we learn from her that she has one last audiotape which he made before leaving for the second time. She explains that he could not remember anything when he returned after that first departure, and that she had offered to go with him when he left again. He had agreed; we are reminded of Spyros's wife leaving with him at the end of *Voyage*.

She then speaks with the reporter in the streets of Athens as we see a Nativity scene in a shop window. She explains that she had felt that he was becoming "another man." She had gone with him to a hotel room where he made love to her violently "as if we didn't know each other. Like strangers who meet in a movie theater in the morning"—this sharply echoes the scene in *The Beekeeper* in which Mastroianni makes love in front of a movie screen in an abandoned movie theater to a young woman he has just met. At that point the politician had left for good. His wife and the journalist are standing by an ugly, noisy highway at night, reminiscent of scenes in *Landscape* and *The Beekeeper*. She concludes, "I know he is dead, but I don't know where and when." She adds that many called her from time to time to say he was here or there.

We cut to the snow-filled border town as the television crew films an interview with the wholesaler who sells potatoes to Mastroianni. They then go through the poor refugee section in search of him, hearing babies scream. But they cannot find him.

At a dismal hotel bar that evening with a lonely soft sax music playing, the crew settles in for some relaxation. Crew members dance and drink, but a young woman (Dora Chrisikou) sitting alone at a nearby table stares at the reporter. There is nothing sensual in her stiff-backed pose, her folded hands, her thin frame staring seemingly into the reporter's soul. It is, in fact, an unnerving gaze, cut off from moment to moment by couples dancing in front of the camera.

The reporter then gazes back at her, the two making contact for almost a full sixty seconds of screen time, which feels, of course, like an eternity. The reporter gets up and walks slowly past her as she continues to stare. He turns and they stare again. She rises, and we see she is wearing a long black dress. In very poised, measured slow steps, she approaches him. He leaves the room, and they walk upstairs without talking. They enter his room. There is no sound. They are now stripped. He strokes her hair.

Angelopoulos did not designate *Suspended Step* as belonging to his trilogy of silence. But such a scene illustrates how Angelopoulos has used silence throughout his career to capture moments of such intensity—of mystery, joy, misery, or passion—without spoken language. Clearly part of what he suggests through such scenes is that speech can take us only so far. We are then faced with the nonverbal language of sounds and music, gestures, gazes, and thus the visual.

Much later we see them walk into the empty barroom. There is the sound of a train. As the barroom light is turned out, she explains that she must go. Now there is the sound of church bells. She walks away and then comes back to touch his face.

He walks alone through the snow, coming, finally, to the line of abandoned boxcars where the refugees live. We see Mastroianni now, speaking to a young boy, telling him a story about the future when "The Great Migration" will take place. According to this myth:

> People will leave their homes by any means possible, and all the people of the earth will gather in the Sahara. There, a child will be flying a kite. And all people, young and old, will hold onto the string. And all of mankind will rise high into the sky, in search of another planet. Each one will be holding a plant, a handful of grain, a newborn animal. Others will be carrying books of all the poetry man has ever written. It will be a very long journey.

The boy asks how the journey will end. Mastroianni does not answer. The reporter watches a man in a yellow raincoat fixing an electric power line.

Of course the telling of a myth, in this case dealing with the future, reminds us of the creation myth in *Landscape*. And the function is very similar. In both cases the myths become a blueprint for a brighter (literally in the case of *Landscape*) future, a vision of magical and mysterious hope.

Soon after, we see the young woman the reporter has slept with come to Mastroianni's boxcar home. She puts the young boy—her brother—to bed. She explains that her mother died when they crossed the border. Mastroianni, their "father," returns. We now understand that he has created another life beyond that lived with his former wife (Moreau). Note the echoes to Spyros in *Voyage* who had another wife and children "over there" in the Soviet Union. But in this case it is not completely clear whether Mastroianni is her biological father or not. Either way, however, he is a father in action, concern, and behavior.

Mastroianni explains that he has been working all day to help repair the power lines that cross the border, which have fallen owing to the winter weather. He then invites the reporter to eat with them.

Later the reporter speaks again with the colonel, who tells him that "chaos" is breaking out here as refugee fights refugee for reasons that can never be known because they do not speak. Thus "they cross their borders to find freedom and create a new border here," he observes. Suddenly a lot of refugee women are running by, screaming. The reporter follows to see a refugee hanged by the neck from a huge metallic loading crane. Women wail as the body is lowered, and the women close in on the body in a ritual of wailing that is both ancient and contemporary.

Then the politician's wife arrives on the train. The reporter meets her and explains that her husband buys potatoes every day.

The next morning, after another bar scene that previous evening, the crew film, from a distance, the meeting of the old politician and his wife on a bridge in town. They stand gazing at each other from the perspective of the hidden camera. She turns to the camera and says, "It's not him." Mastroianni also turns to the camera.

But there can be no certainty.

Angelopoulos leaves us no way to know for sure whether Mastroianni is indeed the politician who went on a journey at the end of the century, or if he is simply someone who resembles the politician and who sells potatoes and tells stories of a future migration to another planet. We now have a scene in which the reporter is watching film clips from the politician's career on a VCR set up in the hotel bar. We see a younger Mastroianni addressing Parliament and then walking out. Suddenly the screen goes blank.

Cut to Mastroianni walking along the shore of the border river, looking for fish. The reporter is beside him playing the audiotape made by the politician for his wife when he left. On the tape he explains that none of us has anything to call our own, not even a name, for that we only borrow temporarily before leaving again. Mastroianni shows no sign that he recognizes this voice, though it clearly sounds like him.

Of course, all can be explained if indeed he has, as his wife claims, "become another person," one who has forgotten his past. But we cannot be completely certain. Mastroianni leaves as the telephone repairmen in yellow rainwear walk by.

Back in town, the reporter learns he must soon leave. He shares a meal with the colonel, who has become a friend. The colonel continues to act out his "chorus" role of commenting on the action. He announces that a wedding will take place between a refugee girl and the boyfriend she knew as a child but who is now separated from her by the border. He says, "There's the bride," as Mastroianni's "daughter" walks in. The reporter stands up, completely caught by surprise. Clearly he is emotionally affected by this revelation. As an accordion player plays and circles her, she stands, gazing at the reporter.

Outside, the colonel says, "It's the border that drives them mad. The boundaries." When he leaves, the reporter says out loud to himself, "The only thing I have known is how to film other people [pause] without caring for their feelings." He then sees the girl. She stares and opens the door for him. They both enter the hotel, closing the door behind them, the assumption being that they make love one last time.

Then follows the most sustained scene of the film, the wedding of Mastroianni's "daughter" and her beloved, who lives on the other side of the river—that is, across the border in the other country. The scene is staged at the border river on a gray winter morning with Mastroianni, the bride in a white bridal gown, and several dozen wedding guests standing with them as they look out across the river to the groom surrounded by an equal number of his guests. The memorable wedding in *The Travelling Players*, of course, has previously illuminated Angelopoulos's sense of how this ceremony, which embraces the personal, social, historical, and religious, can become a powerful moment. And, as we shall discuss, this later wedding scene succeeds in doing so. But the scene, which lasts over six minutes, has an unusual power in its use of cinematic time and space alone. Wolfram Schutte has well described this as Angelopoulos's ability to suggest the strength that was possible in silent film: "The beauty of his composition, his depth of focus, the movement and arrangement of his sequence shots" (5).

Into this somber yet surprising tableau, captured in extreme long shot and with no music on the sound track, enters a brief light moment as the priest arrives on a bicycle, dusts himself off, and begins the ceremony. The scene depicts an Orthodox wedding, complete with the blessings, the exchanges of laurel wreaths, and the triple circling made by the priest and bride as the "congregation" tosses rice, silently.

We then see the groom across the river in the other country repeat, but without a priest, the actions performed in Greece.

Throughout the scene, the only sound is that of water flowing. The

12. *The Suspended Step of the Stork*: Mastroianni acts as a father figure at the young woman's wedding

groom comes down to the river and tosses flowers into the water. The priest leaves, and the bride comes down to the river and tosses in her laurel wreath. She kisses Mastroianni. The guests are beginning to greet her with a kiss when a border patrol rifle shot is heard, and everyone scatters.

Finally, only the bride and groom remain, separated by the border, each in a different country. They gaze across at each other. They each raise an arm in greeting, the river flowing between them, and they too, like a suspended stork, remain "suspended" briefly, gazing at each other. We now see that the reporter and his crew, in the bushes farther up the bank, have captured the whole scene on video. As the crew packs up, the reporter remains "suspended" too, staring at the bride—so briefly the reporter's lover—and her groom. The crew notices how tied into the moment he is. They back off, leaving him alone watching the newlyweds. The bride turns and runs back over the hill to Mastroianni, who has been waiting for her. As accordion music begins, father and daughter walk up through a group of bare trees to three trucks full of the wedding guests and climb aboard, the bride sitting at the back of the last truck. The television crew in their truck follows at a distance, down a long dirt road.

That evening Mastroianni dances with his "daughter," still in her wedding dress, as the accordion player stands and plays in the distance. The reporter comes up and dances a slow dance with her as Mastroianni stands silently by. She stops and the music ceases. She explains to the reporter: "My husband and I grew up in the same village. We come from the same race. I feel his hand holding me. One night he'll cross the river and come take me." The reporter says, "I've never felt like this before," and the bride answers, "And me too," as Mastroianni stands, gazing at both, motionless. "I'm in pain," the reporter says. "And me too, very much," she says, as she turns and runs away into the night. Mastroianni then speaks: "Do you hear the river? Do you hear it roar? It roars and beckons like that every night." It is, of course, a line that echoes the young recruit who, during the roll call, spoke of his fear of the river's roar at night. Mastroianni clutches his jacket around him to keep warm while crying quietly. The reporter comes up and pats him on the back. "I couldn't understand," he says, to which Mastroianni replies, "Don't worry about me. I'm happy." The reporter backs away, turns, and, like the bride, runs off into the night. And he keeps on running.

Cut to morning. The reporter is at the border and repeats the "suspended step" scene he acted out at the beginning of the film. On the bridge, with one foot in Greece and the other lifted, he hovers, looking over to Albania, as the border guards watch. He backs off and returns to the army officer, who informs him that Mastroianni has been sighted by a number of people leaving, in different ways and at different locations. But all of these reports claim he was carrying a suitcase and heading for the border. The officer concludes, "Police are unable to confirm any of these stories." The reporter turns to see Jeanne Moreau standing by a car, looking out across the landscape. She climbs into the backseat of the car and the car leaves. The officer follows him too as they see a man in the distance. "I don't know if that is him or not, but I don't think it really matters any more," he says. The man in the distance runs away.

The reporter walks along the levee and sits by the boy, Mastroianni's young "son," who tells him that he last saw his father walking on the water, carrying a suitcase. The boy departs, saying that his father never finished a story he was telling him. "Maybe he wanted you to finish it," the reporter adds.

We return to voice-over as in the beginning of the film. The reporter asks, "Why can't we assume that today is December 31st, 1999?" echoing a line from the missing politician's book.

He begins to walk along the levee and we see a line of telephone poles, each with a man in a yellow raincoat climbing up, stringing phone wires between them. The music is full, serious, and hopeful. The reporter is framed halting in the midst of the thirteen poles, and then, after moments of suspension, moving slowly forward, down toward the river as the camera pulls back to catch the reflection of the poles in the river, creating a visual doubling of poles and men. As the camera pulls back farther, we see the other side of the river, across the border.

THE HEALING OF A TOUCH: TELEMACHUS TRANSFORMED

As I have suggested, the Greek army colonel (Ilias Logothetis) in this film fulfills the role of a Greek chorus. An outsider assigned to his post at this border town, he automatically has a special perspective on events unfolding there. Thus his insight into the fact that because this borderland area is inhabited by so many refugees from everywhere, they create their own world: the realm of the mythical. This world of myth is, as stated at the chapter's opening, a useful guide for the young journalist and for us as we follow the journalist on his quest for a "story" to share on television.

In this perspective, the television journalist, like the filmmaker in *Voyage*, grows as a person during his Telemachian odyssey: he learns to go beyond his medium, television (it was film for the analogous character in *Voyage*), to become personally and emotionally involved with others. When he is able to tell the young bride that he is "in pain," his life has clearly changed. From being the alienated observer of history, he has become an active participant in mythical stories. What he ends up with, therefore, is not a television show—his project is left incomplete and his crew has already departed. Rather he has gained insight into the joy and sorrow of these border people in this "other Greece." He has been touched by the love of a refugee woman, but also by the plight of these people who have been embraced by the politician in his "new" life or, as his wife says, his life as a "different person." And the reporter has been able to reach out and touch others himself. He thus has, by film's end, begun to take the step that will no longer be suspended, the step of border crossing and of making contact with others. He has, we should note, also gone further than Alexander, the film director in *Voyage*, who remains the passive observer, unable to get involved. In *Suspended Step*, the journalist has opened up and expressed himself as Alexander never does.

Let us consider Telemachus transformed more specifically. In Homer, Telemachus's search for his father is, of course, a search for his own identity and emerging manhood. All male youths need the blessing of their father or a father substitute in order to mature, as Peter Blos states: "At the termination of adolescence a new stage in the life of the growing son appears, when the father's affirmation of the manhood attained by his son, conveyed in what we might call the father's blessings of the youth's impatient appropriation of adult prerogatives and entitlements, reaches a critical urgency" (11). In Homer's epic, this blessing is granted as Telemachus not only finds his father and helps him clear Ithaca of the unwanted suitors to Penelope but also learns about himself and what he is capable of accomplishing in each encounter he has on his own odyssey away from home.

In *Suspended Step*, the politician is not literally the reporter's father (we learn nothing of the reporter's background), but it becomes increasingly clear the further the reporter goes into tracking down his "story" that he has gone beyond the limits he usually explores in doing his television documentaries and has entered a personal and emotional world in which he must see the politician as a father/Odysseus figure.

On a simplistic level, of course, a Homeric parallel is more of a contrast than a contemporary updating of the epic. There is no strong embrace and recognition scene as in Homer, for, in fact, "Odysseus's" identity is still in question by the end of the film. And there are no clear enemies/suitors to destroy, for part of the despair at the end of the century is that such a Homeric solution is impossible today.

Penelope, the politician's wife, is also a study in contrast in this version. For ironically she even embarks on her own odyssey to try to find and reclaim her husband, only to ultimately confront failure: "It is not him."

Dante Revisited: The Time to Take a Voyage Has Come

Suspended Step involves, like Homer's *Odyssey*, a double voyage. But Angelopoulos's ending—with the Odysseus figure taking off again, suitcase in hand, and Telemachus, poised on the riverbank, "suspended" once more, between returning to his home and career and setting off himself on a voyage "somewhere else"—reflects Dante's version of the Ulysses theme as described in the *Inferno*. That reference, based, as noted earlier, on a version of the legend predating Homer's epic, has Odysseus setting sail again after his homecoming and reunion with Penelope and Telemachus. And the film's Telemachus—the reporter—sets us up for such a voyage at the beginning of the film in his voice-over, when he quotes Dante's line about the need to set off on a voyage again.

The implications of echoing Dante extend still further. We noted in chapter 3 that to a degree such a reference becomes part of the border crossing Angelopoulos does between Italian and Greek cultures, with their many Mediterranean links as well as differences. But the Dante connection has at least two other resonances felt in this film. Dante's elaborate vision laid out in the *Divine Comedy* mixes history, myth, folktale, and personal narrative into one vision—which is dark (*The Inferno*), middling (*Purgatorio*), and finally, hopeful (*Paradiso*). Furthermore, the whole vision leads to a mystical and ultimately religious (Christian) triumph initiated through his contact with a girl-woman, his beloved Beatrice.

As usual in our analysis of Angelopoulos, there is no need to insist on any rigid doubling of patterns from Dante in *Suspended Step* or, indeed, any systematic and conscious echoing of Dante in the film beyond the general pattern of his view of Odysseus as a voyager who sets sail once more, even from Ithaca itself. But given the direct reference to Dante in the film, we can briefly note several Dantesque elements in *Suspended Step* that contribute even further, I suggest, to its power.

Seen from the perspective of the *Divine Comedy*, the reporter is much like Dante, who, at the beginning of the *Inferno*, has lost himself in a deep wood when in his early thirties. And just as Dante includes himself at the center of his *Divine Comedy* on a voyage of personal salvation, the journalist is, as we know, the central figure of the narrative who actually narrates to us. A major difference, however, is that while Dante acknowledges on his first page that he is lost, we do not actually hear our narrator in *Suspended Step* acknowledge his condition—though we long suspect it through his behavior—until near the end, when he finally blurts out that he has spent his life filming others but not feeling for them as people. His whole life has, in short, been a suspended step.

The role of a woman in leading a man to salvation in Angelopoulos's film also evokes Dante. Homer's Telemachus does not fall in love on his journey to discover his father and himself. Our reporter in Angelopoulos's film, in contrast, comes under the spell of a young woman. Dante makes it clear that it was simply the vision of Beatrice in his childhood that affected him. In his case, of course, the relationship did not go beyond the gaze. And yet that both specify the importance of the gaze, of such deep and lasting affection aroused through the eye, is significant. The meeting scene in the bar is unlike any other man-woman attraction and meeting scene I am aware of in film. The long stare from her to him as others dance and then, finally, from him to her as their eyes join is difficult to explain in words (testimony again to the power of silence in Angelopoulos's work). We cannot discount that there is sexuality, or attraction between a man and a woman, initiated in this case by the woman. But this basic instinct is not centered on the physical or carnal. Something much deeper is taking place, and it is doing so without spoken language or even physical gestures.

Finally, the pain that the journalist experiences from his encounter with the young woman and the Mastroianni figure, together with the plight of the refugees in general, leads him to be the kind of personal witness who reaches out to us as well. For it is his voice and thus his story

that touch us. And it is a story told not in the medium of television reporting he is used to. He has become a border crosser in a number of ways by
the film's ending, even if he himself is not ready to cross the physical border of Greece in search of the Mastroianni character. But the potential is
there. And the Great Migration that Mastroianni described is left as a
possibility.

THE QUEST, ORSON WELLES, AND ANGELOPOULOS

There is a similarity of narrative thrust between *Suspended Step* and *Citizen Kane* that is useful to consider. In Orson Welles's classic the unidentified reporter remains much less an individualized character than the unnamed reporter in Angelopoulos's film (we seldom even see more than the
back of his head, for instance), and his search for his story—the meaning
of "Rosebud" as a key to the personality of the great Citizen Kane—ends
as a complete failure. What Welles leaves us with is one of the most ironic
shots in the history of film. The reporter has failed to uncover the meaning of "Rosebud," but the viewer learns the answer as the camera glides
over the vast remains of Kane's belongings until we see the burning label,
"Rosebud," on Kane's childhood sled. Through the camera itself we
solve the mystery. And the reporter is left not only without a story but
also without a personality or sense of personal growth as an individual.
He has simply been the means by which Welles has opened up Kane's life
for us.

The *Citizen Kane* theme or narrative structure has served a number of
filmmakers well for various purposes since Welles's film opened in 1939.
Perhaps most notable has been Andrzej Wajda's *Man of Marble* (1977).
Wajda uses a young woman's efforts to make a documentary thesis film
for graduation from film school as a means to open up Poland's Stalinist
past and suggest the political and cultural changes that led to Lech Walesa
and the complete transformation of communist society from the bottom
up. Within the "Citizen Kane" structure Wajda's attractive young filmmaker (and it is significant that he chose a woman to be the protagonist
deconstructing totalitarian patriarchy) uncovers the truth that a worker
hero from the 1950s was actually an artificially constructed political
myth used by Polish Stalinists. Wajda's thrust was thus a particularly political one, but as German critic Wolfram Schutte has noted, both Wajda
and Angelopoulos share a similar mission in cinema: to explore history
and culture through the moving image.

Angelopoulos's use of such a Wellesian frame is less specifically political and, as in his other films, more of a "long shot" of history and culture
beyond the particular shifts that have occurred. In this Wellesian light,

Angelopoulos has clearly given us a reporter with more depth who is even more clearly the center of the narrative than the reporter in *Citizen Kane*, since Angelopoulos's film opens and closes with the reporter's voice-over: thus the entire film becomes a part of his experience, which he has narrated and shared with us. Welles creates quite an opposite effect, for he begins and ends outside of the reporter's search by having the camera track into the castlelike Kane estate at the moment of Kane's death in the opening and then tracking away from the castle, past the NO TRESSPASS-ING sign, at the end. The reporter's search in *Citizen Kane* is actually a search within the larger quest of the camera as a metanarrative force to "trespass" and discover. In contrast, for all of his use of long shots and denial of traditional close-ups, Angelopoulos has, nevertheless, centered the film on his Telemachus figure.

Within this perspective, Angelopoulos also suggests that "Rosebud"— the life of the missing Greek politician—changes for the unnamed reporter. He does not finally get his television documentary, the "history" and "reality" he has been trained to create. But he is beginning to go through a transformation by film's end, touched by the young woman and by Mastroianni's ideas (the reporter paraphrases his book in the final scene) that have led him to a personal understanding and acceptance of "Rosebud."

He has, in short, finally been touched and gotten in touch: with himself and others. Think of how many efforts to touch—physically and emotionally—are made throughout the film. The colonel reaches out to the journalist and goes beyond his duty as an assigned official by, for instance, touching his hand in a gesture of sympathy when the journalist learns that the girl he has just begun to love is to be married the next day. The wedding ceremony conducted across the river border is the most obvious case of "touching" beyond the physical. The journalist himself hugs the politician's wife in the streets of Athens when she feels lost in her search for her husband, and he pats the politician on the shoulder when he, likewise, expresses pain.

On a more lighthearted note there is also the marvelous scene of the man by the river sending music tapes across the border in an act of small-scale black-marketeering—a definite form of communication but also of pleasure since the traders actually play the music as it goes across the border.

Finally, the motif throughout the film of the men in yellow repairing the downed phone lines, a group that the Mastroianni figure explains he has worked with, shifts from being a background thematic element to being foregrounded as the major closing image. At one point as the journalist walks alone along the riverbank, there are thirteen poles and thus thirteen men within the frame, each perched at the top of his pole, reaching out to connect the lines between them, which, we have been told by Mastroianni, will be reconnected with lines across the border. In a story that the choric figure has warned us should be taken as mythical, the ending becomes not only that but biblical as well. We have spoken of the influence of Byzantine iconography on Angelopoulos's work. Nowhere is it more apparent than in this closing image. The immediate connection audiences everywhere make, of course, is to the Crucifixion. Just as Jesus willingly went to his sacrificial death, so these men have voluntarily gone up their poles in an effort to help make things better. And beyond the image of the crucifix, for those in the Orthodox tradition there is another historical image evoked: the stylites, those religious figures, male and female, who dedicated themselves to God by sitting on poles or columns in isolation for up to thirty years or more. Luis Buñuel has paid satirical tribute to them in his gloriously irreverent *Simon of the Desert*.

Yet Angelopoulos's image is one of mystery and hope and thus replenishment that transcends the personal pain felt by the journalist. To have ended the film with the journalist standing alone by the river would have been enough to evoke all the other river scenes, most especially the wedding scene. But it would have emphasized his personal odyssey almost to the exclusion of any wider theme. With the telephone men filling the frame of the final shot, however, we and the journalist are lifted beyond ourselves, beyond himself. This closing image is made all the stronger as an image of an extended touch or communication when we consider the film's opening image: the drowned bodies of the Asian refugees in the sea with army helicopters hovering over them. That image truly does match the politician's book title, *Despair at the End of the Century*.

All of these efforts to reach out add up to new forms of community or, in Angelopoulos's words, the possibility of a "new humanism." We have been told, by the colonel and by the young boy, conflicting stories of where the politician went, but the common theme to the "myth" is that he has crossed the border. Thus the added significance of the final shot, elaborately orchestrated by Angelopoulos to show us the reporter approaching the river as the camera itself crosses the river. We cross the border in a reverse tracking shot as if invited, like the reporter, to go further. The camera work itself is offering the healing touch of movement beyond boundaries.

Part Three . . .
CONCLUSIONS

It is hard for anyone to study Angelopoulos properly. The films deserve large screens—but one would settle for wretched video versions.

(David Thomson, *A Biographical Dictionary of Film*)

Reject everything about the real that does not become true. (Robert Bresson, *Notes on Cinematography*)

Chapter Nine

Ulysses' Gaze: "We Are Dying People"

To Know a Soul

> *And thus the soul too, if it wishes to know itself,*
> *will have to look into the soul.*
> (Plato)

A T THE END of *Suspended Step*, the young reporter is standing in Greece, by the border river, looking across to the other country where the politician played by Mastroianni has disappeared. In *Ulysses' Gaze* (1995), Angelopoulos crosses the border himself, literally and metaphorically, taking us, the viewers, with him. He deepens his concern with and for Greece. But he does so by leaving Greece and exploring the rest of the Balkan nations and their connections to his protagonist's personal journey. "We Greeks are dying people," says the Greek taxi driver to the main character, a Greek-American filmmaker played by Harvey Keitel, before he crosses from Albania into the Former Yugoslav Republic of Macedonia. It is this "dying" Balkan culture that Angelopoulos explores for signs of hope as well as of decay and death in *Ulysses' Gaze*. The line "We Greeks are dying people" is once more an echo of Angelopoulos's favorite poet, George Seferis. Placed early in the film, the line sets a tone and a context within which we must consider the rest of the journey that follows.

This latest film begins where *Suspended Step* left off and goes much further as it becomes a personal quest through the Balkans by a filmmaker who much resembles Angelopoulos himself. *Ulysses' Gaze*, which won the Grand Prix at the 1995 Cannes Festival and has gone on to wide distribution, begins its narrative in Greece and travels through Albania, the Former Yugoslav Republic of Macedonia (known as the Republic of Skopje to the Greeks), Bulgaria, Romania, Serbia, and finally through Bosnia to war-torn Sarajevo. Furthermore, the film embraces the familiar *Odyssey* theme that we have met in so many of Angelopoulos's films. In this case it is announced quite visibly for the first time in the title.

Angelopoulos also evokes Plato, as represented in the quotation above, which appears at the beginning of the film, and thus he calls on a Hellenic tradition of contemplation and philosophical inquiry. Angelopoulos is alluding to a modern Greek cultural heritage as well, for the line from Plato

13. *Ulysses' Gaze*: Harvey Keitel in the Sarajevo film archive

is actually quoted in the George Seferis poem we explored in chapter 1. That Seferis references Plato's line suggests that the modern poet—and filmmaker—have brought together two very different traditions: that of Homer and his epic worldview and that of Plato and the spirit of philosophical questioning, doubt, and thought. Put more directly, the title, *Ulysses' Gaze*, evokes Homer, and thus a poetic world of storytelling and the full range of the human imagination. But the quotation from Plato that appears on the screen asks us to take this journey as one toward an inner self, no matter the exterior landscapes represented.

Finally, in pointing to these Hellenic traditions before beginning his own contemporary journey, Angelopoulos is also asking us, in a sense, to consider how and to what degree such classical references can help and, dare we say, nourish our own quests in landscapes filled with war, hatred, destruction, death, and unresolved passions and memories. If at all.

Critics have been swift to see each of Angelopoulos's films since *Voyage* as "anthology" works that allude to all of his previous films. *Ulysses' Gaze* surely, and richly, solidifies our sense of what I have called in this study the Faulknerian element, that is, the existence of a fictional universe that is referenced from work to work in terms of characters, location, actions, themes, and situations. In this light, consider a contrast of directorial approaches. When I wrote my study of the American director George Roy Hill, whose films include *Butch Cassidy and the Sundance Kid*, *Slaughterhouse Five*, *The World According to Garp*, and *The Little Drummer Girl*, Hill told me that he took great pleasure in doing projects so seemingly different from each other that none of the critics could "tag" his style or his vision of filmmaking as a constant. Much of the pleasure particularly of *Ulysses' Gaze* derives from just the opposite stance. While Angelopoulos has consciously shaped his films knowing that many will not have seen his previous works, he has also made each as an organic narrative deeply related to all of his previous movies. Thus for Angelopoulos "veterans," this latest effort casts the viewer in much the same role as that of the director protagonist himself: a person so full of "images" from the past that he or she seeks renewal too in this journey through the souls of those in the Balkans today.

The film begins with direct lines of dialogue from *Suspended Step*, thus interlocking his "Balkan period." And Angelopoulos goes further to make direct reference to the controversy his actual filming of this previous work created with the local bishop of the town of Florina in northern Greece. Thus, more directly than in any of his previous works, Angelopoulos has built in an autobiographical element. This dimension is even more apparent since the protagonist is a middle-aged filmmaker named "A."

Ulysses' Gaze is also a first for Angelopoulos in two important ways. It is his first film that has been placed predominantly outside of Greece. And it is his first film a major portion of which has been shot in English (see below).

In My End Is My Beginning

In preparing the synopsis for his latest film, I had the advantage for the first time in my writings about Angelopoulos of having his original script. As a professional screenwriter and professor of screenwriting myself, I cannot help but add a note on my interest in the very "European" approach to the written text that Angelopoulos has taken. First, it is a given in Hollywood that scripts average 120 pages, give or take a few, on the supposition that a page is roughly a minute of screen time. Angelopoulos's original script for *Ulysses' Gaze* is 69 pages for a film that is just under three hours in length. And even this three-hour version did not include some of the scenes from the original script that were actually shot, as we shall discuss. Of course you do not need to be a screenwriter to realize that a page is not a minute on the screen for Angelopoulos; on the contrary, one Angelopoulos page equals more like four or five minutes of screen time. And while Hollywood has developed a very strict code of rules for format, Angelopoulos certainly does not follow them in any rigorous manner. Thus even on the written page, an Angelopoulos project stands out as quite different from an American film.

What of the extensive use of English, for the first time, in his film? The film was conceived to be in Greek, with Harvey Keitel dubbed in Greek, much as Mastroianni's dialogue had been dubbed in *The Beekeeper* and *Suspended Step*. But once the editing process began, Angelopoulos realized that Keitel had given such powerful performances in English that the whole film should be reconceived to include English where it seemed to fit, given the multilingual situations that take place in this multinational journey. It was a fortuitous decision, I believe, for English furthers the sense of the effort to reach across borders to communicate with those in other Balkan cultures.

In terms of narrative and character development, the use of Keitel added one more dimension to the original script I have studied: the director became a Greek-American figure rather than a purely Greek director (in the story, he was born in Greece but has been away for some thirty-five years). Angelopoulos says of his choice of Keitel: "The choice was a sort of provocation. It was the challenge of using an American actor, but in my own way. He is known for his portrayals of gangsters, but he possesses something very sensitive" (*Ulysses' Gaze* press package). Even in casting, then, Angelopoulos has reached beyond boundaries, as far, this time, as the United States. Yet Keitel's family came originally from Romania; thus, ironically, his casting for this film is quite appropriate in geographical terms.

The film opens, after the quotation from Plato, with an old silent film of village women weaving. In voice-over our protagonist (Harvey Keitel) explains in English, "*Weavers in Avdella, a Greek Village*, 1905, the first film made by the brothers Miltiades and Yannakis Manakia. The first film ever made in Greece and the Balkans. But is that a fact? Is it the first film? The first gaze?"

Angelopoulos has thus immediately established that by "gaze" he means not only the look that one person can give another, but also that "to know" in the philosophical sense is to gaze into another soul, and furthermore that cinema itself is a process of gazing. Cinema, Platonically conceived, therefore, can become a means of knowing other souls.

In tinted black and white, we see an old man with an early-model camera by the sea photographing a sailing ship drifting by on the sea. As color bleeds into this image, the old man dies and is caught by another narrator, who is explaining what happened to the Manakia brothers, these early pioneers of Balkan cinema. As we watch the same sailboat, now in a luminescent blue, continuing to sail by, the camera tracks to reveal the same older gentleman speaking to Harvey Keitel, with the harbor of Thessaloniki in the background. We learn more about these filmmakers, including the fact that three reels of their films were never developed. "How is this possible?" muses Keitel as he looks out at the sailboat gliding by.

Note that Angelopoulos has begun this latest odyssey using the same "time-destroying" technique developed in *The Travelling Players*. In a single tracking shot we have covered some sixty years, with Keitel, in the present, standing on the same spot the dying Manakia brother occupied and with the same sailboat drifting by. Quite simply, this scene cues us that the "inner" journey has begun. This Greek-American director has begun to gaze into a soul, the soul of early Balkan cinema. We have, once more, thus embarked on what the poet George Seferis called a "mythical story."

The credit sequence then follows together with another splendid score by Eleni Karaindrou, which sounds decidedly more "Balkan" than Greek and which embraces a feisty folk tune at its core.

Cut to a dark rainy night in Florina, the northern Greek town featured in *Suspended Step*, with the film director (never named in the film, but called simply "A" in the script) arriving. In voice-over he explains that it has been years since he has been home. There is a demonstration going on, and a young man rushes over to inform the director that there is an angry protest over one of his films. The best the young man can do under the conditions is to project "A's" film in a local kafeneon with speakers outside for those who cannot get in.

As we enter the town square, we hear Mastroianni's lines from *Suspended Step*: "*We've crossed the border, but here we still are. How many borders do we have to cross before we reach home?*" But this time we hear the lines in English, along with the musical score from the film.

A young woman from the organizing film club committee comes out and leads "A" through the crowd and through the kafeneon to a deserted street beyond. He pauses, as if lost in memories, and begins to quote lines from *The Travelling Players*.

Soon a procession of religious fanatics march through the streets from the church in protest of "A's" film. He remains quite calm in the midst of all. The film club officials urge him to leave. He quips ironically: "I used to dream this would be the end of the journey. But isn't it strange? Isn't this the way it always is? In my end is my beginning."

We understand immediately that "A" is not your typical commercial director, for his last line, for instance, is from another of Angelopoulos's favorite poets, T. S. Eliot. Furthermore, the choice of "A" as a name not only recalls Kafka's use of one-letter names in his fables; it has, for Angelopoulos, a "cinematic" meaning as well. He comments: "Why 'A'? It's an alphabetical, autobiographical choice. Every filmmaker remembers the first time he looked through the viewfinder of a camera. It is a moment which is not so much the discovery of cinema but the discovery of the world. But there comes a moment when the filmmaker begins to doubt his own capacity to see things, when he no longer knows if his gaze is right and innocent" (*Ulysses' Gaze* press package).

The man in charge of the film archives follows with a warning to this returning Greek-American director, "You've been away all these years and then back in Europe doing a new stint. Hasn't all this taught you that the Balkan jungle is worse than the jungle you found in America? You are about to wade into dark waters." "A's" response is simple: "This is a personal journey."

We again see the fragment of the Manakia brothers' documentary, *Weavers in Avdella, a Greek Village*, simply showing village women weaving in the courtyard of a farmhouse.

Then we cut back to the building tension of the Florina protesters. Keitel is about to leave in a taxi when he sees a woman in her forties (the first of several roles in the film played by Romanian actress Maia Morgenstern) watching the film being projected. We hear another line from *Suspended Step*, this time the framing line from the reporter narrator, "If I should take just one step, just one step . . ." The woman is clearly an old love, and "A" speaks to her as we hear one of the closing lines of *Suspended Step*, "Why not suppose this is the 31st of December, 1999?" as the film's musical score sweeps through the square drowning out the protesters.

He follows her, explaining that "something holds me back" from simply taking her now, as it did also in the past when he left, promising her he would return. Note that at times Keitel uses Greek, as any returning native would; thus he makes use of whichever of the two languages the situation calls for.

We now have a montage of images from other Manakia films but with the weavers' film in the background continuing. We end this montage with images from the Big Fire of Thessaloniki, images that finally fade to a stretch of gray sea and a lonely pier. What follows is a setup for the rest of the film.

In the dark streets, a confrontation has developed, as a large group of umbrella-carrying protesters march down a street, toward several lines of shield- and club-wielding police. A group of citizens is behind them. Add to this a kind of religious chant being intoned by one group and the ingredients for angry violence are clear. Instead of showing us the confrontation, however, Angelopoulos leaves us watching these three faceless mobs poised on the brink of violence, appearing both as a spectacle of some sort and also as a menacing force. This scene is an embodiment of "carnival gone wrong"—a street gathering motivated by hatred rather than by what Mikhail Bakhtin defines as the essence of carnival, "the feast of becoming" (4), which we will glimpse by the end of the film.

Cut to bright white. But instead of sunshine, we realize that this is a cloudy winter's day in the snow as "A's" taxi arrives at the Albanian border. There "A" sees a short, elegant old lady (played by the well-known Greek actress Dora Volanaki) standing with a suitcase; she asks if she can get a ride since she is searching for a sister she has not seen for forty-five years. "A" helps her into the taxi, and they cross into Albania.

It is a scene of "total anarchy" (Angelopoulos's words in the script). Illegal emigrants are everywhere, carrying packages. What follows is a wordless, masterful traveling tableau of poor refugees in the midst of a winter landscape. We track, in the taxi, past a wasteland in which hundreds of men with baggage in hand stand like statues, waiting to start on yet another effort to cross the border illegally into Greece. And the script tells us what "A" is thinking, thoughts we do not hear in the film, as he looks out at Albania, "A country without past, without present, without future."

They enter the town of Korçë (Korytsa in Greek). "The town has not changed since the beginning of the century," writes Angelopoulos in the script. They stop in the middle of the empty square, and "A" helps the old lady out. They then drive off, leaving her there, as we hear a Muslim prayer on the sound track.

"A" in the taxi is being driven toward the Former Yugoslav Republic of Macedonia, through a snowstorm. The driver, played by Greece's favorite comic actor of the past forty years or more, Thanassis Vengos, stops and begins to speak about Greece as a dying country. "*We Greeks are dying people*," he reports, "*We've completed our appointed cycle. Three thousand years among broken stones and statues, and now we are dying*"—words that are very close to lines found in Seferis's poetry, as we have noted. The driver makes it clear that he wishes to become friends with "A" and begins to play music from Epirus, the area of northern Greece where Angelopoulos's first film, *Reconstruction*, was shot. He passes "A" a bottle of a potent mountain brandy. The driver then points to the border between Albania and the Former Yugoslav Republic of Macedonia (called "Skopje" in the film). When the driver asks "A" what he is looking for, "A" replies, "Something that may not even exist." The driver explains that he respects the snow, stands on a snowbank, and calls out to Nature herself, throwing her a "biscuit"! The moment is both touching and tinged with humor, especially since it is the comedian Vengos who is tossing the biscuit at the universe in an absurd gesture of frustration.

Why did Angelopoulos cast a leading comic actor for this serious role? He explains: "I have always felt that great comic actors are somehow more outstanding than those who mainly specialize in dramatic roles. I think there is, after all, something deeply dramatic inside each comedian and this is certainly true of Vengos" (interview, Athens, July 1995).

The moment is also significant because it is the second time we see the expression of real friendship and trust (the first being "A's" brief encounter with the film archivist in Florina). These pockets of friendship become the basis for a shared sense of community, that essential human expression which, as Angelopoulos shows so clearly, has broken down throughout the Balkans.

Cut: "A" is now on a crowded Macedonian bus headed for the town of Monastiri in the Former Yugoslav Republic of Macedonia. With some trouble, "A" finally locates the original home of the Manakia brothers. He stands motionless before it like a pilgrim at a shrine.

The color drains out, and the scene becomes part of a documentary made by the Yugoslavs about the Manakia brothers in 1956. We then crosscut between "A" in color and archival footage in black and white. There are interviews with Miltiades Manakia speaking about his work. Manakia appears as a true representative of the Balkans as he says: "See this street? All the armies of Europe have trudged through it. And with each war they changed its name. Now it's called Marshall Tito Street. But we called it Forty Pianos Street." The old documentary footage continues with Manakia giving a tour of the town, pointing out one site after another, including where the old cinema burned down during a Chaplin screening.

The house is a museum now, and a young female guide, Maia Morgenstern in her second role, comes up to ask if she can help "A." When he explains his search for the missing films, she walks away, coldly.

On the train to the city of Skopje that night, he sees the woman from the Manakia museum again. He begins speaking to her about what happened to the Manakia brothers' property after their death. She explains that she is Kali, which is, of course, short for Calypso, the goddess who held Odysseus captive on her island for seven years.

"A" explains his interest in the Manakia brothers: "The Manakia brothers went around photographing and filming things. They were trying to record a new age, a new century. For over sixty years they recorded faces, events, in the turmoil of the Balkans. They weren't concerned with politics, racial questions, friends, or enemies. They were interested in people."

This is obviously the text from the documentary we had been watching, a fact that is underscored as Kali joins in repeating the lines of the text. She continues the words from the documentary to the effect that the brothers filmed "landscapes, weddings, local customs, political changes, village fairs, revolutions, battles, official celebrations, sultans, kings, prime ministers, bishops, rebels." And "A" completes the passage: "All the ambiguities, the contrasts, the conflicts in this area of the world are reflected in their work."

In Italo Calvino's playful novel, *If on a Winter's Night a Traveler* (1979), a romance begins because a male reader and a female reader are

searching for the same missing book. Similarly (and it is worth remembering that the Italian screenwriter Tonino Guerra contributed to this script),
but in a much more serious vein, Angelopoulos brings a film-loving man
and film-loving woman together through their interest in the same missing films. Can this whole film, *Ulysses' Gaze*, be thought of as a "love
story": love of film and of person to person, man to woman? "Yes!" replies Angelopoulos (interview, Athens, July 1995).

Kali remarks that the film archive in the city of Skopje does not have
what he is looking for. They part at the Skopje train station as "A"
stands, suspended, on one foot, much like the protagonist in his own film,
Suspended Step. But she returns and then "A" tells her of an occurrence
he had witnessed on the ancient island of Delos two years before. Keitel,
aboard the train, talks about an ancient olive tree that toppled over and
fell. As he speaks, Kali begins to walk alongside the train as it is pulling
out of the station. He explains that where the tree landed, a crack opened
in the earth from which an ancient head of a statue rose from the ground,
rolling through the ruins of the ancient city and falling into the sea.

The statue's head is something more as well. Its function in Angelopoulos's film is very similar to that of the marble head in the poem by George
Seferis discussed in chapter 1. It becomes for the film director protagonist
what it was for Seferis: an emblem of an ancient past that must be dealt
with but which offers, in and of itself, no clear solutions.

At this point, Kali is literally running to keep up with "A" and his
story. He reaches down and pulls her aboard as the train pulls out of
Skopje. They have clearly made a commitment to share a journey. He
continues to explain that while there on the island of Delos, he took Po-
laroid photos of a pond with a palm tree by it, but nothing came out on
film. The blank Polaroids seem to him to be his own lost "glance." Thus
when he heard from the film archive, for the first time, about the lost
Manakia films, he became obsessed, feeling that these films were not only
"a lost gaze, a lost innocence," but also his own first gaze lost long ago.
The nature of his personal journey is now clear.

Kali is moved by his story as "A" pulls her toward him in a passionate
kiss.

As they approach the Bulgarian border, customs officials force "A" off
the train with Kali following him. The past and the present begin to merge
once more in this "mythical story" as a magistrate dressed in turn-of-the-
century clothing begins to examine "A" in a shabby border train station.
Through the official, we learn more about the Manakia brothers: they
were condemned to death by Bulgarian officials in 1915, accused of trea-
son and terrorism against the state of Bulgaria. The Bulgarian official
talks to "A" as if he were one of the brothers. "I don't understand," protests "A," as he is blindfolded and dragged out to a field for execution.

At the last moment a messenger arrives with a reprieve from King Ferdinand of Bulgaria. Yannakis Manakia's penalty is reduced to exile for "the duration of the war."

Keitel is then allowed to cross into Bulgaria, where Kali is waiting for him. Thus, much as in *Voyage*, the line between the real and the imaginary or cinematic narrative breaks down: imagination becomes both reality and cinema for a film director obsessed with a mission. There is also the parallel here with Homer's Odysseus who is always described as a "man of many ways." This director, as is true of a number of other Angelopoulos figures, becomes more than one person. By falling into the story he is trying to unravel, "A" clearly becomes a man of numerous identities.

"A" continues to talk about Yannakis Manakia while Kali seems confused, yet drawn to him. They board another train. The next day they arrive in Bucharest, Romania. Kali explains that there is no reason to be there since the Romanians never received the films of the brothers from the Bulgarians. But "A" feels driven to visit the city.

Suddenly a young woman in 1940s dress comes by and speaks to "A" as if he were a young boy. "A" and the woman walk together as "A" calls her "Mother." They board a bus full of people in 1940s attire. "A" apologizes for missing her funeral. Russian soldiers from World War II are outside the window. "Mother" tenderly rocks "A" to sleep. We have clearly entered "A's" childhood.

They travel by bus, arriving at their "home" in Kostantza, a Black Sea port town. There, they enter their old family home and the table is set, much as in *Voyage* when Spyros returns to his village. But in this scene, most of "A's" dead relatives are there, dancing. They greet him as if he were a child. And he goes to each one, calling them by name. Then a man in rags appears. It is his "father" home from prison. Father and son are united in yet another Odysseus-Telemachus embrace. The celebration of the homecoming and of the New Year, 1945, begins.

Now in a style familiar since *The Travelling Players*, this single scene, lasting more than fifteen minutes and captured in one continuous shot, covers five years as this waltz takes them through an uncle's arrest in 1948 and, finally, to New Year's Eve of 1950 when the family gains permission to leave for Greece, and they all pose for a huge family portrait. No description of this one scene can do it full justice. Here theater, that is, representation, and history meet in one location and in, seemingly, one continuous time period. What is important is that we now understand that "A's" own memories have become wedded to those of the Manakia brothers.

"A" wakes up in a shabby modern hotel in Kostantza, as if he has dreamed all of the above. Kali is beside him, naked and asleep.

He walks to the port and sees a Romanian barge picking up a huge statue of Lenin to be sold in Germany. The statue is fragmented, and we watch a crane slowly raise and lower the bust of Lenin, placing it on his shoulders and then anchoring him on board. Kali joins him. They are headed, we learn, to Belgrade. They see the statue of Lenin dangle in the air, much like the classical hand rising from the sea in *Landscape* or the classical head rising earlier in this film. Of course we understand: an era has passed and its symbols must be replaced. Dusan Makavejev, the Yugoslav director, had used the dismantling of a huge statue of Lenin some years before this scene in his film *Gorillas Bathe at Noon* (1993), but Angelopoulos has explained that he had not seen the film (interview, Athens, July 1995); this is thus an example of talented artists thinking alike.

Before the boat leaves, "A" breaks into tears. He will leave by himself. "I cannot love you," he says to her, echoing the lines Odysseus speaks to Calypso in the *Odyssey*, as he climbs on board leaving her grieving and surprised on the shore.

"A" is on deck as the barge carrying Lenin moves up the Danube. There follows one of Angelopoulos's well-orchestrated traveling shots, mirroring in many ways the Albanian taxi tableau. Here, it is the barge sailing past hundreds of people standing in awe and curiosity on the riverbank as the fragmented statue of Lenin travels up the river. As in the Albanian segment, there is music but no dialogue.

"A" speaks, as if he were one of the brothers, in a monologue, much like those in *The Travelling Players*. He explains that in 1905 Yannakis went to London to buy a movie camera. The river is, of course, the border as well between Bulgaria and Romania, and Romania and Serbia. They reach the Serbian border, which is called the Iron Gates, recalling the Clashing Rocks in the *Odyssey*.

Before the arrival in Belgrade, Angelopoulos's camera tracks completely around the statue, exploring the shattered Lenin from a variety of perspectives as if saying farewell to all that Lenin was, suggested, and became. Once more, there is a meditative and melancholy mood established as we both feel and think about what has passed. It is as if Angelopoulos is following Plato's command: he is attempting to gaze into the soul of Lenin, but what we realize is that this soul is made up of broken stone, not flesh.

They arrive in Belgrade at dawn in the mist. "A" gets off alone. As he passes through customs, he is met by an old friend, Nikos (played by a well-loved Greek stage, TV, and film comedian, Giorgos Michalakopoulos), a war correspondent, who says, "*When God created the world, the first thing he made were journeys,*" paraphrasing, once more, a line from George Seferis. "A" completes the thought: "And then came doubt and nostalgia."

Nikos explains, as they ride a drab Belgrade trolley, that he has been there since the beginning of the Yugoslav war and may stay and settle down and even marry. "A" is surprised that Belgrade shows no signs of the war. They enter an old folks home. There they meet an old man in pajamas watching television. The man used to be in charge of the Belgrade Film Archive. The old man explains that he had the missing films at one time. He explains that for twenty years they tried to develop the films, but they did not know the chemical formula necessary to do so. Finally, the old man comments that a friend at the Sarajevo Film Archive took them because he knew more about developing old films. On television is footage of Tito and a sound track of old Partisan songs.

They enter the Association for Foreign Correspondents office. As Bosnian news is heard in the background, Nikos and "A" drink to "all our busted hopes, to all our lost daydreams" as they list lost loves and dead friends, including several who are personal friends of Angelopoulos ("Kazuko," for instance, is the wife of Angelopoulos's Japanese distributor, and "Mikis" is the art director who, before his death, worked on so many of Angelopoulos's films). Clearly, in terms of the Odysseus myth, Belgrade is the descent into Hades to meet old comrades and to learn what must be learned to complete the journey. Outside, in the night, they continue drinking and toasting everyone from Charles Mingus and Tsitsanis (a rebetika bouzouki player) to Orson Welles and Eisenstein.

Then "A" makes it clear that he must get to Sarajevo. Nikos explains that there is only one way—"to follow the rivers"—and he promises to find someone to help.

That night a woman (Morgenstern in her third role, this time as Circe, the Homeric sorceress) leads him to the river and a boat that is waiting. The screen is now black-and-white, and the time is again the First World War, the time of the Manakia brothers. The woman and "A" find escape down the river. At dawn they reach a destroyed village and begin to walk past shattered houses, stopping at one. It is the woman's house, and we learn she is Bulgarian. There is a turn-of-the-century wedding photo in the ruins. That evening they eat at a table set in the middle of the rubble with the sound of gunfire in the distance.

The next morning the woman brings him fresh clothes from her missing husband. She is singing as she begins to break up the barge boat with an ax. Then she comes to him as if he is her dead husband and makes love to him. It is clear that this "Circe" wants, like Homer's sorceress, to hold on to Odysseus for her own purposes. But it is also apparent that "A" wishes to continue his own odyssey.

Later "A" awakes and hears gunfire. He sneaks out and down to the river only to discover that the woman is already there with a boat for him.

She is letting him go. She cries and says, "The Aegean Sea": she knows where he must go. He drifts off.

At dawn he wakes to find himself in Sarajevo. The city looks destroyed. People rush around, silently. He has the address of the film archive, but he gets lost in the rubble. "A" finally finds the archive building, and a young boy leads him to a beer house where he finds Ivo Levy, the Jewish director of the archive (Erland Josephson, who appeared in so many Ingmar Bergman films).

He is in line for water along with many other people. Machine guns crackle and all run. As they hide in a bombed-out refuge, "A" tells him what he has come for. Ivo is amazed that he has made it to Sarajevo. He says that to come so far in such danger, "You must have great faith or is it despair?"

They continue their conversation despite the shelling going on, speaking across a street, hiding in doorways. The archivist explains how difficult it was to come up with the right chemical formula. When the coast is clear, the young boy leads them back to the archive, to the basement, past shelves of films, into a sizable room, complete with a large poster of Humphrey Bogart from *The African Queen*, where the old man has obviously been living.

We can hear shelling in the background. He talks about restoring the film as "a kind of birth." "A" says that the old man has no right to keep "the first gaze" locked up. "It's the war," the old man states. The old man offers "A" the mattress to sleep on.

When he wakes up the next morning, a young woman who looks like Kali brings him a package. She is the old man's daughter, Naomi Levy, who is also played by Maia Morgenstern. The girl, a modern-day Nausicaä, according to Angelopoulos's intent, explains that she cannot wait since she lives on the other side of town, and the bombs will go off soon. The woman seems familiar to "A." She blushes and says he looks so familiar. She then disappears.

"A" looks around the lab. He notices that while he has been sleeping, the old man has managed to get the lab working again. As he begins to open a can of Manakia film, the old man and boy return with food and a car battery. The old man sees that "A" is perhaps becoming ill with cold and exhaustion. Ivo is now prepared to finish his job. "*What am I*," he says, "*if not a collector of vanished gazes?*" He then enters his lab and closes the door. Later he emerges saying he needs more water for his work.

"A" finally goes out to get some with the young boy. The city is deserted. They pass corpses on the way to the beer house. More shelling. The boy and "A" take shelter near a psychiatric hospital. The patients, finding the door open, spill into the street, talking and gesturing, completely heedless of the war.

"A" and the boy finally make it back to the archive. Later the boy begins to shiver and cry. The old man comes out of the lab, reassures the boy, and puts him down on the mattress to sleep. The archivist explains to "A" that the boy is a "war child" and cannot or perhaps will not speak.

In the middle of the night, the archivist wakes "A" and takes him into the lab to view the small screen there. He has found the formula! Their joy is mutual, and they embrace, both realizing the importance of the moment. Then "A" notices that the boy is gone. There is fog everywhere. The old man comes up and explains that the film needs a few hours to dry. He tells "A" not to worry about the boy, "He'll turn up suddenly, like an angel of the Lord." Then the archivist explains why the fog is "man's best friend" in Sarajevo since the war began. Without visibility, the snipers cannot shoot, and thus "foggy days are festive days here." And they speak of how this is an important event, the setting free of a gaze held captive since the beginning of the twentieth century.

Soothing music is playing somewhere. The old man explains that it is a band made up of children, Serbs, Croats, Muslims, who play together. They both go into the streets in the fog. And Keitel sees that the old man is right. It is now a festive, transformed city. People greet each other as the music plays. There is even a makeshift production of *Romeo and Juliet* in progress, and Keitel supplies the answering lines, in English, to Juliet's famous lines from her balcony. Ivo and "A" arrive at the cemetery, so full of new graves now. A Muslim funeral procession carrying a body passes them.

Cut to a gentle rock tune in the fog. We vaguely see a number of young girls and boys dancing to the music. Naomi is there. She greets her father and takes "A" to dance. "I did not expect this," he says, obviously delighted, "dancing in Sarajevo!" He makes her laugh, and then the music becomes a number from the 1950s, and they become serious. As they dance a slow dance, they break into Greek, both of them this time, as Naomi has become the Penelope the director left behind in Florina so many years ago. She promises to wait. No explanation is given as to Naomi's transformation, but we understand by now that "A"—who has already "become" the Manakia brothers, at least in his mind as he conducts his odyssey in search of the missing films—has also projected his past lovers into each woman he encounters.

The rest of Ivo's family members show up in the fog and are reunited. Grandchildren included. It is a joyful moment. They walk toward the river, the family getting ahead of Ivo and "A." The film archivist appears worried about how easy it is to get separated and lost in the fog. Then

14. *Ulysses' Gaze*: the youth orchestra of Sarajevo playing in the mist

there is the sound of a Jeep, and the old man holds "A" back, telling him not to move, "whatever happens." Ivo then goes forward as we hear lines about taking away the children, protests from Ivo's wife, Naomi's cry as she is dragged, and then the killing begins. One after the other, we hear the fire of rifles, and this is all the more terrifying since the whole screen is filled with fog. We do not even see "A's" reaction. There are then commands to dump the children in the river, and we hear the splashes. Finally we hear the Jeep drive off. Complete silence. Complete fog.

And then "A" enters the frame, running through the fog.

He finds the bodies in the snow. "A" rushes over to Ivo, lifting up his head and crying out. Then he sees the body of Naomi and goes to her. "A" embraces the dead woman who represents all the women he loves. He trembles, and then the rage, the anger, the helplessness he feels resound in several heart-wrenching screams that come from the deepest reaches of his soul.

Later, he wanders through the fog with others who are gathering, once more, to hear the orchestra in the mist. Then we see the orchestra again, playing its multiethnic tune.

Cut: the dark ruined cinema. "A's" eyes fill with tears as he looks toward us and thus up at the screen where the lost film has just finished running. As the orchestra plays in the distance in the fog, "A" speaks Homer's words of Odysseus to Penelope:

When I return, it will be with another man's clothes, another man's name. My coming will be unexpected. If you look at me unbelieving, and say, You are not he, I will show you signs, and you will believe me. I will tell you about the lemon tree in your garden. The corner window that lets in the moonlight and then signs of the body, signs of love. And as we climb trembling to our old room, between one embrace and the next, between lovers' calls, I will tell you about the journey, all the night long. And in all the nights to come, between one embrace and the next, between lovers' calls, the whole human story. The story that never ends.

We see the screen "A" is watching. It is the cinematic "snow" on the screen that follows the end of a film. We do not see the film itself.

Fade out on "A" as he sits there in this ruined cinema in a Balkan culture that has destroyed itself from within. Has he completed his odyssey or begun yet another?

FILM IN A VIOLENT WORLD: TOWARD A NEW HUMANISM

Two important statements are made about cinema in the opening minutes of *Ulysses' Gaze*. The protest in the small Greek town that divides the whole population suggests the power film can still have, Angelopoulos suggests, to touch people's lives. Of course he is referring not to a typical Hollywood product but to a film such as the ones he has made. And second, with the inclusion of an old black-and-white documentary, Angelopoulos suggests that to go forward, we must first evaluate and learn from the origins of cinema (Balkan cinema in this case). To know a soul we must look into a soul.

I once asked Angelopoulos if he felt that the time for making films had passed. After all, we are living in an age of "post-television" as the computer screen will become our movie theater, our television, our shopping mall, our bank, our library, our school, and our post office all in one. Why make films such as *Ulysses' Gaze* that demand much of their audiences and evoke troubling, strong emotions about issues that have no simple solutions and certainly no "happy endings"? Furthermore, why continue to make films that cry out to be seen on the big screen, the bigger the better, for the full effect of their framing, cinematography, choreography? Angelopoulos answers all of this quite simply but also with a definite sense of purpose: "The world needs cinema now more than ever. It may be the last important form of resistance to the deteriorating world in which we live. In dealing with borders, boundaries, the mixing of languages and cultures today, I am trying to seek a new humanism, a new way" (Horton, "National Culture" 29). *Ulysses' Gaze* definitely lives up to this bold vision for the role of cinema as the century and the first hundred years of cinema end.

Ulysses' Gaze is a triple odyssey: on one level it is a search for the roots of the cinema of the Balkans and, really, of cinema itself: its power, potential, and history. Second, it is also a voyage through the history of the Balkans leading up to and including the ongoing tragedy of Bosnia. And finally, it is an individual journey for a man through his life, his loves, his losses.

It is not possible to put into words the emotion I personally felt when seeing the film for the first time in Athens during August 1995, on the big screen. The summer of 1995 was the summer of *Batman Forever*, *Waterworld*, *Die Hard 3*, and *Power Rangers*. It was also the summer of the Croatian attack on the Krijena territory previously held by the Serbs, of the renewed Bosnian Serb attack on Sarajevo, and of the UN's strike back at the Bosnian Serbs.

Before going into the theater to see *Ulysses' Gaze*, I was carrying with me all of the above information plus my own reading of the screenplay for the film, all of my studies of Angelopoulos's previous work, and my years of travels through the former Yugoslavia including Sarajevo, which I have always felt was one of the most beautiful and exciting cities I have visited anywhere. But even with all of this background, I was not prepared for the emotional power of the film's ending as Keitel screams into the Sarajevo fog over the bodies of the Levy family spread out in the snow before him.

Whatever is meant by a "new humanism," it can be seen as beginning in this film, Angelopoulos suggests, in such an agonizing and cathartic cry at the horror and loss and stupidity and perhaps inevitability of the kinds of forces that have led to the current Balkan war. The new humanism is grounded, as the quotation from Plato reminds us, in the guidelines of the past. And certainly part of the power of *Ulysses' Gaze* is that it purposely pulls back from the documentary approach to current history that television has brought us daily.

Angelopoulos understands that his journey is a mythical story, that the root word in Greek, *istoria*, means both "history" and "story." He has created his own Sarajevo, literally (he was not allowed to shoot in Sarajevo because of the real shooting!) and figuratively. There is no film archive in Sarajevo and never was, and there is no youth orchestra of Muslims, Croats, and Serbs playing in the mist in defiance of snipers in the surrounding hills. But, once more, what Angelopoulos is after is the inner voyage, spiritual truth.

The other films of the summer of 1995 also suggest violence, from *Waterworld* to *Die Hard 3*, but the difference is that unlike its depiction in Angelopoulos's films, the violence they depict is not attached to the real world as we know it. Following in the Hellenic tradition to which he belongs, Angelopoulos has placed the actual violence off-camera and allowed us the space to contemplate the meaning of that violence. The result is the cathartic scream of his protagonist, Harvey Keitel, followed by the final scene, a return to Homer, to words that, although thousands of years old, are given a fresh meaning because of the new context. What if Ithaca itself is the war zone?

For Angelopoulos has stated that the lost film which Keitel locates in Sarajevo is his immediate "Ithaca" (interview, Athens, July 1995).

In Homer's epic, Odysseus can finally settle down after the bloody slaughter of the suitors. Peace is a probable reality at the end of the *Odyssey*. Not so in *Ulysses' Gaze*. The war continues, Keitel is still in Sarajevo, and those he has loved are dead. Furthermore, we are aware of bitter irony wrapped in bitter irony. The tribulations of the Manakia brothers point not only to the troubled history of cinema in the Balkans but to the cyclical nature of conflict in the Balkans. World War I, after all, started in Sarajevo. And that the family members who die at the end of the film are Jewish compounds the horror of the slaughter: the Jews suffered unspeakable sorrow in World War II, and they too are suffering again even though the conflict is "theoretically" not about them. Once the monster of "ethnic cleansing" has been unleashed, Angelopoulos suggests, there can be no strict boundaries to delineate who shall live and who shall die.

The scream at the end is also for all of the women he has loved and lost. Angelopoulos played with the idea of having each character play two roles in *Voyage*. But here Maia Morgenstern is very effective as four of the Homeric tale's women: Penelope, Calypso, Circe, and Nausicaä. Homer does well in exploring the mixture of eroticism and love, *eros* and *agape*, and Angelopoulos builds on this heritage to make the most of the cinematic ability to present the same actress in varying roles.

This is, of course, once more in keeping with his concept of "reconstruction," or of playing with the boundaries between performance and reality or portraying reality as performance. But the bitter irony in relation to the Homeric epic is also clear. It is a brilliant stroke to make Naomi both Nausicaä, the young princess who admired Odysseus and vice versa, and also Penelope, for Angelopoulos succeeds in presenting us with our tendency to find others in the character of those who are before us. And that, unlike the young princess in the *Odyssey* and Penelope herself, this woman who is murdered suggests how corrupted the myth has become in the midst of the current Balkan war. This is not an adaptation of the *Odyssey* but, as Angelopoulos has said, "a pattern that is often used more for contrast than for imitation."

We can say, I think, that the tragic ending of *Ulysses' Gaze* is not a depressing one, for a catharsis such as Aristotle describes in the *Poetics* has taken place. In the scream and in the final Homeric speech, we feel that the emotions of pity and fear are given release. Furthermore, as Angelopoulos explains, "It's important that the lines from Homer are aimed at the future. 'When I return.' . . . So his journey will go on. It is not over. The journey to find a 'home' continues. And this is a kind of hope. For he is, in those closing moments, beginning to be at peace with himself and the world."

Insofar as he is a Greek, Angelopoulos's view of a "new humanism" must necessarily involve the Greek heritage. But Angelopoulos is clear on what he feels it means to be Greek:

> I do not believe that Greece is only a geographical location. That is not what is important or interesting to me. For me, Greece is much larger. It extends much further than the actual borders of the country, for it is the Greece for which we search, like a "home." So this Greece that is in my mind is the Greece I call home, not this office or this place here in Athens where I am sitting talking to you. (Interview, Athens, July 1993)

The unidentified filmmaker who is the protagonist of *Ulysses' Gaze* is Greek. But he is a Greek who has lived in America for more than thirty years and who has, once more, wandered beyond Greece into the heart of the current Balkan crisis in order to find his own renewal. And he finds it, there, in Sarajevo. His renewal takes place in the one spot that would seem to offer no hope, no salvation, no solace. He becomes true to himself and true to his Greek heritage in the larger sense of being a Greek that Angelopoulos embraces. For the Keitel figure, therefore, the new humanism is the knowledge gained and the catharsis experienced in the midst of a very ugly war.

Add one more irony. Angelopoulos was not able to shoot any of the Sarajevo scenes in Sarajevo, even though he tried for two years to get permission. But he did make three trips to Bosnia and neighboring Serbia and Croatia to film in Mostar, Vukovar, and the Krijena area. To the question of why he would go to such extremes to shoot "on location," given the dangers and difficulties involved, Angelopoulos responds: "I believe something special happens on location, in the real place, and I do not mean just the ability to photograph the decor, the landscape. But it is more that when I am in the place I have set the film, all five of my senses are working. I become more *completely aware*. I therefore feel I am living the experiences I want to film" (interview, Athens, July 1995).

Thus even in his concept of production, the location helps evoke the inner journey, the "feel" for the story that using a studio or a substitute location would not call up. He understands, in contrast, that *Casablanca*, for instance, echoes in our memories in large part because we immediately understand that the Casablanca we see on the screen has almost no connection with any real Casablanca. It announces itself in almost every way as Hollywood's version of Casablanca. We feel quite differently, however, about the street scenes in *Ulysses' Gaze*, which are clearly "real." Dare we add that, perhaps subconsciously, we register the fact that there is a special artistic and moral "madness" at play in a film that took itself seriously enough to shoot in a war zone while the war was still being fought? (Angelopoulos offered no stories or worries that the crew or cast were ever in any real trouble.)

THE CINEMATIC GAZE: ANGELOPOULOS AS *KINODIDASKELOS*

To see film as a way to help achieve a new humanism is to view the arts as having a high moral function. In this light, as I have suggested earlier, Angelopoulos is in complete agreement with Czech novelist Milan Kundera that all great art is moral. This entails a view of film as a way toward enlightenment and thus as a form of teaching. And, once more, this attitude belongs to the long Hellenic tradition. Even Aristophanes, the ancient comic poet, claimed that his basic worth and purpose was to be a "teacher through comedy" (*komodidaskelos*). In a similar vein Angelopoulos can be seen as a *kinodidaskelos*: a teacher through cinema. Not a preacher, but a teacher. And as we have discussed, the attention to the visual and to silence places his work in the same moral "teaching" role as that fulfilled by Orthodox icons, frescoes, and mosaics. These spiritual images do not preach to us. Yet they are there for us as *representations* of another world. They invite contemplation and comparison with our everyday world, and, finally, they provide inspiration.

This is not a role that he admits to publicly, but it is there quite clearly in his films and in his commentary on his work. For it has always been the role of teachers, including Socrates, to help individuals understand themselves and the world around them. It is not the role of the teacher, finally, to be dogmatic or to preach.

In this sense *Ulysses' Gaze* offers no simple political moral concerning the Bosnian war. Of course Angelopoulos has his own view on what is taking place: "Two years ago, I had the hope that all of this would end at some point in the near future. But as the people we met while filming in the various countries of the Balkans told us, this war, these problems, will not end in ten years or even in our lifetime. I share their dismay and their evaluation of events" (interview, Athens, July 1993).

What *Ulysses' Gaze* succeeds, finally, in doing is to universalize the crisis and to provide the hope that insight and renewal can come even at the worst of times and in the most dangerous places. We are not allowed to become entangled, like the warring parties, in the particulars of day-today hatred and combat. And we are definitely lifted beyond the level of CNN-style coverage of the war throughout 1995, when the film was released: news bites sandwiched in between coverage of the O. J. Simpson trial and broadcast sports events. We are left at the end of *Ulysses' Gaze*, as the last image fades, with the hauntingly appropriate music played in the mist by the orchestra of young Serbs and Croats and Muslims, joined by their art to a single cause.

The gaze we must exercise in watching *Ulysses' Gaze* thus binds us to Angelopoulos's protagonists and voyagers, establishing yet another "community," the community of those who gaze and those who are the object of the gaze. Just as the Harvey Keitel character is at last united with the work of the Manakia brothers from the beginning of the century while he gazes at the end of the century, so we are joined with the whole contemporary and yet ageless journey Angelopoulos has presented.

Having gazed into this corner of Angelopoulos's soul, we now have a moral duty to learn more about our own soul. Homer and Plato, referenced respectfully in the title and the opening quotation, suggest a direction for a cinematic gaze, for both filmmaker and film viewer, to begin to form a new humanism. After all, as this book goes to print, the possibility of a new peace in the Balkans seems within reach: the Bosnian war has stopped, NATO troops and relief agencies are working together to help insure that peace, and other trouble spots—including the unresolved disagreements between Greece and Albania and Greece and the Former Yugoslav Republic of Macedonia—appear to have quieted down as well.

Conclusions

From the Cinematic Gaze to a Culture of Links

ET US BEGIN to conclude with Angelopoulos's own words. The
following edited interview took place in Theo Angelopoulos's simple office in Athens, not far from the National Museum, during July
1993. At this point he was deeply into preproduction for his latest film,
Ulysses' Gaze. No casting had yet been done. A cigarette in one hand,
Angelopoulos sat at his uncluttered desk next to a bulletin board display-
ing a Xeroxed photo of Mastroianni from *The Suspended Step of the
Stork*. Throughout the interview, Angelopoulos was most expressive,
using his free hand and, sometimes, both to make a point. The interview
was conducted in Greek.

HORTON: Can you say something about your new script, *Ulysses' Gaze?*
ANGELOPOULOS: It concerns a filmmaker who has lost the will to make
    films. One day while he is visiting the sacred island of Delos, the birth-
    place of Apollo, from a crack in the ground a marble head of Apollo
    mysteriously rises from the ground and shatters into many pieces. The
    filmmaker tries to take a picture of this event, but when he develops it,
    he sees that nothing appears. You see, the head had emerged from the
    spot where Apollo, the god of *light*, had first appeared. The light at
    such a spot, the source of light, was too strong for the camera!
    (Angelopoulos smiles.) This event leads him to think about the first
    films ever made in the Balkans and he learns that there was one film
    that was never developed. The film then becomes the filmmaker's
    search for this film and for his own need for inspiration, across the
    Balkans: Bulgaria, Greece, Skopje, Albania, Romania, Belgrade, and
    finally Sarajevo. (He details a few more plot turns.) Finally in Sarajevo
    in the bombed-out film archive as bombs go off around him, he is able
    to see this first film, which a film archivist in Sarajevo at last develops.
    It is a 1902 black-and-white silent film of an actor playing Odysseus,
    washed up on the shore of Ithaca at the end of his voyage. The actor-
    Odysseus looks out at the filmmaker and across the twentieth century:
    Ulysses' Gaze is completed!
HORTON: Obviously in taking on all of the Balkans, you are extending
    your concern for borders, refugees, and all of the changes in these coun-
    tries today, which you began in *The Suspended Step of the Stork*.
    Could you comment on how you feel about the tragedies unfolding in
    Bosnia and elsewhere today?

ANGELOPOULOS: I feel all of this—the ethnic cleansing, destruction, the civil wars, everything—shows us there is a vacuum in Central Europe now and in the Balkans in particular. One era is ending and another is about to be born. We are very much "in between," all of us here. People need a new sense of community, politics, beliefs. The old labels—Left, Right, communist, socialist, etc.—are finished. I don't know what will happen now. But a new epoch is beginning. Borders, attitudes, relations, nations, all will change.

HORTON: Since last year when we spoke, the situation in Bosnia has gotten much worse.

ANGELOPOULOS: Bosnia is a question of problems going back at least to the fourteenth century. We must go back to the spread of the Ottoman Empire. When Islam came to the Balkans, various problems were created everywhere. And there will never be complete and final solutions to these problems. More recently, since World War I, the major powers have determined much of what has happened in this area. Russia, for instance. Personally, I am hopeful that *something* will come from all of this confusion. But we must be willing to be *patient.*

HORTON: Yugoslav director Srdjan Karanovic has said he comes from a country that no longer exists and that as an artist, his position as one who should *create* is difficult in a culture that is bent on destruction.

ANGELOPOULOS: It is a very difficult time for artists of all kinds and writers of course too in the Balkans today. Nobody wants to listen. Nobody. With the killing, the wars, the struggles, troubles, no one *can* listen, *and art, true art, demands listening.* So, in the midst of all of this, what am I to do? Simply, I can make films for those who *do* appreciate my work.

HORTON: What are the biggest problems you face on your new film? Are you worried about shooting a film in Sarajevo?

ANGELOPOULOS (smiling): It is difficult to cast my film because actors of course worry about the problems of Bosnia and so on. I am interested in Holly Hunter, for instance. But my biggest problem is that I cannot find film insurance companies anywhere to insure this film! This is a German, French, Italian, Greek coproduction, but no company will insure me!

HORTON: Why do you feel a need to make such "un-Hollywood" films?

ANGELOPOULOS: There are all kinds of films out there for people to watch. But there are almost no films that truly show what is going on, especially in this part of Europe. Part of what I wish to show is that each individual's life—his thoughts, work, even lovemaking, *everything*—is affected by these terrible problems we face that are larger than we are. We are conditioned by what is "in the air" around us. *I wish to capture something of the melancholy we feel today*, surrounded by murder here and there, and catastrophes in general.

HORTON: One Greek critic has written that in *Voyage to Cythera*, you have created a journey into Greek history. Do you agree?

ANGELOPOULOS: I don't agree completely. I think my films are about voyages we all take, anywhere in the world. The problem is a universal one of not having a place, a home to call our own. I believe this strongly about any film, book, or work of art. If I read, for instance, Thomas Mann's *Magic Mountain*, I cannot say, "This is just a German situation." *No.* In Mann's book I learn something about myself, about all people. I feel the same with my films. That's the role of art. And I feel the deeper one goes into one's particular place—Greece for me—the more universal it will become for others. What I don't like are those films that try to please everyone with a little bit of everything but which wind up being nothing in particular.

HORTON: For example?

ANGELOPOULOS (smiling): For example, we call such films "Euro-pudding"! They have no one strong taste. The point is that a Turkish film should be in Turkish and about Turkish subjects. And a French film should be in French and about French concerns.

HORTON: Jean Renoir came to much the same conclusion.

ANGELOPOULOS: Exactly. A John Ford Western is very much a part of America and the West. But his distinct voice speaks to everyone everywhere through his landscapes and characters. Thus his films mean a lot more to audiences everywhere than, say, American films that try to be European.

HORTON: It seems Europe in particular is worried about the strong domination of Hollywood over "home" film industries in each country. And yet in Greece, especially on television, I hear that old Greek movies by the comic Thanassis Vengos and the romantic Aliki Vouyouklaiki, for example, are even more popular than Hollywood films. Do you agree?

ANGELOPOULOS: It is true the younger Greek generation, like young people everywhere, I think, are now interested in films/styles/music from the 1950s and early 1960s. This is, of course, a desire for lost innocence and a nostalgic movement. In Greece, the young see these past times as "magic" and innocent. Life seems so simple and good in these old comedies and romantic melodramas. But the issue is more complicated, for we must realize that people everywhere now watch a lot of television, including countless commercials, and lots of Hollywood films. There is no real way to control this. It seems futile to me, for instance, to try to place quotas in a country on how many Hollywood films can be shown in a year. You can't or shouldn't dictate what people want to see. That's why the young Greek generation's interest in old Greek movies is interesting: it suggests they are, in part, fed up with the latest Hollywood films and with too much television. Their return to these films is coming from a romantic logic.

HORTON: Your first feature, *Reconstruction*, is generally written about as a fictional film wrapped in a "documentary" (the opening voice-over "documentary" commentary, for instance). But the splendid opening folk song of "Bitter Lemons" suggests we might also consider the film as a kind of cinematic folk song.

ANGELOPOULOS: Yes, indeed. The song is not just a folk song but it belongs to that northern Greek tradition of *mirologia* chants [simple but haunting tunes sung at funerals or in memory of the dead].

HORTON: And in *Voyage to Cythera*, you have the folk song about "red apples" playing an important role.

ANGELOPOULOS: Exactly. Manos [Manos Katrakis, the famous actor who plays the central character, Spyros] sings this song and in a sense it represents him, an old man who, like a rotten apple, is "overripe," finished!

HORTON: Spyros is a returning Odysseus, but his homecoming is very different from Homer's ending.

ANGELOPOULOS: I am friends with Alberto Moravia [the Italian novelist] and I spoke to him about this script while I was writing it. I told him that he was an influence on me. And I think that influence was that Spyros as Odysseus is much closer to Dante's vision of him than to Homer's. For Dante really draws from a much earlier tradition of the Odysseus myth than did Homer. As you remember, Homer has a "happy ending" whereas Dante emphasizes that Odysseus continues to wander and dies at sea.

HORTON: At the end of *Reconstruction* the wife, Eleni, who has murdered her husband, echoing the Agamemnon myth, is taken away in a police Jeep. But as they are driving away, she is attacked by a group of old ladies who seem either like the Furies themselves (in Aeschylus) or like the old ladies stripping the widow's house at the end of Michael Cacoyannis's *Zorba*. Was this your intention?

ANGELOPOULOS (smiling deeply): There are those similarities, but it was not really planned that way. You see, on that first film, we had a very tight shooting schedule. Thus there was a lot of quick thinking going on from day to day. For that particular shot I simply went to the local church in that village and asked for the women to be in the scene. The only direction I gave them was to react to "that woman" who had just murdered her husband and taken up with a local man. That was all they needed to hear. They suddenly attacked her, they *charged*! And I was afraid they might *really* strangle her!

HORTON: Much of what is important in your films happens off-camera. Could you comment on this?

ANGELOPOULOS: "Off space," as we call it. Yes, on one hand it is part of the ancient tradition of Greek tragedy. We never see an actual death or violence on stage. It is always "off." The same is true of Chinese and Japanese theater. And much of Brecht as well. You see that with *Reconstruction* and its ending, I began to use this approach quite obviously, for you see the main characters go into the house, you know that the murder will take place inside, you see people come and go in the yard, the children come and play and leave, but you do not see the murder, the event itself. And of course I use this a lot in *The Travelling Players*.

HORTON: You seem to have a very strong interest not only in the Greek landscape but also the Greek village.

ANGELOPOULOS: The village is a complete world in miniature. The old Greek villages had a spirit, a life, full of work and play and festivity. Of course Greek villages began to depopulate by the turn of the century, but it was really World War II and the subsequent civil war in Greece that completely destroyed the reality and concept of the Greek village. Our whole way of life was changed by these two catastrophes.

HORTON: Would Greece still be a village-centered nation without these two wars?

ANGELOPOULOS: Of course villages would have changed anyway. But not so drastically. The changes would have been made in a much more gradual and gentle way. You have to understand that part of the result of these wars was that in the 1950s over 500,000 village men went to Germany in particular, but also America and Australia, etc., to become guest workers. That meant a big shift in village life. Suddenly the men were gone and the women remained. With all these changes, the *spirit* of the villages began to die.

HORTON: What is your hope? Do you feel Greeks should return to the villages? Should half of Athens move out?

ANGELOPOULOS: No! I have no such desires or hopes. It's just that I am concerned that something beautiful died here. It is like the death of a strong love affair—you want to remember it, think about it, examine it. It is hard to let go of! (Pause.) What do I want to happen? I simply want our life here to become more human. As you know we have lost so much in Athens. Crime, pollution, traffic, the impersonality of the city, so much. We need to return to those places to find much of what is still important, authentic to our lives.

HORTON: Aristophanes says in one of his plays that he is a *komodidaskelos*: a teacher through comedy. Are you a *kinodidaskelos*: a teacher through cinema?

ANGELOPOULOS (laughter, shakes his head): Aristophanes was . . . Aristophanes! I don't know. What I can say is that there is a generation of Greeks (and foreigners) that has grown up on my films. When I was shooting *The Suspended Step of the Stork* in Florina [northern Greece], I had something of a mild heart problem and went to the hospital. The doctor there, thirty-eight years old or so, told me I was responsible for his becoming a doctor. "How so?" I asked. "I was studying in Italy," he replied, "and I saw *The Travelling Players*, and it made such an impression on me that I knew I had to become a doctor and return to northern Greece where you shot your film, and try and help 'my' people!"

I have had many people tell me similar stories.

HORTON: The village in *Voyage to Cythera* that Spyros returns to. Where is it?

ANGELOPOULOS: In Macedonia, not far from Mount Olympus. (Smile.) Of course they never get to Cythera, the real island.

HORTON: And at the end of *Landscape in the Mist*, the children cross the border between Germany and Greece, yet no such real border exists.

ANGELOPOULOS: True. It is an allegorical border.

HORTON: Are the children dead or alive at the end of *Landscape*? It seems we could take the ending either way.

ANGELOPOULOS (laughing): We only hear *one* bullet!

HORTON: The theme of fathers and sons or the search for a father seems important to many of your films. Can you comment?

ANGELOPOULOS: In all of my films there are characters looking for fathers. I don't just mean real fathers, but the *concept* of the father as a sign or meaning or symbol of what we dream of. You see, the father represents what we want or what we believe in. That is, the search for a father is really a question of finding one's own identity in life.

HORTON: The Bosnian director Emir Kusturica said that for him "joy" is everything, that joy includes pain as well as pleasure. Many of your scenes, such as the one in *Voyage to Cythera* when Spyros dances on the tomb of his old friend, seem to suggest a similar large view of "joy."

ANGELOPOULOS: Yes, the idea of dancing on the tomb of friends is an old custom involved in the celebration of death in the Ponti [part of Asia Minor] and northern Greece. When someone dies, you eat, drink, laugh, dance, celebrate.

HORTON: Like a jazz funeral in New Orleans.

ANGELOPOULOS: Like a jazz funeral! It is a kind of victory of life over death or perhaps of acknowledging that beyond the sadness of death, there is the realization of the *freedom and release* that death means. The soul is free and that means more than just that the body is dead.

Theater and film director Peter Brook speaks of there being three major "cultures" in a person's life. The first is "the culture of the state," which is the culture that is imposed upon us (236). The second is "basically that of the individual" and thus has to do with the world we create as we either turn within ourselves or reach out to others. The third culture he speaks of as "*the culture of links*" (239): it is the force that can counterbalance the fragmentation of our world. *It has to do with the discovery of relationships where such relationships have become submerged and lost*—between man and society, between one race and another, between the microcosm and the macrocosm, between humanity and machinery, between the visible and the invisible, among categories, languages, genres.

The cinema of Theo Angelopoulos is a cinema that crosses the borders of the first two areas of culture—the state and the individual—to explore this third "culture of links." His films show us such a variety of fragments. There are the hands rising from the sea, the theatrical performances left unfinished, the journeys to Cythera that never take place, the suspended steps that are never completed. But it is a tribute to his cinematic art that the concept, style, structure, framing, and *texture* of his films provide us with the means to transcend the fragmentation and thus enter into a culture of links.

And yet part of what is absolutely distinct about the cinema of Theo Angelopoulos is that he leaves the act of actually creating these links to us.

What does a hand rising from the sea signify? What do we make of friends and family applauding as they stand around a fresh grave? What kind of marriage would be carried out across a river that is a border between two unfriendly countries? What do we understand from an extended shot of hundreds of silent, statuelike refugees standing as if frozen in their Albanian landscape as they move toward illegally entering Greece once more?

A film can end with a character's isolation, as in Chaplin's films as he wanders down the highway, alone. Or it can suggest, in one form or another, an embrace and thus a sense of shared experience, an effort at creating a community. Angelopoulos's endings belong to the latter category. Clearly his films cross borders to establish links which create an embrace of the fragments that leads to a sense of community.

Even in the dying horse scene, Voula is there to hold and comfort Alexander. And as the film ends, whether they are dead or alive, they are together, embracing a seemingly magical life-giving tree in a bright landscape without mist. Finally, even in *Ulysses' Gaze*, despite the horror of the current Bosnian war and the personal loss the protagonist feels, he is not alone. We leave him united with the film he has sought and thus with a whole heritage of history and culture not only from this century but ranging over several thousand years back to Homer and beyond.

Angelopoulos is a rare and distinct voice in an increasingly faceless cinematic mass market. His inner odysseys presented on film remind us, at the close of the twentieth century, of what his favorite poet, George Seferis, had written years ago:

I want no more than to speak simply, to be granted this grace.
Because we have burdened song with so much music that it is gradually sinking
and we have adorned our art so much that its features have been eaten away
   by gold
and it is time to say our few words because tomorrow the soul sets sail.
      (From "An Old Man on the River Bank," in *Four Greek Poets* 62)

Filmography

THE BROADCAST (E EKPOMBEI) 1968

SCREENPLAY: Theo Angelopoulos
CINEMATOGRAPHY: Giorgos Arvanitis
EDITING: Giorgos Triantafillou
Black and white. 23 minutes
1968: Salonika Film Festival, Critics' Prize

RECONSTRUCTION (ANAPARASTASIS) 1970

SCREENPLAY: Theo Angelopoulos, with the participation of Stratis Karras, Thanasis Valtinos
CINEMATOGRAPHY: Giorgos Arvanitis
EDITING: Takis Davlopoulos
SOUND: Thanasis Arvanitis
CAST: Toula Stathopoulou (Eleni Gousis); Yiannis Totsikas (Christos Grikakas); Michalis Photopoulos (Costas Gousis); Thanos Grammenos (Eleni's brother); Alexandros Alexiou (Police Inspector); Theo Angelopoulos, Christos Paliyanopoulos, Telis Samandis, Panos Papadopoulos (Journalists)
PRODUCER: Giorgos Samiotis
Black and white. 110 minutes
1970: Salonika Film Festival—Best Director, Best Cinematography, Best Film, Best Actress, Critic's Prize
1971: Georges Sadoul Prize as "Best Film of the Year Shown in France"
1971: Best Foreign Film at the Hyères Festival

DAYS OF '36 (MERES TOU '36) 1972

SCREENPLAY: Theo Angelopoulos, with the participation of Petros Markaris, Thanasis Valtinos, Stratis Karras
CINEMATOGRAPHY: Giorgos Arvanitis
EDITING: Vassilis Syropoulos
PRODUCTION DESIGN: Mikis Karapiperis
SOUND: Thanasis Arvanitis
MUSIC: Giorgos Papastefanou
CAST: Kostas Pavlou (Sophianos), Petros Zarkadis (Lukas), Christophoros Nezer (Director of the Prison), Vassilis Tsanglos (Guard), Yannis Kandilas (Kreezis), Thanos Grammenos (Sophianos's brother)

PRODUCER: Giorgos Papalios
Color. 130 minutes
1972: Salonika Film Festival—Best Director, Best Cinematography
1972: FRIPESCI (International Film Critics' Association) Best Film, Berlin Fest

THE TRAVELLING PLAYERS (O THIASOS) 1975

SCREENPLAY: Theo Angelopoulos
CINEMATOGRAPHY: Giorgos Arvanitis
ASSISTANT TO ARVANITIS: Vasilis Christomoglou
PRODUCTION DESIGN: Mikis Karapiperis
EDITING: Takis Davlopoulos, Giorgos Triantafillou
SOUND: Thanasis Arvanitis
MUSIC: Loukianos Kilaidonis with Fotos Lambrinos, Nena Mejdi, Dimitri Kamberidis, Kostas Messaris
CAST: Eva Kotamanidou (Electra), Aliki Georgouli (Mother), Stratos Pachis (Father), Maria Vasileiou (Chrysothemis), Vangelis Kazan (Aegisthus), Petros Zarkadis (Orestes), Kiriakos Katrivanos (Pylades), Grigoris Evangelatos (Poet)
PRODUCER: Giorgos Papalios
Color. 230 minutes
American distributor: New Yorker Films
1975: FRIPESCI (International Film Critics' Association) Best Film Award, Cannes Festival
1975: Best Film in "Forum" at Berlin Festival
1979: Best Film of the Year, London; Awards in Portugal, Japan, etc.
1975: Salonika Film Festival, Greek Critics' Association—Best Film, Best Director, Best Screenplay, Best Actor, Best Actress
Italian Critics Association: Best Film in the World, 1970–1980
FRIPESCI: One of the Top Films in the History of Cinema

THE HUNTERS (E KENEGE) 1977

SCREENPLAY: Theo Angelopoulos, with the participation of Stratis Karras
CINEMATOGRAPHY: Giorgos Arvanitis
PRODUCTION DESIGN: Mikis Karapiperis
EDITING: Giorgos Triantafillou
MUSIC: Loukianos Kilaidonis
SOUND: Thanasis Arvanitis
CAST: Vangelis Kazan (Savvas), Betty Balassi (his wife), Giorgos Danis (Yannis Diamantis), Mary Chronopoulo (his wife), Ilias Stamatiou (Antonis Papdopoulos), Aliki Georgouli (his wife), Nikos Kouros (the General), Eva Kotamanidou (his wife), Stratos Pachis (Giorgos Fantakis), Christophoros Nezer (the Politician), Dimitris Kamberidis (the Communist)
PRODUCER: Theo Angelopoulos with the participation of INA

Color. 165 minutes
1977: Cannes Film Festival, Special Recognition
1977: Chicago Film Festival, Golden Hugo for Best Film
1977: Prize from the Greek Film Critics' Association

ALEXANDER THE GREAT (O MEGALEXANDROS) 1980

SCREENPLAY: Theo Angelopoulos, with the participation of Petros Markaris
CINEMATOGRAPHY: Giorgos Arvanitis
EDITING: Giorgos Triantafillou
PRODUCTION DESIGN: Mikis Karapiperis
MUSIC: Christdoulos Chlaris
CAST: Omero Antonutti (Megalexandros); Eva Kotamanidou (his daughter); Michalis Yiannatos (Dragoumanos); Grigoris Evangelatos (the Schoolteacher); Christophoros Nezer (Mr. Tzelepis); Mifanta Kounelaki (Mrs. Tzelepis); Ilias Zafeiropoulos (Young Alexander); E. Gkotsis, Ch. Pisimisis, Y. Kovaios, Ch. Timotheou, Ch. Stamatelos (Bandits)
PRODUCER: R.A.I., Z.D.F. (Germany), Theo Angelopoulos Productions
Color. 165 minutes
1980: Venice Film Festival, "Golden Lion" (Best Film)
1980: FRIPESCI (International Film Critics' Association) Award
1980: Salonika Film Festival, Greek Critics' Association Prize

ONE VILLAGE, ONE VILLAGER (CHORIO ENA, KATEKOS ENAS...) 1981

CINEMATOGRAPHY: Giorgos Arvanitis
EDITING: Giorgos Triantafillou
SOUND: Thanasis Arvanitis
PRODUCER: YENED (Greek Television) Color. 20 minutes

ATHENS: RETURN TO THE ACROPOLIS (ATHENA, EPISTROPHI STIN AKROPOLI) 1983

SCREENPLAY: Theo Angelopoulos
CINEMATOGRAPHY: Giorgos Arvanitis
PRODUCTION DESIGN: Mikis Karapiperis
EDITING: Giorgos Triantafillou
SOUND: Thanasis Georgiadis
MUSIC: Manos Hadzidakis, Loukianos Kilaidonis, Dionysios Savopoulos
POETRY: George Seferis, Tasos Levaditis
CLIPS FROM: *The Travelling Players*, *The Hunters*, *Megalexandos*
PRODUCER: Trans World Film, ERT-RTV ELLENICA, Theo Angelopoulos
Color. 43 minutes

VOYAGE TO CYTHERA (TAXIDI STA KITHIRA) 1983

SCREENPLAY: Theo Angelopoulos, Thanasis Valtinos, Tonino Guerra
CINEMATOGRAPHY: Giorgos Arvanitis
EDITING: Giorgos Triantafillou
MUSIC: Eleni Karaindrou
PRODUCTION DESIGN: Mikis Karapiperis
CAST: Manos Katrakis (Old Man [Spyros]), Mary Chronopoulou (Voula), Dionyssis Papayannopoulos (Antonis), Dora Volanaki (Spyros's wife), Julio Brogi (Alexander)
PRODUCER: The Greek Film Centre, Theo Angelopoulos Productions
Color. 137 minutes
1984: Cannes Film Festival, Best Screenplay
1984: FRIPESCI (International Critics' Association) Award, Cannes Festival, Best Film
1984: Greek National Award—Best Film, Best Script, Best Actor, Best Actress
1984: Rio de Janeiro Festival Critics' Award, Best Film

THE BEEKEEPER (O MELISSOKOMOS) 1986

SCREENPLAY: Theo Angelopoulos, in collaboration with Dimitris Nollas; special collaboration also by Tonino Guerra
CINEMATOGRAPHY: Giorgos Arvanitis
EDITING: Takis Yannopoulos
MUSIC: Eleni Karaindrou
CAST: Marcello Mastroianni (Spyros), Nadia Mourouzi (young girl), Serge Reggiani (the sick man), Jenny Roussea (Spyros's wife), Dinos Iliopoulos (Spyros's friend)
PRODUCER: The Greek Film Centre, Marin Karmitz Productions, ERT-1 TV (Greece), Theo Angelopoulos Productions
Color. 120 minutes

LANDSCAPE IN THE MIST (TOPO STIN OMICHLI) 1988

SCREENPLAY (from a story by Theo Angelopoulos): Theo Angelopoulos, with the participation of Tonino Guerra, Thanasis Valtinos
CINEMATOGRAPHY: Giorgos Arvanitis
EDITING: Yannis Tsitsopoulos
MUSIC: Eleni Karaindrou
PRODUCTION DESIGN: Mikis Karapiperis
CAST: Tania Palaiologou (Voula), Michalis Zeke (Alexander), Stratos Tzortzoglou (Orestes)
PRODUCER: The Greek Film Centre, Greek Television (ERT-1), Paradis Films (Paris), Basicinematografica (Rome), and Theo Angelopoulos Productions
Color. 126 minutes

American distributor: New Yorker Films
1988: Venice Film Festival, Golden Lion Award
1989: Felix (European "Oscar" award)

*THE SUSPENDED STEP OF THE STORK (TO METEORO
VIMA TOU PELARGOU)* 1991

SCREENPLAY: Theo Angelopoulos, Tonino Guerra, Petros Markaris, in collaboration with Thanasis Valtinos
CINEMATOGRAPHY: Giorgos Arvanitis, Andreas Sinanos
ART DIRECTION: Mikis Karapiperis
EDITING: Yannis Tsitsopoulos
MUSIC: Eleni Karaindrou
ARCHITECTURAL DESIGNS: Achilleas Staikos
CAST: Marcello Mastroianni, Jeanne Moreau, Gregory Karr, Ilias Logothetis, Dora Chrisikou, Vassillis Bougioclakis
PRODUCER: The Greek Film Centre, Theo Angelopoulos Productions, Arena Films (France), Vega Films (Switzerland), Erre Produzioni (Italy)
Color. 126 minutes

ULYSSES' GAZE (TO VLEMMA TOU ODYSSEA) 1995

SCREENPLAY: Theo Angelopoulos, with the participation of Tonino Guerra, Petros Markaris
CINEMATOGRAPHY: Giorgos Arvanitis, Andreas Sinanos
ART DIRECTION: Giorgos Patsas, Miodrac Mile Nicolic
EDITING: Yannis Tsitsopoulos
MUSIC: Eleni Karaindrou
SOLO VIOLA: Kim Kashkashian
MUSIC PRODUCTION: Manfred Eicher
CAST: Harvey Keitel ("A"), Erland Josephson (Ivo Levy), Maia Morgenstern (the Woman in Florina / Penelope, Kali / Calypso, the Widow / Circe, Naomi Levy / Nausicaä), Thanassis Vengos (the Taxi Driver), Giorgos Michalakopoulos (Nikos), Dora Volanaki (Old Lady in Albania), Mania Papadimitriou, Angel Iavanof, Ljuba Tadic, Gert Llanaj
PRODUCER: Theo Angelopoulos, The Greek Film Centre, Mega Channel, Paradis Films, La Générale D'Images, La Sept Cinéma, with the participation of Canal +, Basicinematografica, Instituto Luce, RAL, Channel 4
Color. 180 minutes
1995: Cannes Film Festival, Grand Prix

Bibliography

Aeschylus. *Agamemnon*. Translated by Richard Lattimore. Chicago: University of Chicago Press, 1953.

———. *The Oresteia*. Translated and introduced by David Grene. Chicago: University of Chicago Press, 1960.

Angelopoulos, Thodoros. *O Thiasos* Published screenplay in Greek. Athens: Themelio, 1975.

———. "Première ébauce d'une scene des *Chasseurs*." *Positif*, no. 200 (1995).

———. *Ulysses' Gaze*. Unpublished screenplay, 1994.

Arecco, Sergio. *Anghelopulos*. Florence: La Nuova Italia, 1978.

Bacoyannopoulos, Yannis. "The Promise of a Young Cinema." In *Cine-Mythology: A Retrospective of Greek Film*. Athens: The Greek Film Centre, 1993.

Bakhtin, Mikhail. *Rabelais and His World*. Translated by Hélène Iswolsky. Cambridge: MIT Press, 1968.

Bazin, André. *What Is Cinema?* Vol. 1. Edited and translated by Hugh Gray. Berkeley and Los Angeles: University of California Press, 1967.

Biro, Yvette. "*Voyage to Cythera*." *Film Quarterly* 41, no. 1 (Fall 1987): 49–58.

Blos, Peter. *Son and Father: Before and beyond the Oedipus Complex*. New York: The Free Press, 1985.

Bresson, Robert. *Notes on Cinematography*. Translated by Jonathan Griffin. New York: Urizen Books, 1977.

Brizio, Montinaro. *Diaro mecedone Journal de tournage D'Alexandre le Grande*. Milan: Edizione II Formichiere, 1990.

Brook, Peter. *The Shifting Point: Forty Years of Theatrical Exploration, 1946–1987*. London: Methuen, 1988.

Burch, Noel. *To the Distant Observer: Form and Meaning in the Japanese Cinema*. Berkeley and Los Angeles: University of California Press, 1979.

Butterworth, Katharine, and Sara Schneider, eds. *Rebetika: Songs from the Old Greek Underworld*. Athens: Komboloi, 1975.

Cacoullos, Ann. Speech to a Loyola University Study Tour in Greece. Athens, Greece, June 1993.

Cavafy, C. P. *The Complete Poems of C. P. Cavafy*. Translated by Rae Dalven. 3d ed. London: The Hogarth Press, 1966.

Ciment, Michel, and Hélène Tierchant. *Theo Angelopoulos*. Paris: Ed. Edilig, 1989.

———. "Theo Angelopoulos." In *Theo Angelopoulos*. New York: The Museum of Modern Art Retrospective Program, 1990.

Corliss, Richard. "Cannes Goes Under." *Time*, June 12, 1995, 68–70.

Danforth, Loring M. *The Death Rituals of Rural Greece*. Princeton: Princeton University Press, 1982.

Demus, Otto. *Byzantine Mosaic Decoration: Aspects of Monumental Art in Byzantium*. Boston: Boston Book and Art Shop, 1964.

De Santi, G. *Il Cinema di Angelopoulos*. Pesaro: Comune di Pesaro, 1979.

Dimopoulos, Michael, "Greek Cinema." Program booklet. London Film Festival of Greek Films, 1975.

"Dossier Theo Angelopoulos." *Positif*, no. 370 (December 1991): 5–19.

Durgnat, Raymond, "The Long Take in *Voyage to Cythera*." *Film Comment*, November–December 1990, 43–45.

Eder, Richard. "Film: Electra Reflected: *The Travelling Players*." *New York Times*, September 5, 1975.

Eisenstein, Sergei. *The Film Sense*. Translated by Jay Leyda. New York: Harcourt, Brace & World, 1970.

Elley, Derek. "The Travelling Players." *Film and Filming* 22, no. 9 (June 1976): 31–32.

Esteve, Michel. "Theo Angelopoulos ou Le refus de l'idée totalitaire." In *Le Pouvoir en question*. Paris: Ed. du Cerf, 1984.

Eudes, Dominique. *The Kapetanios: Partisans and Civil War in Greece, 1943–1949*. Translated by John Howe. New York: Monthly Review Press, 1973.

Finley, M. I., ed. *The Portable Greek Historians*. New York: Penguin Books, 1989.

Holden, Stephen. "A Moody Search for a Fictive Father: Landscape in the Mist." *New York Times*, September 14, 1990.

Horton, Andrew. "The Beginnings of a New Greek Wave." *Athenian*, April 1975, 22–24.

———. "Conversation with Angelopoulos." *Pilgrimage*, April 1976, 35–36.

———. *The Films of George Roy Hill*. New York: Columbia University Press, 1985.

———. "Greek Films vs. Films Made by Greeks." *Pilgrimage*, June 1976, 27–29.

———. "History as Cinema and Cinema as History." *Athenian*, October 1977, 36–37.

———. "National Culture and Individual Vision: An Interview with Theodoros Angelopoulos." *Cineaste* 19, nos. 2–3 (1993): 28–31.

———. "The New Greek Cinema and Theodore Angelopoulos' Melissokomos." *Modern Greek Studies Yearbook*. Vol. 3. Minneapolis: University of Minnesota Press, 1987.

———. "*O Thiasos*: Not So Much a Film as an Experience." *Athenian*, December 1975, 31–33.

———. "*O Thiasos*: The Most Original and Important Film of 1975." *Pilgrimage*, April 1976, 34–36.

———. "The Poetry of George Seferis and Constantine Cavafy." Master's thesis, Colgate University, 1969.

———. "Theodor Angelopoulos and the New Greek Cinema." *Film Criticism* 6, no. 1 (Fall 1981): 10–20.

———. "Theodore Angelopoulos, The New Greek Cinema and Byzantine Iconology." *Modern Greek Studies Yearbook*. Vol. 2. Minneapolis: University of Minnesota Press, 1986.

Houston, Penelope. "*Days of '36*." *Sight and Sound* 41, no. 3 (Summer 1973): 52.

Jaehne, Karen. "Theodore Angelopoulos." In *World Film Directors 1945–1985*. New York: H. W. Wilson, 1988.

Kael, Pauline. *Kiss Kiss Bang Bang*. New York: Bantam, 1971.

Kaplan, Robert D. *Balkan Ghosts: A Journey through History*. New York: Vintage Books, 1993.

Kazantzakis, Nikos. *The Odyssey: A Modern Sequel*. Translated by Kimon Friar. New York: Simon and Schuster, 1958.

Kazhdan, Alexander, and Giles Constable. *People and Power in Byzantium: An Introduction to Modern Byzantine Studies*. Washington, D.C.: Dumbarton Oaks Center for Byzantine Studies of Harvard University, 1982.

Keeley, Edmund, and Philip Sherrard, eds. *Four Greek Poets*. Harmondsworth, England: Penguin, 1966.

Klima, Ivan. *Love and Garbage*. New York: Penguin, 1990.

Kolovos, Nikos. *Thodoros Angelopoulos*. Athens: Aigokeros, 1990.

Koning, Hans. "*O Thiasos*." *Film Quarterly* 30, no. 3 (Spring 1977): 46–50.

Kousoumidis, Marinos. *Istoria tou Ellinikou Kinimatograou*. Athens: Kastanoiti, 1991.

Kundera, Milan. *The Art of the Novel*. Translated from the French by Linda Asher. New York: Grove Press, 1988.

Lake, Steve. "Covering the Waterfront: Eleni Karaindrou's Music for Films." Notes to the CD *Eleni Karandrou: Music for Films*. Munich: ECM Records, 1991.

Lévi-Strauss, Claude. *Tristes Tropiques*. Translated by John and Doreen Weightman. New York: Atheneum, 1975.

Liehm, Mira, and Antonin J. Liehm. *The Most Important Art: Soviet and Eastern European Film after 1945*. Berkeley and Los Angeles: University of California Press, 1977.

McBride, Joseph, and Michael Wilmington. *John Ford*. New York: Da Capo, 1975.

Megalos, William. "The Filming of *O Megalexandros*." *Athenian*, July 1980, 22–25.

Mercouri, Melina. *New Greek Cinema*. Athens: The Greek Film Centre, 1991.

Michelson, Annette. "The Kinetic Ikon in the Work of Mourning: Vertov's *Three Songs of Lenin*." Paper delivered at the Society for Cinema Studies Conference, New York University, June 1985.

Mitchell, Tony. "Animating Dead Space and Dead Time." *Sight and Sound* 50, no. 1 (Winter 1980–1981): 30–33.

Mitchell, W.J.T. *Iconology: Image, Text, Ideology*. Chicago: University of Chicago Press, 1986.

Mitropoulou, Anglae. *Ellinkos Kinimatographos*. Athens: Kedros, 1980.

Murphy, Kathleen. "Angelopoulos: Children of Paradise." *Film Comment*, November–December 1990, 38–45.

Nichols, Bill. *Blurred Boundaries: Questions of Meaning in Contemporary Culture*. Berkeley and Los Angeles: University of California Press, 1995.

Olson, Elder. *The Theory of Comedy*. Bloomington: Indiana University Press, 1968.

Orati, Daniela. *Thodoros Angelopoulos*. Venice: Circuito Cinema Quaderno 9. Ed. Comune di Venezia, 1982.

Pappas, Peter. "Culture, History and Cinema: A Review of *The Travelling Players*." *Cineaste* 3, no. 1 (Winter 1976–1977): 36–39.

Paul, David W. *Politics, Art and Commitment in the East European Cinema*. New York: St. Martin's Press, 1983.

Pera, Alberto. "Theo Angelopoulos, una creacion desde la tragedia." *Assij de teatre*. Barcelona: Revue de l'Universite, December 1994.

Quandt, James. "*Landscape in the Mist*," *Theo Angelopoulos*. New York: The Museum of Modern Art Retrospective Program, 1990.

Rafalidis, Vasilis. *Kinomatographika Themata 1984–85*. Athens: Aigokeros, 1985.

Ruggle, Walter. *Theo Angelopoulos: Filmische Landshaften*. Baden, Switzerland: Verlag Lars Mueller, 1990.

Sadoul, Georges. *Dictionary of Films*. Translated and edited by Peter Morris. Berkeley and Los Angeles: University of California Press, 1972.

Schuster, Mel. *The Contemporary Greek Cinema*. Metuchen, N.J.: Scarecrow Press, 1979.

Schutte, Wolfram. "Land-Surveyor and Time-Traveller: The Greek Film Director Theo Angelopoulos." Notes to the CD *Eleni Karaindrou: Music for Films*. Munich: ECM Records, 1991.

Seferis, George. "Mythical Story." In *Four Greek Poets*, translated and edited by Edmund Keeley and Philip Sherrard, 43–54. Harmondsworth, England: Penguin, 1966.

Segal, Charles. *Interpreting Greek Tragedy: Myth, Poetry, Text*. Ithaca: Cornell University Press, 1986.

Sklar, Robert, and Charles Musser. *Resisting Images: Essays on Cinema and History*. Philadelphia: Temple University Press, 1990.

Snell, Bruno. *The Discovery of the Mind: The Greek Origins of European Thought*. Translated by T. G. Rosenmeyer. New York: Harper & Row, 1960.

Soldatos, Yiannis. *Istoria Tou Ellinkou Kinimatografou*. Athens: Aigokeros, 1982.

Stanford, W. B. *The Ulysses Theme*. Ann Arbor: University of Michigan Press, 1968.

Stenzel, Samatha. "Composer Who Probes the Soul: Eleni Karaindrou." *Athenian*, December 1990, 40–41.

———. "An Interview with Thodoros Angelopoulos." *Athenian*, June 1981, 34–35.

Stratton, David. "*Ulysses' Gaze*." *Variety*, May 29–June 4, 1995, 53.

Tarr, Susan, and Hans Proppe. "*The Travelling Players*: A Modern Greek Masterpiece." *Jump Cut*, nos. 10/11 (1976): 5–6.

Themelis, Constantine A. "An Artist Has No Biography: His Biography Is His Work. An Interview with Theo Angelopoulos." Translated and edited by Yiorgos Chouliaras from the original printing in Greek in *Periodiko #39*, Athens, August 1989. In *Theo Angelopoulos*. New York: The Museum of Modern Art Retrospective Program, 1990.

Theo Angelopoulos. New York: The Museum of Modern Art Retrospective Program, 1990.

Theo Angelopoulos. Paris: Etude cinématographiques, nos. 142–145, 1991.

Thomson, David. *A Biographical Dictionary of Film*. 2d ed. New York: William Morrow, 1981. 3d ed. New York: Knopf, 1995.

Tyros, Andreas. "The Greek Vision: Gloom and Splendor." In *Cine-Mythology: A Retrospective of Greek Film*. Athens: The Greek Film Centre, 1993.

Underwood, Paul A. *The Karije Djami*. Vol. 1, *A Historical Introduction and Description of the Mosaics and Frescoes*. London: Routledge, 1967.

Vickers, Brian. *Towards Greek Tragedy*. London: Longman, 1973.

Weaver, Mary Anne. "The Greek Who Filmed His Country's Tragedy." *Washington Star*, April 25, 1976, 14.

West, Rebecca. *Black Lamb and Grey Falcon*. Harmondsworth, England: Penguin, 1941.

White, Hayden. *Tropics of Discourse: Essays in Cultural Criticism*. Baltimore: Johns Hopkins University Press, 1986.

Wilmington, Michael. "Angelopoulos: The Power and the Glory." *Film Comment*, November–December 1990, 32–37.

Wilson, David. "Interview with Theo Angelopoulos." *Athenian*, June 1981, 15–17.

———. "Out of a Dead Land." *Sight and Sound* 57, no. 1 (Winter 1987–1988): 64–65.

Woodhouse, C. M. *The Story of Modern Greece*. London: Faber and Faber, 1968.

Index

About the Author

Andrew Horton is Professor of Film and Literature at Loyola University in New Orleans. He is the author of *Writing the Character Centered Screenplay, Russian Critics on a Cinema of Glasnost, Comedy/Cinema/Theory*, and co-author, with Michael Brashhinsky, of *The Zero Hour: Glasnost and Soviet Cinema in Transition.*